THE MODERNIST ENTERPRISE

The Modernist Enterprise

FRENCH ELITES AND THE
THREAT OF MODERNITY,
1900-1940

Marjorie A. Beale

STANFORD UNIVERSITY PRESS
STANFORD, CALIFORNIA

Stanford University Press
Stanford, California
© 1999 by the Board of Trustees of the
Leland Stanford Junior University
Printed in the United States of America
CIP data appear at the end of the book

Pour Gérard Grisey (1946–98),
en souvenir d'une longue amitié

Acknowledgments

W riting this book has been a long, at time arduous, but often festive process as well, in the course of which I have incurred an enormous debt of gratitude to friends and colleagues, and to the institutions that have funded my research. The John D. and Catherine T. MacArthur Foundation, in conjunction with the Social Science Research Council, provided financial support for my initial period of research in France in 1986–87, as did the Cultural Services of the French Embassy, with a Bourse Chateaubriand. Subsequent research support has come from the University of California, Irvine's humanities research and travel funds, and the Center for German and European Studies at the University of California, Berkeley. Support for writing was provided by the Doreen B. Townsend Center for the Humanities in 1989–90, the Rutgers Center for Historical Analysis, and career development funds in 1993–94 from the School of Humanities at University of California, Irvine, which also funded a sabbatical quarter in 1994–95.

In its initial form my work benefited tremendously from the comments and suggestions of the community of historians at Berkeley in the late 1980's. My thanks go first of all to Susanna Barrows, who directed my dissertation, for her innumerable and unfailingly gracious contributions over the years as editor, counselor, hostess, and friend, and to her daughter Alexandra, for all she has taught me over the years about the realm of the surreal and the pleasures of writing. I am grateful, too, to Martin Jay for his insightful comments on my work and his unwavering support of my various intellectual projects. Thomas Laqueur provided invaluable assistance when I first began writing by reading the earliest drafts of my work in epistolary form; he has remained a faithful friend and an esteemed reader. The graduate experience at Berkeley in the 1980's bore considerable resemblance to participation in a mass movement. Thanks to my *camarades* David Barnes, Michael Bess, Joshua Cole, Sarah Farmer, Sheryl Kroen, Catherine Kudlick, Ben Lapp, Mark Meigs, Maura O'Connor, Sylvia Schaefer, Vanessa Schwartz, Regina Sweeney, Matt Truesdale, and Jeff Verhey for taking the time to focus their considerable intelligence, both collective and individual, on my work.

At Rutgers (and in Berkeley) John and Tina Gillis were unstinting in their hospitality and unflagging in their moral support. John Gillis, Victoria de Grazia, Gene Lebovics, Mara Miller, Phil Nord, and Bonnie Smith read large portions of the original manuscript during my year at Rutgers and made suggestions that have shaped my current work in many ways. I am grateful, too, for the comments of my colleagues at Irvine over the years. Ann Blair, Alice Fahs, Thelma Foote, Jim Given, Karl Hufbauer, Lynn Mally, Carrie Noland, Patricia O'Brien, Ken Pomeranz, Mark Poster, Steven Topik, Anne Walthall, and Jon Wiener read all or part of the manuscript in its various states, offering advice and encouragement. Colleagues at the Ecole des Hautes Etudes en Sciences Sociales, where I was a visitor in 1994 and 1998, were an ongoing source of intellectual stimulation. Patrick Fridenson fundamentally transformed my research project by telling me about the Fonds Coutrot at the Archives Nationales. Luc Boltanski first suggested that I consider the role of social Catholicism in French technocratic thought during the interwar years. Yves Cohen's work has broadened my knowledge of twentieth-century labor movements, while Marie Cheyssel's research has helped to refine my understanding of the emerging advertising profession in France. Most of all, my discussions with Jacques Revel, Maurizio Gribaudi, and Sabina Loriga led me to reconsider many of my most basic assumptions about the ways ideas are transmitted within (and among) intellectual milieus. My thanks to each of them for pushing me to think more deeply about the task of writing intellectual history in a cultural mode.

Conversations with Dipesh Chakrabarty have helped me to think in unconventional ways about the meaning of modernity. Shared presentations with Leora Auslander, Judy Coffin, Bob Frost, Ellen Furlough, and Rosemary Wakeman have compelled me to pay attention to social history in spite of myself. A visit to Cornell was the occasion for trenchant commentaries on my written work from Steven Kaplan, Dominick LaCapra, and their students. Finally, I was fortunate enough to be the recipient of generous and insightful readings of my penultimate draft by Daniel Sherman and Tyler Stovall, who reviewed the manuscript for Stanford University Press. At Stanford, Norris Pope shepherded my work through the review process in the most supportive and efficient way imaginable. John Feneron was a dream of an editor. My thanks to both of them for their patience and their faith in my project. Marc Kanda and Amelia Lyons helped to ease the final throes of the manuscript preparation, reading the page proofs aloud in their entirety, making the index, and contending with the author's endless demands on their time.

Many, many friends have offered their hospitality over the years during the periods I've spent in France. Thanks in particular to Susanna Barrows, Catherine Kudlick, and Vanessa Schwartz for kindly sharing their apartments, and to Gérard Grisey, Mireille Guigui and Raphael Grisey, Valerie and Peter Humphrey, Vincent and Youkali Rotgé, Reneé Rousso, Denyse de Saivre and Christopher Miles-Thomas, Sybille Oettinger-Slattery and Michael Slattery for years of their friendship and forbearance during my visits to Europe. I am grateful, too, to Bob English and Anna Zara, Hu Ying and Michael Phelan, Ken Kambara, Susan Klein and Joe McKenna, Joan Levinson, Amy Nestor, Carrie Noland and Christopher Beach, Pamela Paradowski, Lori and Michael Pond, Kathy Ragsdale and Michael Fuller, Katharine Streip and Anne Walthall for the ongoing gift of their friendship. And finally, thank you to Bill Bird and Judith Vida for helping me to bring this project to completion.

Paris, July 1999

Contents

THE MODERNIST ENTERPRISE

Introduction

As philosophers and critics proclaim the end of the modern era,[1] modernity remains an elusive concept, one that defies definition and resists precise historical situation. Scholars have argued for the emergence of a distinctively "modern" sensibility as early as the scientific revolution[2] or the famous French literary *Querelle des Anciens et des Modernes* of the late seventeenth and eighteenth centuries.[3] For the purposes of most contemporary historians, though, the modern era begins in the late Enlightenment, with the beginnings of bourgeois liberalism, the first stirrings of industrial capitalism, and the ascendancy of a scientific worldview. One classic presentation of modernity's character and transformative scope occurs in the opening section of Karl Marx's *Communist Manifesto* (1848), where Marx first describes the appearance of the bourgeoisie on the stage of world history.

> The bourgeoisie has put an end to all feudal, patriarchal, idyllic relations. It has pitilessly torn asunder the motley feudal ties that bound man to his "natural superiors," and has left remaining no other nexus between man and man than naked self-interest, than callous "cash payment." It has drowned the most heavenly ecstasies of religious fervor, of chivalrous en-

thusiasm, of philistine sentimentalism, in the icy water of egotistical cal-
culation.

. . . Constant revolutionizing of production, uninterrupted disturbance of all social conditions, everlasting uncertainty and agitation distinguish the bourgeois epoch from all earlier ones. All that is solid melts
into air, all that is holy is profaned, and man is at last compelled to face
with sober senses, his real conditions of life, and his relations with his
kind.[4]

Marx here establishes a clear demarcation between the dynamic,
forward-looking realm of the modern and the changeless domain of
tradition, hierarchy, and devotion that it left behind. On one side of
the great divide lies the newly emergent bourgeois social order with its
dependence on rationality and the cash nexus, while on the other lies a
world, now forever inaccessible except to memory,[5] in which the reality of domination was softened by sentiment, by faith, and by notions
of duty, loyalty, or personal engagement all too readily cast aside in
the modern era as irrational and irrelevant. Ever since Marx, then, this
stark pair of images, the before and after, the pre- and postlapsarian,
has served as a fundamental point of reference for all later discussions
of modernity.

Despite its future-oriented projects and its utopian schemes to
transform the world, modernity is figured in the passage above as a fall
from grace, a loss of wholeness. For Marx, of course, this fall was
merely one uncomfortable stage in an ongoing dialectical process, a
transient episode that would soon be subsumed by the movement of
history and ultimately transcended. Nonetheless, it has become a
commonplace for commentators on the modern from Marx onward
to analyze the social and cultural phenomena of modernity in terms
tinged with nostalgia: for the modern sensibility, reflection on society's present or its future has come to be almost inseparable from some
form of meditation on its relationship to the past.

Many of the major twentieth-century essays on the meaning of
modernity have been produced under the signs of nostalgia, regret,
and loss. For the German sociologist Max Weber, who set out to rethink Marxian categories in cultural and political terms, the modern
era was characterized by what he famously called "the disenchantment

of the world," that is, the banishment of human values from a realm of public discourse and action increasingly dominated by instrumental rationality. The account of modernity that emerges in Weber's writings is sharply at odds with any progressive notion of history: in his view, the progress of means-end rationality in Western societies had created a world in which bureaucratic institutions proliferated at the expense of any single individual's ability to act in a publicly meaningful way or to fully grasp the complexity of contemporary social problems. The deep irony of modernity, then, was that while instrumental rationality appeared to make Western man ever more the master of his social environment, the losses entailed by that mastery were considerable; as Weber put it, "the ultimate and most sublime values have retreated from public life either into the transcendental realm of mystic life or into the brotherliness of direct and personal human relations." [6] What had disappeared in the modern era was the possibility of a genuine and active engagement with public life.

The philosophers of the Frankfurt School posed the problem of modernity in slightly different terms, but returned once again to the theme of loss.[7] For T. W. Adorno and Max Horkheimer, modernity was divided against itself from its inception as a result of what they called the "dialectic of Enlightenment." Bourgeois liberalism, they argued, was founded on Enlightenment rationality's quest for clarity and knowledge as a means to collective emancipation. Over the course of the nineteenth century, however, as bourgeois social institutions began to triumph, it slowly became apparent that the rationalist ideals of Enlightenment had engendered a number of unintended cultural effects. Most prominent among these was bourgeois society's fascination with technique and technology as the solution to every imaginable sort of intellectual, social, or aesthetic problem. As a result, Adorno and Horkheimer observed, bourgeois culture itself had taken on an increasingly technical aspect, an industrial and mass-produced quality that made it ill-suited to represent genuine human concerns. What was lost in this instance, then, was the possibility of a literature, an art, a music, or a philosophy that could move beyond the sentimentality and cliché of mass cultural products to address the full range of human specificity and human emotion.[8]

Even Jürgen Habermas, the Frankfurt School's contemporary philosophical heir, casts his account of the evolution of the bourgeois public sphere (and thus bourgeois modernity) from the Enlightenment to the present day as a tale of decline, constraint, and compromise.[9] Habermas's sociology of communication is built around the notion of free and open public discourse as the foundation of bourgeois liberalism. His earliest major work, *The Structural Transformation of the Public Sphere* (1961), traced the history of Western society's attempts to institutionalize that ideal. In general, he has noted, a free and open space for public discussion can only be achieved on the basis of some measure of exclusion: if a forum for public exchange is to remain free of coercion, it must first be protected from potentially disruptive influences. Ironically, over time this reliance on protection and exclusion has tended to compromise the discursive space itself, to an extent that has transformed Habermas's notion of "communicative rationality," or noncoercive public communication, into something more closely resembling an ideal category than an observable social phenomenon. For Habermas, modernity is characterized precisely by its inability to sustain a free forum for public consultation about matters of civil governance. Once again, the modern era is figured as "disenchanted" in almost the Weberian sense to the extent that the liberatory aims and restrictive practices of bourgeois liberalism can never be fully reconciled.

What follows is an attempt to bring some of the concerns of Marx, Weber, the Frankfurt School, and even Habermas to bear in an empirical study of the cultural practice of modernity as it took shape in Paris from the turn of the century to the fall of France in 1940. For the elites of pre–First World War and interwar Paris, modernity presented itself in the form of a series of questions about France's place in a newly competitive industrial world and their own position as the leaders and managers of a mass society. What was the optimal form of governance in a mass democracy? What new roles would there be for elites? How could public opinion best be shaped and regulated? And above all, how could France's cultural identity be preserved against an onslaught of foreign influences?

This book differs from much of the existing literature on the intellectual and cultural history of modernity[10] in its attention to a variety of individuals who are not generally recognized as major intellectual figures in their own right or even as notable representatives of important scientific, philosophical, or aesthetic tendencies. Instead, I have concerned myself here with the way that ideas were transmitted within the French elite and how they were deformed to suit the needs of their users once they were taken up in settings outside the immediate precincts of official high culture and the inner circles of the Parisian avant-garde. The central characters in this story are for the most part only peripherally identifiable as intellectuals, with the exception of a few individuals such as Jean Epstein, Victor Basch, and Le Corbusier, who figure prominently in the opening chapter, and perhaps Jean Coutrot, whose life and works serve as the focus of the final chapter. Taken together, their group publications, their speeches and manifestos, their individual writings, and the organizations that they created leave us with a very different perspective on the cultural history of modernity than more conventional intellectual histories have so far provided. *The Modernist Enterprise,* then, is an extended reflection on the ways in which French elites in the early part of the twentieth century responded to modernity's threat and its promise by reinventing their social environment in ways that brought together the alien and the familiar, the innovative and profoundly conservative.

This book begins with the development of advertising and the mass communications industry as a way of engaging with the larger issue of how French elites attempted to rethink their notions of public life in the Third Republic and how they finally came to terms with the reality of mass democracy. The very term *publicité,* after all, places advertising within the context of both literate culture and politics. In French, *publicité* denotes both the public sphere[11] and the means by which a mass audience may be addressed. While a number of authors have discussed advertising in France as a part of commercial culture, a force for economic modernization, and the creation of consumer society,[12] they have paid relatively little attention to the attempts of the advertising profession to establish itself within French high cultural traditions. Until the period after the Second World War, when French advertising firms began to emulate their American counterparts, French advertisers saw themselves as businessmen engaged in a pursuit that combined economic concerns and high cultural projects. My aim in beginning with the history of *publicité,* then, is to draw attention to advertising as one focal point for French thinking, at a variety of cultural levels, about the significance of the public sphere and the problem of communicating in a society as yet only uneasily committed to egalitarian values.

In subsequent chapters, I show how a traditionally educated elite meets the threat of modernity and mass culture. In the early years of the twentieth century, French elites in business and communications were confronted by a series of challenges to the old order brought on by the establishment of a mass democracy in France. Old cultural values were on the wane: where elites had once been the undisputed leaders of public opinion, they now found that leadership challenged by a newly vocal public of workers and consumers bent on leading France away from its aristocratic heritage and into the brave new world of American-style consumer capitalism. *The Modernist Enterprise* tells how professionals from the worlds of advertising, journalism, and industrial management struggled to use new communications techniques. They reached out to the mass public while still hoping to contain it and to divert it from the temptations of American-style mass democracy and the consumerist values that inevitably accompanied it.

The first chapter, "Advertising as Modernism," describes the beginnings of scientific advertising in France around the turn of the century. During the nineteenth century, French advertising was characterized by its utter lack of attention to such issues as consumer psychology and marketing. As French industrialists faced increasing competition from Germany, England, and the United States, such a divergence became insupportable. Pressure mounted for the business community to look outside for models of marketing success. The United States was the most obvious model for emulation, since scientific advertising—the creation of ads in accordance with the latest insights of modern experimental psychology—was already a highly developed commercial practice there. However, French industrialists and advertisers balked at the prospect of adopting American techniques, fearing that it would mean the wholesale adoption of American cultural values and the concomitant destruction of everything French. And so they set about the quixotic task of devising a science of advertising rooted entirely in the French tradition.

Unlike their American counterparts, French ad men drew on philosophy, often-antiquated theories from academic psychology, and other high cultural sources to develop a home-grown science of persuasion. Remarkably enough, they succeeded in developing effective methods: at least, they managed to persuade industrialists that their methods were worth trying. Even more remarkable was the fact that their efforts were paralleled by a group of avant-garde painters, writers, and architects led by Le Corbusier who felt that the time had come to create a science of perception in the arts. Despite their differing aims, elites in fields as diverse as art, advertising, and management were drawn to a similar range of solutions for managing public opinion. The plight of advertisers confronting a mass audience for the first time was in many ways emblematic of two larger issues that faced French elites in the dawning era of mass democracy and consumer culture: first, the urgent matter of learning to manage the public sphere and, second, coming to terms with the realization that such management was critical if the elite wished to maintain its grasp on cultural and political power.

The second chapter, "Commercial Warfare and the Critique of the French Press," takes up the problem of public opinion once again, this time as a catalyst for the modernization of journalism in France. It demonstrates how the language of paranoia and suspicion that contaminated wartime propaganda was transformed through the efforts of a radical journalist into a vehicle for critique and reform.

In the years leading up to the First World War, the French newspaper business was a veritable school for scandal. The editors of the major Parisian dailies were notorious for their lax ethical standards, both in their editorial policies and in their approach to their contractual agreements about commercial advertising. Their reputation for slovenly standards became far more egregious during the war itself. In 1916, a young investigative reporter, Eugène Letailleur, discovered that a German ad agency had managed to take control of the advertising space in every one of France's most influential papers through a Swiss holding company. While the editorial pages of these papers denounced the Germans as swine, the ads they ran allowed German manufacturers to dump their excess merchandise on the French market, disguised under French brand names. In the scandal that ensued, advertisers and newspaper publishers were forced to reconsider the careless standards that had prevailed for so long in their business. As the French civilian economy slowly rebuilt itself after the war, advertisers led the way to a series of ambitious, if never entirely successful, efforts to rationalize and modernize publicity in the French press.

The third chapter, "The Culture of Business," examines the issues regarding mass society and culture that first surfaced in chapter 1 in an entirely new setting, among the management specialists who adapted American theories of scientific management for use in French factories and offices. As France set about rebuilding her industrial base in the wake of war, factory owners and their managers quickly concluded that the future belonged to those who adopted American methods of organization. As in the case of the ad men, though, these would-be proponents of Taylorean efficiency studies and Ford-inspired assembly lines worried that these practices relied too heavily on American beliefs about the value of egalitarianism in the workplace. French workers, their managers claimed—or perhaps hoped—were accustomed to performing their tasks in a more hierarchical setting, and they would find it difficult to function in an American-style factory. Moreover, some social commentators feared that exposure to American practices would produce a more demanding workforce.

Henri Fayol, a former naval engineer and the protagonist of this chapter, set out to rethink Taylorism in a way that made sense in French cultural terms. By combining Taylor's organizational insights with ideas about the aristocratic nature of leadership drawn from the writings of nineteenth-century French military leaders, Fayol produced a theory of organizational psychology that brought the concerns of cultural traditionalists into an uneasy harmony with more forward-looking productive aims.

The fourth chapter, "Catholicism and Modernity," describes the contribution of the French social Catholic movement to the elaboration of a science of communication in mass society. This seems at first glance improbable. We tend to think of French Catholicism as a highly conservative and antimodern force, but the social Catholic movement of the interwar period frequently invoked science as a means to Christian social action. Pope Leo XIII's encyclical on modernity, *De Rerum Novarum,* had long encouraged Catholic intellectuals to seek out a new place for Christian ideas and values in a society increasingly geared toward mass production and consumption and seemingly devoid of more spiritual concerns. Activist Catholics formed the backbone of many secular institutions designed to reintroduce "the human factor" into the social experiments of the 1930's. Their contributions to the debates on scientific management and consumer society provide yet another example of the way that paternalist social and spiritual values could be infused with the flavor of the modern.

The final chapter, "Jean Coutrot and the Art of Social Engineering," focuses on one exemplary case that displays the tension between tradition and modernity in a particularly compelling way. Coutrot frequently wrote on aesthetic issues and was equally welcome as a contributor to such established literary journals as the *Nouvelle Revue Française* as he was to more venturesome avant-garde publications. At the same time, Coutrot's professional life was dominated by his intensely technocratic vision of France's future: he was trained as a military engineer and worked variously as a factory manager, an expert on scientific management techniques, and eventually a Popular Front official in charge of overseeing the state's efforts at industrial rationalization.

This archetypical technocrat founded a Christian humanist institute, the Center for the Study of Human Problems, which sponsored high-level conferences and research groups devoted to the study of scientific techniques for social control. His attempts to develop a science of social management, taking into account cultural and spiritual issues, provide a case in point of the claims made earlier on about the struggles of the elite to come to terms with mass culture. Ultimately, this chapter argues, Coutrot found himself in an impossible position, for the scientific and cultural alchemy he hoped to effect proved elusive. His efforts, like those of the French elite more generally, to find a way of reconciling classic high cultural values with the democratizing impulses of the new age left him vulnerable to authoritarian solutions to the dilemma. In his case, his efforts to reconcile aristocratic ideals with mass democracy through science ended in a problematic flirtation with fascism.

In France more generally, what did not end in fascism ended in chaos. Although the Vichy regime did manage to forge a precarious alliance between modern industrial organization and traditional values, it succeeded in doing so only at huge cost to democratic ideas. After 1945, France modernized along American lines with the help of the Marshall Plan, in many ways fulfilling the direst prophecies of interwar commentators. In other respects, though, elite—even aristocratic—values have lived on and continue to permeate French society at every level. The culture wars continue today, albeit in altered forms, as the French attempt to mediate between the imperatives of their elite cultural traditions and the challenges of mass society in a global era.

CHAPTER I

Advertising as Modernism

I n the years directly following the First World War, French artists, businessmen, and social psychologists began to see their public with new eyes. Before the war, it had been a journalistic commonplace to describe the French as a nation of critics, rationalists, and skeptics who were not easily taken in by anything; they could scent even the best-concealed fraud as though it were a round of Tomme ripening in some Savoyard closet. The French were internationally known as, and knew themselves to be, a nation of tough customers, trained from father to son and mother to daughter to do business only with people they knew they could trust and to make discerning choices in every aspect of their lives as consumers and connoisseurs.

While it would be difficult to assess the actual effects of the war on local standards of taste and patterns of consumer behavior, it is clear that the experience of the war produced a marked change in the self-image of the French. The newly victorious nation found itself burdened with debt, overwhelmed by the task of reconstruction, and anxious about its ability to compete in the world market with its allies, or even with the Germans, who, according to the best French intelligence sources, had begun rebuilding in the last year of the war in the hope of defeating the French in an economic war after the armistice. Over and over in the first years after the Great War, the relative openness of the French economy—and French society—to modernizing influences became a topic for heated debate. In the weeks and months immediately following the war, political and journalistic discussion tended to focus less on the problems of physical reconstruction than on the more fundamental work of moral regeneration that remained to be achieved before France could truly recover from the war. Prewar French society was routinely criticized and condemned as decadent, frivolous, and self-indulgent. Moreover, the experience of war had altered so many aspects of daily life and manners that the years leading up to 1914 now seemed strangely distant and most decidedly part of the past. As Marcel Proust observed in *A la recherche du temps perdu*, both the high style and the intellectual refinement of salon life before the war now seemed strangely tired and dated—they were *passé* in every sense of the term. The world of the future belonged not to aesthetes and aristocrats but to social planners and leaders of men, energetic and determined individuals who would force the traditionalist French to come to terms with modernity.

In the arts, the predominant movements before the war—analytic cubism, futurism, and the coloristic experimentation of the *fauves*—were supplemented and, in the early 1920's, supplanted by purism, whose practitioners were less fascinated than their artistic predecessors with indeterminacy, relativity, and the complex interplay between human perception and objects as they exist in time and space.[1] They abandoned modernist perspectivism almost entirely, concentrating instead on simplicity and purity of form in their paintings and on solidity, functionality, and reproducibility in their work as designers. They were also deeply concerned with questions about the social role of art in a way that clearly distinguishes them from their more subjectivist predecessors. It is surely no accident that one of the primary exponents of purism, Charles-Edouard Jeanneret (known for most of his career as Le Corbusier), later became an internationally famous architect and urban planner. The purists and their associates were most interested in the social dimensions of artistic practice, and they saw their fundamental project as one of helping to reorder the visual culture of their compatriots, training them to appreciate the clean lines and pure forms generated within industry, and to judge art not for its representational power or ornamental qualities but for its economy of expression and pure, unimpeded formal and emotional impact.

The desire to regroup and embrace modernity was certainly not limited to the artistic community. In the economic sphere, businessmen began to call for a strategic restructuring of the economy based on techniques developed in the United States for managing labor more effectively, organizing production to match demand, and stimulating demand through professionally planned advertising campaigns. Louis Chambonnaud, a professor of business at the newly established Haute Ecole Commerciale in Paris, responded to the challenge of postwar economic renovation by inaugurating a series of textbooks on organizational psychology, salesmanship, marketing, and publicity, beginning with *Les affaires nouvelles*, which appeared in 1919. Chambonnaud's introduction to the book and to the series makes amply clear the importance of modern business techniques in a competitive international marketplace. He begins with several tales of German commercial infiltration of France during the war that highlight the strategic importance of advertising. Among German businessmen, he claims, it was a common practice to identify a popular French product with a high sales volume (often a food item) and then begin producing and distributing a comparable item with a similar trade name and logo in an attempt to flood the market and supplant the original product. Sales of the German product would often outstrip those of the original French article because the Germans would take care not to reveal its national origin and because they did a much better job of advertising, marketing, and distributing the product than the French.[2] After a few weeks of this, there would normally be an uproar in the press over the fact that one company was attempting to usurp the trade name of another. A legal battle might even ensue, but according to Chambonnaud, the wily Germans were expert in profiting from scandal. They recognized it as an opportunity for more publicity, which they exploited to the fullest, while the French concern was left to pay the legal bills.

Worse still, through a series of complicated maneuvers involving a Genevan holding company and the unwitting participation of the Agence Havas, a German posting company had managed to secure the posting concession for all the walls of Paris and control over most of the advertising space in the five largest Parisian dailies. In the words of politician Victor Cambon, "If we had not paid attention at the last minute, the public announcement of French mobilization would have been handled by German business interests. There was as much treacherous forethought on one side as there was blind thoughtlessness on the other."[3] The relative backwardness of French commercial organization had taken on the importance of a national security matter in more than one sense. In the aftermath of the war, French politicians and businessmen were thoroughly self-conscious in their use of battle metaphors as they attempted to describe the economic task that lay ahead.

In the French advertising industry's principal trade journal, *La Publicité,* the war had a slightly different significance. For the editors, the task of reconstruction meant that the French had to begin sizing up the competition and taking modern business methods more seriously if they hoped to regain their prewar economic standing. Before the war, modernizing trade journals such as *La Publicité, La Publicité moderne,* and *Mon Bureau* (which offered advice on increasing office efficiency, training salespeople, and preparing advertisements) all flirted with the notion of scientific advertising. In an issue of *La Publicité* from 1909, Octave-Jacques Gérin complained that French advertising was years behind the American profession technically and conceptually because the French had not yet managed to develop their own science of advertising. At that time, in fact, most advertising materials were designed by poster artists (Toulouse-Lautrec and Chéret are two familiar examples) or, in the case of newspaper advertising, by typesetters and their assistants.

Even attempts on the part of journals like *La Publicité* to professionalize the production of advertisements stopped short of the kinds of scientific experimentation that had been taking place in the United States from the turn of the century onward. Gérin argued that the French advertising profession should follow the lead of the United

States by developing a more systematic and ultimately more scientific approach to the creation of advertising images and texts.

Advertising should be suggestive, and not in the current sense of the word, but in its scientific sense. Given the substantial spending on advertising that takes place today, it is essential that this money not be squandered. [In advertising,] our assault [on the public] must be mathematical.

Thanks to the theory of suggestion, advertisers can now achieve this. Their budgets can be planned with the assurance that advertising expenditures will produce a maximum return.[4]

Gérin envisioned the advertisement of the future as the result of a highly developed technology of persuasion that could produce predictable and reliable responses from consumers.

Pierre Clerget, a professor at the Ecole supérieure de commerce in Lyon, published an essay in 1908 about the potential applications of the new dynamic psychiatry in the advertising profession, citing Alfred Binet's research on automatic behavior and Théodule Ribot's *La psychologie de l'attention.*[5] For Clerget, the truly modern advertisement would be designed for maximum suggestivity and memorability. The advertising profession, then, had certainly entertained the possibility that scientific studies of human perception and memory might provide the basis for more systematic and rational forms of mass communication. However, Clerget and Gérin were somewhat ahead of their times, since the majority of advertisements created in the years before the war were still composed with only minimal attention to visibility, suggestive power, and other qualities that scientific research had determined would influence their effectiveness.

As for the critical sensibilities of the French, these apparently remained intact and reemerged in the postwar press, albeit in a slightly altered form. What had been a national virtue now posed a peculiarly French problem for anyone who wished to address the public at large. In advertising periodicals and modernizing business journals, various commentators argued that while American psychological techniques, based largely on shock and affront, were marvelously successful in attracting and retaining the attention of credulous, tasteless Americans, they could only be offensive and repugnant to more refined French audiences. Thus, if modern business techniques were to succeed in France, they would have to be redesigned to suit their target audience. And redesigned they were, in the image of the French science of the unconscious.

The ideas of psychologists and philosophers such as Henri Bergson, Ribot, and Hippolyte Bernheim were part of the cultural background of most educated members of the middle and upper classes in France at the beginning of the twentieth century, and as such, they left their traces in many different areas of French life. Several recent works have produced a substantial body of evidence to suggest that basic concepts from French dynamic psychology were put to use in a broad spectrum of activities, ranging from politics and medicine to the arts and artisanal production.[6] In some ways, contemporary discussions of advertising techniques provide us with a cultural artifact that records the extent to which ideas about human perception and recollection first derived from dynamic psychology had entered the working vocabulary of nonspecialists.

The literature on scientific advertising in France after the turn of the century certainly provides an index of the cultural power of academic psychology. In the United States, the relationship between the advertising business and academic researchers in psychology was structured according to the needs of advertisers. The best-known and most influential psychologists tended to be those (e.g., Walter Dill Scott or Daniel Starch) who made the study of advertising their professional specialty. By contrast, French ad men looked to the experts for advice on more general problems in psychology, such as identifying the conscious and unconscious mechanisms that allow one person to influence another or determining how human perception works. In France, advertising practices tended to follow the theoretical formulations of the academicians, while in the United States, although advertisers were certainly interested in unraveling the mysteries of suggestion and perception, the kind of work that research psychologists actually did for them was dictated strictly by such pragmatic concerns as sales volume and cost-effectiveness.

The French were rather more hesitant about the actual business of making money. Their interest lay in legitimating advertising both as a practice and as a profession by fully integrating it into French culture. In addition, they were often tremendously anxious about the potential effects of advertising on French culture, both as an agent of modernity and as a force for Americanization. Gérin was willing to embrace the influence of the Americans, at least to a certain degree. He argued that the French advertising profession should follow the lead of the United States by developing a more systematic and ultimately more scientific approach to the creation of advertising images and texts. However, for Gérin, following the American example did not entail slavish imitation of any sort, in terms of either graphic design or scientific methodology. He remarked that France had its own school of dynamic psychiatry whose research findings were perfectly suited to the needs of advertisers: "I am indebted to the Ecole de Nancy," he claimed, "and to the work of Bernheim and Liébault for having enabled me to understand advertising and establish precise and unambiguous rules for it. Given that these rules concern the human brain, they allow for great flexibility in their application, depending on the moment, the social milieu, and the individuals in question."[7]

Fortunately for advertisers and the business community at large, the French literature in psychiatry and clinical psychology from the 1880's onward proved to be rich in materials that might provide the basis for a more scientific approach to mass communications. Even before the Great War, a certain number of basic psychological concepts had made their way into common parlance—and into advertising journals. Contributors to trade publications such as *La Publicité* and *Mon Bureau* proffered advice on how to increase the suggestive power of advertising copy and speculated about the effectiveness of repetition in "hypnotizing" potential clients.[8] However, the use of such terminology probably does not reflect a concerted attempt by advertisers to incorporate contemporary psychological theories into their sales methods since, as Henry Ellenberger notes, by 1900 the terms *suggestion* and *hypnosis* had both come to be used so carelessly that they lost their more specifically clinical meaning.[9] The prevalent view among advertisers at this time seems to have been that the consuming public could best be understood and addressed as a collective entity that functioned as a group. The notion that consumers made decisions not as a group but as individuals came only *much* later. In consequence, the first advertising manuals tended to rely heavily on the pronouncements of well-known figures in crowd psychology, such as Gustave Le Bon, who wrote on advertising and the mind of the crowd, or Gabriel Tarde, a noted criminologist whose work on the spread of ideas and fashions in society provided an early model of consumer behavior.[10]

Despite the suggestions of writers like Clerget and Gérin, psychiatry came into its own as an influence on the advertising profession only at the end of the war, when *La Publicité* rediscovered the work of Dr. Hippolyte Bernheim, founder of the Ecole de Nancy. Bernheim was in some ways a natural choice for advertisers, because his work spoke directly to some of their central concerns. In the 1870's and 1880's, he had been one of the first clinicians to popularize hypnosis as a technique for treating medical problems other than hysteria, and he wrote extensively about the uses of suggestion and hypnosis with psychologically normal subjects. He was also tremendously interested in the role that visual images played in normal human thought processes. The results of his experimentation with hypnosis and suggestion in Nancy marked a significant departure from the findings of his major professional competitors, the researchers at the Salpêtrière, headed by Jean-Martin Charcot. Charcot and his colleagues were convinced that suggestibility and susceptibility to images were unique to hysterics, and they viewed Bernheim's work as fundamentally flawed. However, for advertisers, a theory of human suggestibility that departed from the usual focus on abnormal cases had the potential to revolutionize advertising psychology, transforming it from a hodgepodge of hit-or-miss practical strategies into a rational discipline with a coherent view regarding the laws of human perception.

Bernheim argued that suggestibility was an essential element in normal mental functioning. In his *De la suggestion dans l'état hypnotique et dans l'état de veille* (1884), he describes suggestion as a dynamic process based on "the brain's ability to receive or call up ideas and its tendency to transform them into acts."[11] Suggestion, then, is intimately linked to action in Bernheim's account: the brain is organized so as to transform external stimuli into dynamic mental images which, in their turn, engender action. Bernheim referred to this process as the law of *idéodynamisme*. This conception of the thought process was particularly appealing to advertisers because of the central role it accorded images in transforming external stimuli into a form the brain could more easily assimilate.

In Bernheim's view, the normal individual experienced the world as a flow of images incessantly bombarding his consciousness with potential suggestions. Vision thus became less a matter of selection than of passive reception, at least initially.[12] However, Bernheim argued that ultimately the process of visual suggestion "is not simply a passive occurrence, a simple deposit of a psychic image within the brain." Instead, "the psychic brain takes an active part . . . in the process of transforming impressions into ideas, and elaborating them: each idea suggests others, and these ideas transform themselves into a variety of sensations, emotions, and images. This association of ideas, sensations, and images results in a suggestive synthesis which each individual accomplishes in his or her own fashion."[13]

This analysis awakened advertisers to the power of images themselves to generate mental and physical activity. A well-designed advertising image could provide a kind of shortcut into the psyche by presenting itself in a form that allowed the mind to assimilate it more readily, converting it into a series of associational elaborations and, eventually, into action. The truly successful advertisement would be a forceful and coherent visual stimulus that was likely to produce a clear and uncomplicated chain of associations. Thus, a lot of early advertising literature emphasized clarity, unity of composition, bright colors, repetition, and simplicity in design. Bernheim's ideas were also of interest to advertisers because they indicated that suggestion could take place through the use of images with little or no involvement of the conscious mind. Imagistic suggestion worked by engaging an automatic process that produced an act or a will to act before the conscious mind even had time to reflect on it.

Bernheim's work, then, laid the foundation for a science of persuasion ideally suited to the critical French. Where a contemporary American advertisement would play on the emotions, evoking the conscious and unconscious desires and fears that provided motivations to buy, the first scientific advertisements in France were designed to by-pass feeling altogether. Instead, they were based on neurological data about the psychology of perception, and sought to induce automatic visual sensations.

Another central point of reference for advertising psychology was Théodule Ribot's work on attention. Like Bernheim, Ribot believed that suggestibility was an important part of normal mental function-ing, and like both Bernheim and Bergson, he was an exponent of the view that mental representations tended to translate themselves into action. His research focused on the different ways in which individu-als pay attention and the sorts of attention that produced a mental state receptive to suggestion. In his 1889 study, *La psychologie de l'at-tention*, Ribot distinguished between two basic modes of attention. The first, spontaneous attention, arises "naturally" and produces a deep and long-lasting trancelike state, while the second, voluntary at-tention, appears in Ribot's account as an "artificial" result of effort and education that tends to be more transitory and more tiring than spon-taneous attention because of the mental energy required to sustain it. Ribot also suggested that attention was closely related to obsession and that it worked by suspending ordinary mental processes so that all the mind's mental energy could be diverted to the object of attention. Under normal conditions, he believed, the mind experienced "a plu-rality of conscious states, or, to use an expression favored by certain authors, *polyïdéisme*. Attention occurs when this perpetual parade comes to a halt for the benefit of one particular state, *monoïdéisme*."[14] Ribot also argued that suggestions made during spontaneous atten-tion tended to be more effective than those made at other times be-cause the subject was more relaxed and more open to external influ-ence than during voluntary attention.

In consequence, advertisers were particularly interested in finding ways to induce the quasi-hypnotic state of spontaneous attention in their audience. As Edith Weiler noted in her much-praised book on advertising psychology, "Spontaneous attention is the true, primitive form of attention. . . . Advertising appeals first of all to spontaneous attention. It seeks to introduce a given sensation into an area where the mind can visualize clearly. An advertisement thus provides [a sensation] which lasts for an appropriate amount of time and introduces affective and intellectual factors that will help to maintain it."[15] Weiler, who was writing in 1932, eventually departed slightly from Ribot, concluding that in order for spontaneous attention to be truly useful in advertising, it needed to be extended and developed by voluntary attention. As she notes, advertising is never a simple matter of persuasion through hypnotic suggestion. The persuasive process takes place in several stages. First, an ad has to capture and maintain the attention of a future client long enough for the associational process to begin. Next, it must provide some plausible rationale for buying the product in question. The actual act of purchase finally happens as the result of what appears to the consumer to be a conscious and more or less rational decision. Even if suggestion was the primary motivation for purchase, an ad had to be put together in a way that allowed it to address its viewer both as a suggestion and as rational argumentation.[16]

However, Weiler's conclusion was long in coming. At first, advertisers who had read Ribot reasoned that the best way to design a successful advertisement was to create a bold and striking image that commanded the attention of viewers or to introduce a phrase that was rhythmic and easily remembered and then repeat it incessantly so as to produce a kind of obsessive fascination with the image or slogan. Moreover, the advertising profession as a whole had some rather surprising ideas about the sorts of images and texts that might place the spectator in the desired mental state. One theory was that spontaneous attention was most easily provoked and potential clients were most readily hypnotized by loud colors, bold typeface, and attention-getting graphics. As a result, the images that appeared in the daily press could be remarkably unsubtle. One example of this occurred in the well-known ad for shoe polish that showed a man with a nail being driven into his head by a hammer with the legend "[Let us] knock this into your brain!"[17] On other occasions, advertisers would attempt to create obsession with advertisements that resembled a rather ludicrous condensation in a dream, as for example an advertisement for vegetable oil that encouraged potential customers to preserve their health by avoiding excess butter in their cooking. The slogan for the ad, "Gendarmez-vous!" (Protect—or police—yourself) was emblazoned across a line drawing of a chubby *flic* standing in a pot of soup, sipping broth out of a hefty ladle. Admittedly, the fit was not always perfect between the psychological principles that were to inform the construction of a modern advertisement and the actual results of those principles when translated into images. Even so, as the advertising profession developed a clearer and more realistic sense of the potential uses of psychology in design, ad men and women began to incorporate the results of psychological research on perception in increasingly sophisticated ways.

The advertising community in France also took a lively interest in literary and philosophical work on consumer behavior and human perceptual processes. A number of postwar advertising psychologists and business writers derived some of their ideas on human behavior from novelists (favorite references were Gustave Flaubert and Emile Zola). They also made frequent reference to such academic figures as Gabriel Tarde and Henri Bergson in their discussions of the relationship between perception and action. At times, authors used references to Bergson primarily as a sign of their own erudition or sophistication. This was certainly the case in Pierre Herbin's *Comment concevoir et rédiger votre publicité*, where the author quotes Bergson at some length on the creative process in a section on how to prepare oneself psychologically for the task of creating the perfect image or slogan.[18] In other instances, though, Bergson's ideas were an integral part of more technical arguments about the ways in which individuals experience their surroundings. In the February/March 1920 issue of *La Publicité*, Jules Lallemand used Bergson as the centerpiece for an essay on applied psychology in advertising. "Bergsonian introspection," he wrote,

> captures something of the *spontaneity* or *immediacy* of *consciousness* in which we recognize the tools of the teacher or the advertiser. . . . Thanks to his magical style, BERGSON . . . has managed to reproduce [the experience of] life with words in much the same way that the cinema re-creates movement from static images, or that the phonograph reproduces the sublime wail of the Stradivarius. The study of dream and reverie have made it possible to gracefully reconstitute the spontaneity of consciousness, which is so difficult to capture in its ceaseless *becoming* and endless dynamism.[19]

For Lallemand, Bergson's work was of use to advertisers in at least two distinct respects. First, his explorations into the lived experience of consciousness provided a working model of the mind in its most receptive state, the mind advertisers hoped to address. Second, his writings lent a certain legitimacy to the advertising psychologist's attempts to institute a science of commercial persuasion. Bergson himself was prestigious as a scientific thinker, and even his prose style emerged in Lallemand's treatment as a kind of precision instrument which, like the motion picture camera or the phonograph, faithfully records sensory impressions.

In looking to Bergson for help in understanding conscious (and unconscious) mental processes, Lallemand, Herbin, and others were remarkably consistent, because Bergson's ideas on the relationship between perception and action, imagistic thinking, and the dynamic power of images closely resemble those of Bernheim. Bergson and Bernheim shared a common background of clinical experience with hypnosis. Bergson's first encounters with hypnosis came during his tenure at the University of Clermont-Ferrand (1883–88), where he attended the hypnotic sessions of Dr. Moutin as an observer. In 1886, Bergson designed and carried out his own experiments concerning the influence of hypnosis and suggestion on perception, publishing the results in the *Revue philosophique*.[20] The hypnotic state also figured centrally in one of Bergson's most important works, the *Essai sur les données immédiates de la conscience* (1889), where he described receptivity to aesthetic experience as a state akin to hypnosis and aesthetic influence as similar to hypnotic suggestion.

For Bergson, art produces aesthetic sentiment in much the same way that a skilled physician produces the various stages of hypnosis. The real aim of art, in his account, is to relax the spectator so as to facilitate the process of imprinting in his or her mind the basic formal and dynamic elements of an artist's visual ideas. "The aim of art," he writes, "is to lull the more active and resistant aspects of our personality into sleep, thus placing us in a state where we sympathize with the sentiments it expresses. In artistic methods we find an attenuated, refined, and almost spiritualized form of the processes through which the hypnotic state is ordinarily achieved."[21] With this statement, Bergson places art and hypnotic suggestion along a single continuum, transforming artistic expression into a more "refined" and "spiritualized" version of a crude clinical procedure for implanting messages in the brain. As we will see, this assimilation of artistic communication to a medical or scientific technique was to have some important practical ramifications for the development of advertising strategies in France during the 1920's and 1930's.

Bergson also shared Bernheim's belief that a significant portion of our mental processes occur through the mediation of mental images. In the opening pages of the *Essai*, Bergson draws a sharp distinction between the mind's analytical capacities and its more spontaneous emotional capacities. Analytic understanding, he claims, occurs primarily in language and is based on a fundamentally spatial apprehension of the world, while emotional experience is much more immediate and takes the form of dynamic multilayered mental images. Using language forces us to imagine distinctions between ideas where, in fact, none exist. Spatial thinking and language also encourage us to approach concepts according to a set of physical principles that have very little to do with the way ideas exist in the mind and the way they interact with one another.

One essential part of Bergson's project in the *Essai* is to use his ideas about imagistic thought as an argument against deterministic views of human behavior. Bergson claims that much of human psychological reality is composed of emotions, which cannot be described in quantitative, spatial, or linguistic terms because we experience them as qualitative, temporal, and imagistic. He further contends that the temporal and nonquantitative character of emotional experience guarantees that our actions cannot be entirely determined. Once temporality (*la durée*) is correctly understood as perfectly heterogeneous and nonquantifiable, it becomes clear that there is no way to imagine oneself into the emotional state that would be the precondition for a given action without actually being in the situation for the first time.

Ultimately, a curious paradox emerges in Bergson's discussion of the way we respond to art. The very conceptual device that allows him to slip out of the deterministic bind, the dynamic mental image, also leads him to describe aesthetic response as automatic and to argue that one person's emotional experience can be successfully reproduced in another individual. In fact, he sees this re-creation of the artist's sentiments in the viewer as the basis for all aesthetic communication. In a discussion of the reception of poetry, Bergson identifies the poet as

> one whose sentiments develop in images, and whose images translate themselves into words subject to rhythm. As we watch these images pass before our eyes we re-experience the sentiment which was their emotional equivalent. However, these images could not come into being as powerfully for us without the regular movements of rhythm. . . . The plastic arts produce a similar effect in the sudden fixity they can impose on life, which is communicated to the attention of the spectator through a kind of physical contagion.[22]

The artist's task, then, is to translate his or her emotional and aesthetic experiences into concrete imagistic forms (whether the images concerned are visual or linguistic) which will induce similar sensations in those who encounter the work of art. However, in this account, artistic communication remains a one-way process in which the artist imposes on the viewer or listener both the images and the subsequent chain of associations that ultimately reproduce the artist's original experience.[23]

Rhythm plays an integral part in this process. It addresses the body directly and engages it at the level of automatic neurological response. In an account of dance and the way it affects an audience, Bergson suggests that the dancers' movements draw us in by provoking a kind of physical sympathy which ultimately surfaces in the form of moral or aesthetic evaluations of the spectacle.[24] In this way, rhythm effectively bypasses the conscious mind and works to produce conscious affect and judgment by engaging a series of automatic physiological (and especially neurological) reactions. Bergson also notes that aesthetic experience arrests the attention of the spectator in much the same way that a cataleptic fit arrests the activity of a hysterical patient. The work of art, then, is fascinating to the point of nervous paralysis; it imposes on the spectator a kind of contagious physical mimesis that forces him or her into the appropriate state of receptivity and leaves the artist in complete control.

Bergson's work on perception, recollection, and the experience of time has most often been interpreted as one of the philosophical bases for modernist experiments with simultaneity and the superimposition of immediate impressions, associations, and memories.[25] H. Stuart Hughes characterizes Bergson as a vitalist whose philosophical style was primarily mystical and metaphysical rather than rational. However, rereading Bergson in light of contemporary advertising psychology makes it possible to assess his work and its significance for French culture at the turn of the century in a rather different way. For all that Bergson's philosophy was intuitive and rejected the mechanistic views of time and language endorsed by positivism, his philosophical writings also relied heavily on contemporary medical models of emotional and imaginative experience. After all, Bergson developed his ideas regarding the nature of conscious experience on the basis of extensive reading in the scientific literature on hypnosis, aphasia, and speech impairment.[26]

In the *Essai*, Bergson transforms artistic communication into a technical problem in physiology. In his description of aesthetic experience, he notes that "art seeks to imprint sentiments upon us rather than to express them; it suggests them to us, and blithely abandons the imitation of nature when it finds more effective means [of communicating]."[27] Artistic communication, then, emerges as a means of making a mark or impression on the brain, which Bergson imagines in material terms as a unit of organic matter possessing certain neurological properties. Moreover, as this passage and others in the *Essai* suggest, the key to communication in the arts lies in the ability of images to reproduce specific emotions. Thus, in creating a work of art, the artist seeks out the appropriate techniques that will speak to the automatic parts of the mind, eventually producing the desired physiological response.

Like the work of Bernheim and Ribot, Bergson's writings on automatism may have encouraged advertisers and artists alike to think about aesthetic communication as a unidirectional process: those who created images could imprint suggestions or impressions on the minds of their audiences while ignoring the problem of public reception almost entirely. Beyond his influence on the modernist concep-

tion of time, then, Bergson may have made a second crucial contribution to the culture of modernism in France by using contemporary
psychology to provide a theoretical common ground for artists and
advertisers as they confronted the task of addressing a mass public.

For advertisers, the elaboration of a scientific model of perception
and suggestion was an enormous boon, for it allowed them to legiti-
mize their modernizing efforts in the business world and to identify
themselves as technicians—engineers of public perception whose task
it was to render communication more efficient. Engineering was, of
course, a highly prestigious profession and a field in which France had
a proud heritage, from the designs of Vauban to the Eiffel Tower and
the Suez Canal. In the first flush of enthusiasm for the future of advertising as a technological enterprise, the advertising agency affiliated
with *La Publicité* named itself BTP, the Bureau Technique de Publicité. Similarly, when the advertising industry as a whole began to
lobby with the state for the introduction of a regular advertising curriculum and degree program in state educational institutions, the di-
ploma awarded upon completion of the program was to be named the
Brevet Technique en Publicité, and bearers were to be granted the title
of *technicien*.

As technicians, advertisers came to serve as a model of modernity
for artists and designers in postwar France, for the telegraphic style of
advertising slogans and the hard-hitting, concentrated force of advertising images had come to seem like a paradigm for the communications of the future. Although advertisers themselves were hesitant
about their cultural position as a result of their relationship to the
world of industry and money, it was precisely that connection which
made advertising appealing to the French artistic community of the
early 1920's. Advertising had already permeated the realm of quotid-
ian urban life,[28] and in its ubiquity it promised artists the possibility of
clear, rapid, powerful, and efficacious communication with every sec-
tor of society. The allure of advertising seemed to be especially powerful for the group of writers, artists, filmmakers, and designers who
collaborated on the purist journal *L'Esprit nouveau*. The journal was
founded by a trio of men whose diverse aesthetic interests coincided in
their concern with the problem of clear and efficient mass communi-

cation in the arts and in the world at large. Probably the best known of the three was the designer and architect Charles-Edouard Jeanneret (Le Corbusier); he was assisted by the painter (and future historian of cubism) Amédée Ozenfant and the dramatist and advertising specialist Paul Dermée. Le Corbusier's fascination with the power of advertising was such that he faked advertising copy in the journal as a self-promotion scheme, attempting to attract business for his fledgling design concern with ads suggesting that powerful industrialists had already served as patrons for his innovative architectural projects.[29]

L'Esprit nouveau appeared at irregular intervals between 1920 and 1925, serving as a forum for contemporary debate about a variety of issues. Of course, news and commentary on artistic movements received extensive coverage, and the journal's collaborators devoted a considerable amount of energy to analyzing and criticizing the aesthetic conceptions behind cubism, futurism, surrealism, expressionism, and suprematism. However, the journal's editors saw their primary task as the promotion of modernity in all its forms, and as a result, most issues were not narrowly focused on aesthetic problems. Instead, they contained articles on French politics and foreign policy, psychoanalysis, personal health, film, urban planning, literature, and economics. Le Corbusier's interest in urban planning and the design of objects for everyday use kept his contributions to the journal filled with examples from the worlds of science and industry, while Dermée's background in advertising, journalism, and the psychology of mass communications probably accounts for some of the journal's strength in politics, psychiatry, and literature.

Although advertising was never an object of explicit discussion in the journal, *L'Esprit nouveau* was closely tied to the interests and actors of the advertising profession from its inception because of the influence of Paul Dermée. Dermée was a professional journalist and *homme de lettres* who spent the years between 1920 and 1922 preparing a fascinating treatise on the psychology of advertising and poster design entitled *Les Affaires et l'affiche*. He was widely known in the advertising community as a regular contributor to *La Publicité*, where he published the series of articles that eventually made up his book, and the book itself appeared in the prestigious Chambonnaud series, which means that it was probably consulted by nearly everyone who attended business school or trained in commercial design during the interwar period. Dermée's influence is apparent in *L'Esprit nouveau* in the fact that early issues contained ads for *La Publicité* and its affiliated agency, the BTP, as well as advertisements for products that were being promoted by the BTP. However, it appears that neither Dermée nor anyone from the BTP had "editorial control" over the design of a substantial proportion of the ads that appeared in the first few issues, for many of them were technically weak according to the standards of the time and anything but indicative of the cutting-edge modernism of the advertising profession. The texts made no argument or were merely decorative and contained empty modifiers, while the graphics often lacked any unifying visual principle.

Consider, for example, a Nestlé ad that broke every rule of good advertising design. The ad read, "Une Place au foyer pour les produits Nestlé," and then simply listed the names of three products without providing any images that might indicate their possible uses around the house or provoke mimesis by suggesting the act of purchase. This particular ad also used several different typefaces that made it appear cluttered and visually confusing, two of the cardinal sins in advertising design. However, the BTP's ads were technically perfect and may well have been published in *L'Esprit nouveau* as a lesson in design from the world of industry. Their ad for Omega watches was contained in an oval traced by a heavy line that served to focus the attention of the viewer on the text and that also mirrored the form of the watch in the illustration. The typeface was bold and clearly legible, and the copy made real arguments for the purchase of a watch.[30]

Advertising was more than a physical presence in *L'Esprit nouveau*, for despite the journal's silence on matters directly concerning the production of advertisements, its pages were filled with discussions of the importance of design and packaging for the economy and for public morale. It featured essays on the psychology of communication in the arts that recall articles on effective image design in trade publications from the advertising world. The journal also contained a large number of articles regarding the mechanism of human perception and the need for a new "science of art." Its very first issue opened with a manifesto, "Le Programme de *l'Esprit nouveau*," which proposed that aesthetics be treated as a scientific discipline and suggested that the world of engineering might provide the most appropriate source for artistic ideas truly representative of the modern era. Moreover, in the lead article for this issue, Victor Basch, a professor of "Esthétique et Science de l'Art" at the Sorbonne, advocated a physiological view of aesthetic experience that bears a close resemblance to the work of advertising psychologists in its attempts to explain how images should influence their audience. Basch wrote that "the first task of the aesthetician is to study sensation . . . ; the first science allied with aesthetics is physiological psychology." In this account, then, aesthetics had become a matter for technical knowledge in much the same way as advertising. Basch went on to discuss the importance of understanding where form comes from in art, and argued that we neither *see* nor *recognize* form, but instead *create* it out of our tactile and motor sensations. "Thanks to years of hereditary experience," he said, "this creation takes place so rapidly that we no longer notice the act we perform and believe that we are seeing a form when in reality we are creating it. Beyond the study of direct sensation, then, modern aesthetics takes up the study of the *form* of sensations. Ultimately, all natural objects and all plastic creations . . . can be reduced to [formal] relationships, lines, and geometrical forms."[31]

Basch's search for a systematic and scientific view of aesthetics based on physiology was central to the project of the journal, and it informed both Le Corbusier's art and Dermée's work in advertising. Basch clearly believed that the success of visual communication was largely a function of form. His views are certainly related to earlier psychological views of the perceptual and suggestive process, for those who took up the problem, from Bernheim to Bergson, all described the impact of visual stimuli on the psyche in terms that referred back to the body. There is also some resemblance between their mechanistic interpretations of human automatism and Basch's reductionist view of visual communication. However, in their emphasis on form, Basch's remarks also represented a certain advance over previous theories of human perception because of their potential for practi-

cal application. In this account, visual information was organized and
processed through a grammar of abstract forms that correspond to
specific psychological states. If such a grammar could indeed be identified, it might then be possible to design images that had been engineered to produce specific and predictable emotional responses. In
some ways, Basch's scientific aesthetic was the dream of the advertising profession, for it provided anyone who wished to move or persuade a large, unfamiliar audience with a standardized and somewhat
instrumental conception of visual thinking.

Le Corbusier, Dermée, and other writers for *L'Esprit nouveau* certainly incorporated some of Basch's basic insights into their work for
the journal. They placed great emphasis on the mechanical nature of
perception, maintaining that the subject confronting images was
much more likely to respond automatically to them than to any other
form of artistic expression. This they saw as an advantage of images—
visual communication was truly modern because of its great potential
for efficiency. In an article where Le Corbusier attempted to summa-
rize the principles behind the aesthetic vision of *L'Esprit nouveau*, he
claimed that industrial activity must be the basis for artistic work of
every kind. He further developed this idea by arguing that "the elite
individuals who make up the world of industry and who thus live in
that virile atmosphere where beautiful objects are created imagine
themselves to be quite distant from [any engagement in] aesthetic activity. They are wrong to believe this, *for they are among the most active
creators of [a] contemporary aesthetic.*" He concluded by insisting upon
the central role of the industrial elite as the organizers who manage the
production of a distinctive modern style, and clearly indicating the
importance of the machine aesthetic for this elite: "The art of our age
is in its place when it addresses the elite. Art is not something for the
people, nor is it a common prostitute. Art is a necessary nourishment
for the elite, which must gather its thoughts in order to lead."[32]

Here, Le Corbusier introduced an intriguing complication into
Basch's formulation: the basic principle behind his aesthetic judgment
was that art acts on sensibility in a mechanical fashion. Consequently,
the world of mechanical systems and objects should have been its pri-

mary source for inspiration. Moreover, this mechanical aesthetic was determined by an elite for its own communicative purposes, and it served primarily as a means of preserving aesthetic order.

In a sense, Le Corbusier's version of the mechanical aesthetic functioned in much the same way as an advertising project. Aesthetic vision came from above and helped to further the directorial aims of an industrial elite which, incidentally, inhabited a sphere of virility. This aesthetic, in the form of design, advertising, or art, was then imposed on a feminized (and not simply feminine) public of consumers who were by definition incapable of making sense out of the world in anything but the most rudimentary and mechanical fashion and unfit to make aesthetic judgments for themselves. Le Corbusier's project, then, was to create art for an age of mass communications in which artistic production, like industrial production, must take into account the norms of standardized perception.

The articles published in *L'Esprit nouveau* between 1920 and 1925 attempted to redefine the goals of modernist art in French society by pursuing two distinct but related lines of inquiry. First, they hoped to reach some understanding of the mechanisms underlying suggestibility, aesthetic influence, and the formation of sensibility. The journal's collaborators approached this problem from a number of different perspectives, taking on tasks that ranged from outlining the physiological rudiments of the psychology of perception to speculating about the ways in which film might modernize the perceptual habits of the masses by training them to look at the world as a motion picture camera does. Their second project concerned the social and moral impact of visual communication and design in a modern industrialized nation. For Le Corbusier, as for his colleagues, industrial organization provided a kind of moral lesson for the arts. The factory was a model of order and efficiency in part because the demands of international markets had forced manufacturers to abandon their particularism and come to terms with the need for an international standard for communication, the norm. Its normalized methods of production held the promise of a future in which the national economy would flourish and standards of living would improve because of the expanded opportunities for international commerce. *L'Esprit nouveau* claimed that artists and designers should be similarly courageous in abandoning their own cultural particularism and adopting more universal and standardized techniques of aesthetic expression. Streamlined design took on a certain moral value as a kind of visual pedagogy for the masses. In Le Corbusier's vision, then, the visual renovation of postwar France became a *dirigiste* engineering project which demanded that artists become the technicians of visual communication, a goal which closely resembled the aims of their colleagues in advertising.

This new insistence that art and design were fundamentally technical pursuits resulted in a dramatic transformation of the aesthetic hierarchies inherited from the nineteenth century. If we return for a moment to Victor Basch's essay in the first issue, "L'Esthétique nouvelle et la science de l'art," the problems of establishing a new hierarchy immediately become evident. Basch hoped to sort out the various components of aesthetic experience and judgment, separating the act of judgment itself from the feelings that accompany it, the actual moment of perception, and the emotional associations that immediately attached themselves to that perception.[33] Although he defended personal association as a valuable part of aesthetic response, he also saw it as less essential than standard physiological reactions to images in understanding the way individuals respond to art. This attempt to downplay the role of personal sensibility as a key to understanding the process of aesthetic response and to de-emphasize individual variations in responses to images was typical of *L'Esprit nouveau*'s approach to the problem. Most often, contributors to the journal would adopt a normalizing view of aesthetic receptivity that focused on identifying standard responses to visual communications.

Also typical are Basch's scientific pretensions—he described his conception of aesthetics as "genetic" and even likened himself to Darwin, noting that his technique for the analysis of aesthetic sentiment "is concerned less with reducing the higher to the lower, than in ascending from the lower to the higher, stopping at each distinct step along the way. . . . Before examining the contribution of the so-called superior faculties to this process, and so as to study it more thoroughly and precisely, it is essential to begin with the so-called inferior faculties: sensations, the feeling of a sensation, the perception of elementary forms, without which the larger aesthetic phenomenon could never occur." Basch thus presented sensation and the initial associations attached to it as the lowest stages of perceptual development, while aesthetic judgment and criticism were the highest stages. In a sense, this schema fit nicely with Le Corbusier's view that art was primarily the concern of a masculine industrial elite, for it provided a convenient rationale for associating specific "levels" of perceptual and aesthetic capabilities to groups seen as biologically different—for example, as males and females or as a feminized public and a masculine elite. Basch concluded his article by calling for serious scientific experimentation in the field of aesthetics, since "contemporary aesthetics has at its disposal procedures for measuring the intensity of sensations and of elementary aesthetic sentiments."[34] He saw empirical measurements as the best way of determining the relative strength of perception, association, and judgment as factors that might contribute to the process of aesthetic reception.

Other contributors to *L'Esprit nouveau* were more than happy to accept the possibility that perception could only be understood when broken down into such components. For example, Le Corbusier himself and his coeditor, Amédée Ozenfant, collaborated on an essay which argued that the perceptual process could only be usefully understood once the associational components of perception had been separated out from the physiological act of perception itself. They argued that although association and judgment did contribute something that differentiates one individual's aesthetic responses from those of another, these differences were trivial. In "Sur la plastique," they wrote:

THE SAME FORMAL ELEMENTS TRIGGER THE SAME SUBJECTIVE REACTIONS: this is what makes the language of design universal, the language of a true work of art. . . .

Thus, since we are concerned with the primordial conditions of the *plastic*, it must be understood first of all that if the human value of a work lies in the subjective sensation that it sets off, what mediates between the creative imagination and other men is a system of visual massage:

PHYSICALLY, a painting is a clever massage device.[35]

Artistic communication emerged here as a process akin to physical manipulation with a mechanical device. Further on in the essay, Le Corbusier and Ozenfant criticized all previous aesthetic theories on the grounds that they had granted far too much importance to "the demands of individual sensibility" and not enough to the universal aesthetic principles and correspondences between form and response that make up the "language" of the plastic arts.

Universality comes up repeatedly in *L'Esprit nouveau* as one of the primary criteria for evaluating the aesthetic success of a work. Maurice Raynal, a poster artist and critic for the journal, introduced *universality* as a term of approbation in his review of a show of paintings by Le Corbusier and Ozenfant. He wrote that the particular merit of their work

> is to have insisted, in works of admirable purity, that these methods must be *universally* human above all else, and based not on human weakness (which we know in the form of sensitivity, affectation, preciosity, sensuality, licentiousness, and disordering of the senses) but on the purest strength . . . [that of] sensibility that does not allow itself to be encumbered by the cult of human imperfection.[36]

In this account, the purity of form in the paintings in question (which bear a certain resemblance to Malevich's early attempts to represent the essence of forms) lent them a certain moral superiority because their creators had managed to detach themselves from the decadent particularism of Romantic and Symbolist conceptions of the artist's psyche and attained to the expression of the universally human.

Universality appeared once again as a criterion for aesthetic (and commercial) excellence in discussions of the qualities that had made American and German films more successful than French films in the world market. In Louis Delluc's celebrated essay on the photogenic, Hollywood set design was praised for its neutrality and the relative austerity of its lines because these characteristics made the decor of American films more typical and more readily assimilated by a variety of different publics.[37] Similarly, the noted film critic Emile Vuillermoz suggested that German film companies had succeeded in conquering the French and even the American markets for film because of their studied attempts to eliminate all idiosyncratic elements in direction and acting from their films in order to achieve a more uniformly palatable cinematic product. Even the lovemaking in these films had a strangely universal character, according to Vuillermoz, because savvy heads of production recognized that

> audiences in different places have well-established prejudices that it is best not to disturb. The kisses, caresses, tender gestures and sentimental nuances of French lovers prove laughable or offensive to the Kansan, Japanese or Australian couples who contemplate their actions on the screen. German technicians have had the sense and the know-how to avoid this trap. Their interpretation of love is simple, healthy and universal. It would provoke no resistance, even from the cultures furthest removed from this norm, and can insinuate itself into every social milieu. German film has attempted to create an international visual language.[38]

Thus the act of love in the age of mechanical reproduction. The very romantic complexity and specificity (or so we suppose) of French love scenes made them culturally unsuitable for export and even vaguely unhygienic by comparison with German films. According to Vuillermoz, the only way for the French film industry to increase its market share was by learning to de-emphasize the detail and produce a more standardized and universally palatable version of romance.

Particularity and detail also came under attack in *L'Esprit nouveau* with the partial reprinting of Adolf Loos's seminal 1908 article, "Ornament and Crime." Loos argued that the urge to cover an object with ornamental details was a sign of a primitive or childlike mentality or even an inability to successfully contain (or sublimate) one's own erotic drives. "To the degree that the culture of a civilization has developed," said Loos, "ornament disappears from everyday objects."[39] The inclusion of Loos's piece in the second issue of the journal was a telling choice, for Loos made the same sort of economic argument against ornament in everyday objects and in works of art as Delluc, Vuillermoz, Le Corbusier, and Ozenfant. He claimed that the absence of ornament was closely tied to modernity and economic progress, since ornamental detail was no longer linked to culture or the condition in a necessary (he said "organic") way. Ornament, or excessive attention to nuance (as in the case of the French cinema), created an economic problem for two reasons: first, it required an unjustifiable expenditure of labor hours, tools, and materials that could be better put to use in more productive activity, and second, it resulted in products that were overly individualized and therefore unsuitable for too many markets. Gender distinctions also became an issue in Loos's critique of ornament, although they were not present in the essay as it appears in *L'Esprit nouveau*. In his essay "Ladies' Fashion" (1902), he associated ornamentation with a particular form of economic oppression, suggesting that women were forced to resort to deceitful uses of ornament because they had no economic power and needed to attract and keep a "big, strong man" in order to survive. In his view, ornament would disappear with the advent of economic independence for women, since "woman's value or lack of value will no longer fall or die according to the fluctuation of sensuality."[40]

This condemnation of ornamentation came out in a slightly different form in Le Corbusier's and Ozenfant's writings on the importance of universality in art, for they did not attribute the taste (or need) for ornament and individualistic detail exclusively to women. However, as their remarks cited earlier would indicate, they were sharply critical of what they would term aesthetic effeminacy, and they saw the salvation of visual culture in the masculine sphere of industry. In their writings, they established a systematic opposition between what they saw as the decadent and effeminate particularism that grew out of excessive attention to detail and the healthier masculine capacity for mastery and self-restraint in the use or appreciation of detail. In an essay denouncing the Prix de Rome, Le Corbusier concluded that detail posed a positive danger to the creative virility of young artists and designers. Those whose sensibilities were not yet fully formed were truly endangered by the seductive power of style, whether it emerged in the form of Baroque ornaments, a Romantic landscape, or "charming" ruins.[41] Ultimately, Le Corbusier and Ozenfant concurred with Loos's more general argument, for they believed that detail and ornament were most appealing to groups who were economically or aesthetically powerless, for example, as bad or unformed artists or the effeminate, kitsch-loving masses.

In their view, the visual habits of the masses were in desperate need of reform, and as a consequence they saw the social task of artists, architects, and designers as one of instruction and organization. The artist possessed of "l'esprit nouveau" would be a convinced modernist committed to the creation of a new visual language that communicated clearly and directly to the public, thereby training it to appreciate economical design.[42] In "La formation de l'optique moderne," Le Corbusier and Ozenfant suggested that urbanization and industrialization had already begun to generate a remedy for the disarray of contemporary visual culture. The development of modern industrial society had changed the way individuals looked at the objects that surrounded them in everyday life and the ways in which they might respond to the various visual stimuli they encountered in the course of their daily activities. For one thing, modern cities had produced an entire generation whose basic visual points of reference all came from industry. This was not to say that modern viewers had consciously adopted an "industrial aesthetic" of the sort we know today. Rather, *L'Esprit nouveau*'s editors argued that industry had begun to provide the forms, colors, and rhythms that constituted the visually "natural" for city dwellers. As the authors put it, "The changes in the external aspects of our existence have had a profound effect by expanding [the average urbanite's] capacity to assimilate information, and his tolerance for spectacles unknown in earlier times (frequent images, new series of colors presented in new relations to one another as the result of the invention of violent chemical shades, etc.). This is true for the education of the eye as well as the ear."[43]

Le Corbusier and Ozenfant further claimed that the influence of factory-produced streamlined shapes, rapid repetitive motions, chemically synthesized colors, and color combinations not to be found in nature had altered modern perception by combining with the mind's innate love of geometry to produce a new set of visual expectations and desires. In their view, geometry was deeply seductive:

> stores in rows, one after another, impose upon us the endless creations of modern industry. Each object possesses an imperative precision, the inevitable consequence of *machinisme*: articles of every kind are presented in impeccable order; here, geometry brings its seductive power to commerce. Even fruits and vegetables, chickens and whole lambs are organ-

ized into perfect pyramids and friezes. Order and organization are so convincing that they excite our appetite: the produce and animal carcasses that made such a pathetic and deathly still life in the disorder of the village shop windows incite us to joy when we see them in concerted order: [this is the] power of geometry.[44]

The most striking thing about this passage is the consistent linkage of commercial excitement with restraint, authority, and order. The stores themselves were arranged in a strict order, and their displays *"impose[d]* upon us the endless creations of modern industry" rather than offering them or presenting them in a more neutral fashion. The influence of industry made precision "imperative" in the presentation of commodities, and Le Corbusier and Ozenfant described this new commercial precision as a "fatal consequence of *machinisme*."

Perhaps the strangest thing about this passage, though, was the discussion it contained of consumer desire. Le Corbusier and Ozenfant treated consumer appetites as though they were subject to the dictates of order and geometry. By their reasoning, once commodities were displayed in accordance with the principles of the new industrial aesthetic, the business of selling would become a rational and predictable process. Well-trained consumers would succumb to the appeal of order, rather than to irrational and unpredictable desires. This rationalist fantasy of predictable desire echoed some of the fondest hopes of the advertising profession in the early 1920's. As we have seen, the advertising community at this time had turned to psychology in the hope of discovering reliable techniques for arousing and containing consumer desire. The dream of a suggestive technique that produced predictable results was in part motivated by a hope that advertising might eventually lessen the impact of economic fluctuations by steadying demand and making it more reliable. A true science of advertising would allow manufacturers to stimulate or curb demand at will.[45] The negative image of this utopia of mass consumption would appear from time to time in the trade journals. *La Publicité*, for example, contained numerous accounts of consumer desire run amok—small business horror stories in which an ill-planned advertising campaign was too successful at the outset, and generated such an enormous popular demand for the product advertised that it outstripped the manufacturer's ability to produce. Uncontrolled consumer desire could easily lead to bankruptcy and ruin, especially when coupled with a poorly organized marketing infrastructure and unreliable distribution. Anxiety about the risks of expansion, then, drove ad men and their clients to hope that the scientific study of techniques in advertising and mass communication would provide them with greater protection against the risks of doing business.

For the editors of *L'Esprit nouveau* as for the advertising community, the best way to ensure that one's techniques for visual communication were thoroughly reliable and scientifically documented was to attempt to ground an aesthetic and a theory of communication in research in medicine, biology, and neurology. Le Corbusier and Ozenfant's use of medical terms to describe the pressing need for greater purity in the arts was not merely metaphorical. In their view, visual communication could best be understood as a physiological process. In "Esthétique et purisme," Le Corbusier and Ozenfant set forth several of the basic principles of their science of aesthetics. First, they argued that artistic practice should derive from what science would recognize as the most universal aspects of human response to visual stimuli. They also distinguished between primary (universal) responses to images and secondary (particularistic) responses, adding that the former were "practically identical since our senses are moved by identical agents," and that, while secondary responses do explain the differences in individuals' reactions to what they see, "the spectacle of simple geometry provides the most imperative direction for judgment because it provokes such a pure response." They concluded that before art can become perfectly communicative ("transmissible" in French), it must "make use of techniques based on geometry, means whose result is well-defined, for . . . the language adopted must be as universal as possible. Research has thus provided us with a kind of physiological language which allows us to trigger constant [predictable] physiological sensations in the spectator."[46]

Thus, Le Corbusier and Ozenfant believed that there was a fundamental language of physiological response to images which they proceeded to catalog: straight lines caused the eye to move continuously and produced a calming effect on the mind and body; broken or jagged lines forced the eye muscles to contract and relax repeatedly, causing changes in blood pressure and a sense of cadence; circles produced a continuous eye movement and were soothing, while curves provided an "unctuous massage." They also likened art to machinery, describing a painting as an "affect machine" (in French, "une machine à émouvoir").[47] For Le Corbusier, the Parthenon was another such machine, and he claimed that in our encounters with it, "We enter into the realm of implacable mechanism. There are no symbols attached to these forms; they provoke categorical sensations; we do not need a key to understand [them]."[48]

Later, in "La formation de l'optique moderne," they argued (as elsewhere) that a viewer's emotional response to a work was fundamentally conditioned by his or her physiological response to color, form, and line. "The emotion provoked by a work of art is powerful," they wrote, "because it results from a disturbance of our senses triggered by optical phenomena. No personal coefficients come into play, as in literature, for example."[49] The distinction they made here between literature and the visual arts is telling: images were presented as more effectively universal because they produced a direct and unmediated physiological response in a way that language could not. In the visual arts, there were no "personal coefficients" that needed to be factored out of the viewer's response. Images communicated more efficiently and with less obstruction than words ever could, especially if they had been constructed with some attention to the basic laws of optics. For Le Corbusier and Ozenfant, the truly modern image was one that possessed no style, an impersonal scientific production designed to evoke a specific set of responses. This echoed Bergson's description of the work of art, and it also bore a significant resemblance to the conception of the ideal advertisement that appeared in the writings of Paul Dermée, Louis Chambonnaud, Edith Weiler, and Jules Lallemand, among others. Moreover, once stylistic neutrality and the ability to evoke a specific response became the defining characteristics for modernist works in the visual arts, it became very difficult to distinguish between art and advertisements.

Paul Dermée's work on poster design in *Les Affaires et l'affiche* was based on many of the same principles of visual communication, for he took physiology just as seriously as his two coeditors on *L'Esprit nou-veau*. He began his examination of the way an ad draws the viewer's attention by describing Hugo Munsterberg's experiments on atten-tion. Munsterberg, the eminent German-born psychologist who taught at Harvard, found that when a subject is asked to look at some-thing for one second and then turn his head away, the eyes continue to look in the same direction even after the head has moved. Dermée concluded from this that the mechanisms controlling visual attention were not entirely the same as those that control intellectual attention. He then introduced Ribot's distinction between spontaneous and voluntary attention, claiming that both states had visual correlates with analogous characteristics. Like Edith Weiler and others, he thought that advertising should address itself only to the spontaneous gaze, the automatic, thoughtless, involuntary form of visual atten-tion.[50]

Dermée went on to argue that the best way to understand what the average viewer is likely to notice is by imagining the eye as a kind of photographic device. Normally, it becomes fixed on one central object but still picks up a fair amount of detail within a limited sur-rounding area. He quoted a treatise on the physiology of vision, Dr. Jean-Paul Nuel's *La vision* (Paris, 1904), to the effect that "our eye is such an imperfect instrument that I would refuse it if it were offered me by my instrument-maker." He further developed the comparison, noting that "from the outset, the decline in the clarity and sharpness of images occurs much more rapidly than with a camera."[51] For Dermée, then, the visual reception centers in the human brain were like inade-quate film that fails to properly preserve the impressions imprinted upon it of the outside world.

Dermée further suggested that spontaneous attention resembles both shock and monomania and that it produces a mental state in which the viewer's consciousness is dominated by emotion:

> The mechanism of spontaneous attention is a shock, an emotion (e.g., surprise), a halt in the stream of mental representations. Spontaneous at-tention presupposes sensation—and something more: a cause that pro-duces an arrest and a centering of consciousness, an alarm signal. . . . Spontaneous attention is an erection of consciousness that occurs fol-

lowing an extremely rapid perception which instantly freezes the consciousness or sets it boiling, either by *monoïdéisme* or by a flow of more or less numerous mental representations.[52]

Thus, Dermée followed Ribot very closely in his account of the way spontaneous attention brings the workings of the conscious mind to a standstill. His vocabulary in this passage even suggests that he saw some similarity between attention and other more purely physical forms of arousal. More generally, Dermée's discussion of perception and attention in his book on poster design indicates that he was committed to a mechanistic physiological model of visual communication.

Dermée's "scientific" logic informed his writings on aesthetics as well. In his first piece for *L'Esprit nouveau*, "La découverte du lyrisme," he wrote that the psychological discoveries of the last fifty years had helped bring to light "the mechanisms of judgment, sentiment, will, and desire," and he noted that "we could provide a fine defense and illustration of art by using the arguments furnished by science."[53] Dermée's writings on art and advertising reveal his interest in understanding the workings of the unconscious and putting his insights to use in the creation of images. However, his vision of the unconscious remained limited by his dependence on the models of the mind constructed by Bergson, Ribot, or Janet. In his view, aesthetic response was a form of automatism. In his essay on poetic inspiration (what he called *lyrisme*), he cited Pierre Janet, a psychologist who distinguished between the conscious self and "a set of autonomous secondary functions which occur in the absence of any conscious will," automatism, which was at the base of all creative and receptive activity in the arts.[54]

Dermée's interest in automatism and aesthetics allied him, at least to a certain extent, with the surrealists. One major part of Dermée's writing for *L'Esprit nouveau* was a series of articles in which he attempts to define an aesthetic of the surreal. He actually employed the word *surreal* well before the surrealists and became part of an artistic controversy in the mid-1920's by attacking André Breton for claiming the term as his own invention in his book *Manifeste du surréalisme* (1924). *L'Esprit nouveau* published a notice concurrently stating that "our collaborator recalled that he had defended the term 'surrealism,' created by Apollinaire, in the pages of our journal since 1920. . . . In addition, Paul Dermée insisted that the psychological theory of poetic inspiration that M. Breton presented as new was, in its basic argument, no different from the theory he expounded here in 1920 and 1921."[55] The notice also indicated that by 1925, Dermée had abandoned the term *surrealism* in favor of what he called "le panlyrisme," which emphasized automatism, unconscious mental processes, and irrational or spontaneous human behavior in much the same ways that surrealism did. Dermée certainly shared the surrealists' interest in the lyrical possibilities of everyday life. In his essay "Le panlyrisme," he described the enormous potential for surreal experience in day-to-day urban existence. "One can tease out [the lyrical aspect of everyday life] . . . even in the things that seem to be most contrary to lyricism," he said. "So it is that I can clearly perceive the lyric qualities of modern business."[56] For Dermée, then, even commercial activity participated in poetic logic.

Admittedly, Breton, Aragon, and other self-styled surrealists also saw modern commercial life as potentially poetic, but for distinctly different reasons. In Aragon's *Le paysan de Paris*, commerce was surreal because it filled the world with fragments of language addressed to no one in particular (and by implication, everyone) that can be torn out of their immediate context (a poster, a shop sign, an ad) and reframed or reused at will. Aragon took these tag ends of language as aleatory messages from the absolute. They were surreal because they were spontaneous, unexpected, unsolicited—the artist might simply come upon them and make use of them in the same way that (s)he might use material from a dream. In Dermée's account, by contrast, commercial activity was lyrical because of its organization, not because of its spontaneity or unpredictability. Commercial life was so thoroughly organized that it called forth automatic behavior in all the individuals who participated in it in much the same way that order produced stimulation among consumers in Le Corbusier's account of the perfect shop window display. For Dermée, the state of mental spontaneity resulted from the rigorous commercial organization in enterprises that functioned mechanically according to a set of predetermined rules.

This linkage of spontaneity and determination, or inspiration and organization, appeared at other moments in Dermée's writings on the lyrical. In an early essay on aesthetics, "Poésie = lyrisme + art," he wrote:

> Lyricism is a flux shaken from the deepest source of our conscious being; it is normal and occurs with varying frequency and strength in each of us. . . . Both its content and its form are rigorously determined: the waves formed from our subconscious creations flow along the stone banks constructed by automatism.[57]

In this passage, the automatic was figured as a kind of material obstacle to the unmediated expression of subconscious impulses and inspirations. Later in this essay, Dermée outlined a "mechanism of inspiration,"[58] which closely parallels the mechanism of perception he described elsewhere in *L'Esprit nouveau* and *Les Affaires et l'affiche*. Artistic inspiration, like most human perception, was largely a question of physiology and motor habits. As Dermée noted:

> The notions which emerge most clearly in our consciousness during aesthetic reflection on our works, those of others, or our ideas play a determining role in the efforts we will make at creating or changing a work. Because of their predominantly motor character, these ideas exert a deep influence upon us so that after a certain period of thought and testing, they become part of our automatic behavior. Henceforth, we observe a particular rule or follow a particular method as unconsciously and spontaneously as we . . . would spell.[59]

Aesthetic ideas were inescapably tied to motor functioning, activity, gesture, and repetition. Ideas that originated in a variety of outside sources would come to seem spontaneous and original only at the end of a complex process of learning and incorporation in which the execution of a certain technique became automatic, determined, and *therefore* spontaneous. Dermée was thus very close to Ozenfant and Le Corbusier in his account of the mechanism of perception. These passages also suggest that he was perfectly comfortable with the notion that the creative process itself could be explained by analogy with the functioning of a machine.

Ultimately, Dermée argued that the role of modern art was to play with the mechanism of perception in a way that undermined the domination of the rationally constituted self (the intelligence) in favor of automatic behavior. The relationship he posited between lyrical creativity and the liberation of subconscious forces was fairly standard in surrealist writings, but Dermée's account is worth examining in greater depth because of the ambiguity surrounding his conception of automatism and automatic behavior. In his writings, the automatic fluctuated in value between something close to Bergson's *élan vital*, the source of all creative activity, and a state that resembled hypnosis—a kind of defenseless suggestibility and receptivity to every kind of outside influence with no interference from the conscious mind (as in the description from his advertising manual of the automatism of an individual whose attention has been captured by a poster). Dermée's work on the relationship between automatism, suggestibility, and artistic inspiration also merits attention because it pushed at the boundaries between artistic activity and the realm of practical or commercial endeavor in a way that was entirely foreign to the surrealists, despite their interest in the world of the everyday.

The introduction of advertising posed a real cultural dilemma for the French, who hoped to prevent American-style commercialism from contaminating their public sphere and altering the basic character of French culture. The business community turned to French psychologists and philosophers for a scientific alternative to American techniques, and eventually developed a technique of mass communications based on the idea that human perception is fundamentally mechanical and that suggestion is most successful when it is aimed at the automatic components of human consciousness.

At the same time, certain avant-garde artists had begun to investigate the possibility that art, too, might become more scientific. Like advertisers, these artists drew on current psychological research in order to devise new methods of visual communication, so that by the mid-1920's, modernism and advertising substantially overlapped in their views on how best to reach a mass audience. Moreover, the artistic and commercial communities had been placed in greater contact with one another as the result of the burgeoning film industry and the new design concerns of industrial advertisers and department stores. Most traditional accounts of modernism have characterized the movement as one that remained distinct from and critical of the world of commerce. However, in interwar France, the theoretical and practical distinctions between art and advertising had become hopelessly blurred, to the point where artistic strategies for the presentation and representation of objects were nearly indistinguishable from commercial techniques of display and salesmanship. For all that modernist art and advertising differed in their ostensible aims, they shared in a single utopian project: both sought to rationalize mass visual communication, producing a newly objective form of artistic expression and a consistently persuasive style of commercial representation. At a time when mass politics was still an unpredictable novelty that threatened to turn the world of elite governance upside down, Le Corbusier's dream of aesthetic order replicated itself in mass culture and in the new science of communications that was advertising.

CHAPTER 2

Commercial Warfare and the Critique of the French Press

With the outbreak of war late in the summer of 1914, most professional activity in the world of advertising came grinding to a halt. The profession was hurt disproportionately by the war, for advertising tended to attract younger people, and many of the field's greatest innovators were men in their twenties and thirties who were called up to fight. Within months, most of the major trade journals had ceased publication altogether as their staff members were mobilized. Moreover, while the press continued to flourish during the war, fed by heightened public interest in the latest news developments and increased sales, ad placement stagnated. As French industry adjusted to the demands of wartime production and distribution and consumer buying power declined, industrialists began to look at advertising budgets as an obvious place to cut costs.

Despite the retrenchment imposed on the fledgling profession by the war, the period between 1914 and 1918 was profoundly formative for the advertising business in France, in large part as the result of government propaganda campaigns. In Germany, England, and the United States, advertisers were called upon to help create the images that were used to urge men to enlist and to encourage citizens to support the war effort with their savings. In France, however, almost no professional advertisers were engaged to create official propaganda during the war; instead, the War Ministry left the task to the government offices in charge of organizing the national bond drive. After the war, the poster campaign for the Emprunt National was widely ridiculed in the advertising trade press because of its reliance on outmoded images and design techniques. Advertising professionals openly criticized government propaganda officials for avoiding innovation and insisting on traditional techniques in such a strategically important area of the war effort.[1]

For advertisers and other progress-minded businessmen, the government's reluctance to employ modern communications techniques in building popular support for the war effort was emblematic of a much broader resistance to modernity both on the part of the French state and within French society more generally. However, this institutionalized resistance to modern mass communications helped to strengthen the advertising community's sense of itself as a natural ally for other advocates of industrial and commercial modernity and as a force for national economic renovation and reform. The sheer energy devoted to propaganda during the war made it amply clear to advertisers that the mass communications industry would have a crucial role to play in the postwar reconstruction of France.

Most recent discussions of the cultural impact of the First World War[2] have devoted considerable attention to the vexed relationship between the actual state of public opinion during the war and the various attempts of the belligerent governments to shape public sentiment, boosting domestic morale and disheartening their enemies through the strategic use of propaganda and disinformation. Paul Fussell, Jean-Jacques Becker, and others have suggested that while propaganda was effective and closely attuned to popular feeling in the early months of the war, it became less and less so as hostilities dragged on, until nationalist journalists and government propagandists found themselves failing to hold the line against the erosion of public confidence in the war effort. In France, by most accounts, the systematic suppression and distortion of information about the war, combined with the state's indiscriminate use of propaganda and censorship, only served to sharpen the French public's suspicions of official pronouncements and to create a generalized sense of public disillusionment with the government and with the press.

My contention in this chapter is that while wartime propaganda did produce some dramatic changes in the tone of French political debate and increase public mistrust of officialdom and the press, it did not lead the French into apathy or disillusionment with the current state and future prospects of their national press. In fact, one might argue that in France propaganda had a revitalizing effect, for it helped sensitize the French public to the power of the mass media and the dangers of journalistic misrepresentation. Moreover, it was instrumental in convincing the public at large that if republican political culture was to survive after the war, the press would have to be reformed. Ultimately, nationalist propaganda served as the impetus for a movement within the journalistic profession to eliminate fraudulent advertising, raise standards for truth in reporting, and reduce the influence of financial backers on the editorial policies of newspapers.

In the years between the founding of the Third Republic and the outbreak of the First World War, the major Parisian dailies (*Le Matin, Le Petit Parisien,* and *Le Journal,* among others) were often less than reliable as sources of accurate information, whether one consulted them for political and financial coverage or simply glanced at their advertising pages. Advertisements were particularly suspect because at the time there were no official regulations directed against fraudulent publicity. The landmark press law of 29 July 1881, which spelled out the limits to the freedoms of press, posting, and publishing guaranteed in the Constitution of 1875, never really addressed the issue of misrepresentation or fraud in the world of business. This was rather remarkable, for the law included a long list of political offenses for which a newspaper could be fined or indicted. Among them were inciting the public to commit crimes, whether or not any criminal act actually took place, attempting to dissuade members of the military from their duty, insulting the president of the Republic, the Republic itself, or its parliamentary institutions, insulting heads of state and their ambassadors, publishing seditious statements or false information that might disturb the peace, engaging in defamation or libel, and printing offensive material that constituted an "outrage aux bonnes moeurs."[3]

In short, the provisions of the 1881 press law suggest that while Third Republican legislators recognized the power of newspapers to create public opinion within the realm of politics, they were largely unconcerned with, and even unaware of, the role of the press either as a commercial entity or as a motivating force in financial activity and the creation of economic opinion. One result of this was that the advertising pages of French newspapers tended to be something of a school for scandal in the years before the war. Newspapers regularly carried advertisements for midwives and abortionists, despite legal prohibitions against them, and derived a significant proportion of their business from the inventors of patent medicines.

Other forms of fraud and illegality flourished in the pages of the dailies as well. For example, partial shares in lottery tickets were offered to gullible purchasers for unauthorized drawings that never took place. Worse yet, when drawings did occur, it would often emerge that the same shares had been sold to several people who all had equal and conflicting claims on the prize. Another popular gambit was to advertise high-paying unskilled employment. The prospective candidate would report to a given address, only to learn that signing up for work would involve an initial investment in tools or other equipment, such as a sewing machine, as well as a trial period of employment during which (s)he would be paid at a lower apprentice rate. Victims of this ploy would be offered the chance to purchase the necessary equipment on credit, paying it off as they worked their way through the apprenticeship. However, after a week or two, they would usually be let go on the grounds that their work was unsatisfactory. At this point, their erstwhile employers would present them with the options of either coming up with the balance of what they owed on the equipment they had agreed to purchase immediately or forfeiting their pay altogether. Thus newspapers were often the willing instruments and accomplices of small-time urban swindlers who attracted their victims through advertising.[4]

However, deceptive publicity was not always limited to the advertising sections of newspapers, for the boundaries between disinterested reporting and commercially subsidized copy were tremendously fluid in French daily papers at the turn of the century. In most newspapers, the graphic demarcations between publicity and editorial copy were clear enough, since standard layout at the turn of the century relegated advertising images and classified ads to the last page of the paper, a space referred to as "the wall," where advertisements were forced to compete for the attention of potential customers. However, despite the apparent segregation of commercial information from the literary or political content of the newspaper, there was a constant slippage in the pages of dailies between news reporting, features, and financial information and what newspaper editors called "la publicité rédactionnelle" (editorial advertising). This consisted of pieces written to order for commercial clients in which the product or establishment would be mentioned, briefly described, or discussed at length, depending on the amount paid by the client.

The presentation of these pieces varied according to the item or venue in question: pieces advertising a theatrical production would appear in the form of a society column and gradually evolve into an account of *mondain* enthusiasm for the play being promoted, while announcements for more common products such as shoe polish or cheap cologne would be couched within a *feuilletonesque* romantic intrigue. In a typical story, a young man meets a young woman who is drawn to him because of his scent or the shine on his shoes, and then the couple are separated by a series of colorful mishaps, only to find each other at the end because of the characteristic detail of personal hygiene that brought them together in the first place. These advertising messages would be more or less palatable as stories depending on the skill of the writers assigned to produce them, but no matter how transparently commercial they were, French newspapers were generally unwilling to acknowledge their promotional character and presented the articles as part of the publication's regular editorial content.[5]

Advertising affected daily news reporting and commentary in other ways. Many French newspapers derived large monthly incomes from "publicité à la muette" (silent advertising), an arrangement in which the papers received a regular payment for not mentioning a given product or its manufacturers or, more frequently, an investment scheme whose perpetrators hoped to keep potential investors as ill-informed as possible about their activities. Similar arrangements were sometimes made for straight publicity, for commercial advertisers were often willing to pay to keep advertisements from their competitors out of the large-circulation dailies where their own announcements appeared.

Probably the most insidious form of unacknowledged advertising, though, appeared in the financial pages of the major national papers. In the decades before the war, most of the investment information in newspapers came directly from interested sources. Banks, investment houses, and even foreign governments would issue financial reports designed to further their own commercial interests, and the newspapers would print them without labeling them as advertisements or providing any indication to their readers that the reports had not been compiled by their reporters or some other independent agency. In addition, newspapers and the wire service organizations that supplied them with dispatches frequently accepted large sums of money to adapt their national and international news coverage to the requirements of their financial advertisers.

In large part, such arrangements flourished thanks to the quasi-monopolistic structure of the French news industry. The majority of the transactions between the press and financial concerns took place through the mediation of the Agence Havas, an organization which managed the advertising concessions for most of the major French newspapers and ran one of the principal European wire services. The Agence Havas functioned as a source of both news and financial support for the press, contracting with newspapers to provide wire service copy and a guaranteed income from publicity in exchange for exclusive rights to the publication's advertising business. A typical Havas contract would guarantee to increase a newspaper's advertising business by a fixed percentage each year over a period of several years, thus increasing the publication's annual income and the value of its space to the agency.[6] One result of this policy was that the agency was often willing to make substantial loans to its more promising clients. These loans were designed to encourage increased circulation by enabling a newspaper to improve its content or appearance by expanding its news coverage or purchasing new printing equipment. However, they also served to make daily newspapers dependent upon the Havas organization to an extent which left them with little or no bargaining power in further contract negotiations and made it very difficult for them to oppose suggestions the agency might make regarding their editorial policies.

Havas was quick to realize the enormous power it had to influence the content of the French dailies it did business with, and soon used this influence to become an independent agent in the world of financial journalism. In 1889, the Agence embarked on one of its first forays into international investment, contracting directly with the Russian government to handle all the advertising for Russian securities in France over a period of several years. In a letter to the head of Nordbureau, the agency's largest competitor, Edouard Lebey, the director of Havas, wrote:

> The issuing of bonds is always preceded by an advertising campaign designed to call attention to the securities being offered and to highlight the advantages of investing . . .
>
> Since the Agence Havas has a contractual right to manage the publicity that appears in all French newspapers, both in Paris and the provinces, the task of organizing this advertising should naturally fall to it. . . .
>
> Given the importance of the French market to Russia, it is essential that the market be kept in a state of suspense, and that the French public become accustomed to the idea of Russian bonds. A bit of advertising a few weeks before the bonds are issued is not sufficient to accomplish that; instead, the press must constantly discuss Russia, its resources, its future and so forth.
>
> The Agence Havas can achieve this result not only through the use of its regular paid advertising, but also through its wire dispatches, which appear in all the newspapers and which, given current circumstances, could do a lot to promote understanding between France and Russia. In this way, political issues seem to be quite intimately linked to financial questions.[7]

Thus, between 1889 and 1905, the wire service branch of the Agence Havas became quite indistinguishable from the agency's advertising division whenever Russian politics or the state of the Russian economy was in question. Moreover, Havas was not alone in its attempts to manipulate the market. The close relationship between foreign news and domestic financial interests made it all too tempting for such widely read and well-respected publications as *Le Temps* and *Le Journal des débats* to use their international economic and diplomatic coverage as a seemingly respectable form of journalistic advertisement for Turkish and Russian bonds and shares in colonial joint stock companies.

By the time hostilities had broken out between Russia and Japan in 1904, the conflict of interest between news reporting and financial publicity had become so extreme that Havas and several large Parisian newspapers took to actively concealing information about the events in Russia in order to prevent French investors from pulling their funds out of Russian securities in a panic. The Havas wire service, for example, learned almost immediately once the war had been declared because of its close contact with the Quai d'Orsay, but it chose not to release this news until late in the afternoon, after the stock market had closed for the day. In fact, between February 1904 and November 1905, reports of impending Russian defeat and the crisis situation of the Russian economy were systematically discounted or downplayed in the French press, for Havas and a number of the larger daily papers (among them *Le Petit Journal, Le Figaro, Le Matin, Le Journal, Le Français, Le Petit Marseillais,* and *Le Progrès de Lyon*) were receiving money from a representative of the Russian government living in Paris, the economist Arthur Raffalovitch, and from French banks with investments in Russia to provide coverage of the events in Russia that would be as reassuring as possible to the public of investors.

Most often, the subsidies of the Russian government and French banks purchased silence. Thus, in November 1905, when the news of the sailors' uprising in Kronstadt and the strikes in St. Petersburg first began to break, Havas was paid to provide an unsensational and vaguely optimistic account of the events in its wire service bulletin. As Raffalovitch reported to his superiors, "Thanks to the costly arrangement reached with Havas many tendentious news releases have been [entirely] suppressed."[8] However, silence was not the only thing that could be bought from the French press. A long-standing agreement with *Le Matin* stipulated a level of cooperation that went well beyond paid silence, for as Raffalovitch noted in another report, "For this [unspecified] price, we have been promised six months of dependable cooperation. . . . [In the case of *Le Matin,*] this does not mean neutrality, but a reliable service which will consist of counteracting the currents [of popular opinion] and enlightening the public."[9]

The net effect of these complex and costly arrangements was that while the Agence Havas and its client newspapers did keep their readers abreast of the events in Russia, their incomplete financial analyses of the situation led a substantial number of small investors to underestimate the risks of purchasing and holding on to Russian and Turkish bonds. This was a serious matter, for French *rentiers* held a significant portion of state debt for both of these nations, and many private individuals' personal savings were eliminated or seriously diminished in part because of unscrupulous financial publicity.[10] Perhaps the most remarkable thing about the French system of financial advertising, though, was the tenacious grip it had on the press. Even in the wake of a major financial scandal, almost no one seriously entertained the possibility that the whole system of editorial publicity that had helped to precipitate the crisis was corrupt or in need of reform.

Smaller newspapers were dependent on the wire service information furnished by the Agence Havas, and even the largest papers were not always in stable enough financial condition to do without the steady advertising income guaranteed by Havas contracts. By the beginning of the twentieth century, then, much of the French press had evolved into a kind of information cartel centered around the Agence Havas, its affiliates, and a few successfully competing independent newspapers and smaller wire services which had adopted Havas's methods of doing business. Consequently, in the decade before the war, there was very little independence in the national press, tremendous uniformity in the provincial press, and almost no impetus for change or renovation of any aspect of the system. Newspaper editors were still largely unwilling to take responsibility for false advertising or to lose profitable financial publicity as a result of making overscrupulous distinctions between news reporting and advertisements.

In the years directly before the war, the newly formed corps of professional advertisers, which called itself the Chambre Syndicale de Publicité, was one of the only organizations to argue in favor of press reform. In the early 1900's, the modernizing wing of the French advertising profession, mainly young designers and copy writers who aspired to head their own agencies, felt that large-scale advertising had never really taken off in France, in part because commercial clients were not well served by the press. In their view, French newspapers had consistently been more concerned with wringing the last bit of short-term profit out of their advertising clients than with cultivating their business over the longer term. These young advertisers, then, who were grouped around the trade journals *La Publicité, Mon Bureau, Atlas,* and *La Publicité moderne,* hoped to transform the advertising industry, turning commercial publicity into a rational pursuit founded on scientific principles that was worth a substantial investment because it could guarantee results. Logically enough, they spoke up for reform because they feared that the dishonest practices that prevailed in the press had tarnished the reputation of publicity to a degree that made it increasingly difficult to persuade manufacturers, distributors, and other potential clients that advertising should become a regular part of their operating budget.

However, their proposals for change went largely unheeded by the press and those who managed its advertising. As late as 1910, the majority of newspaper owners and directors still balked at the prospect of agreeing on standard pricing of ad space; they even refused to allow a delegation from the central corporate organization to visit their establishments in order to determine accurate circulation figures. Similarly, the ad men's idea that magazines and newspapers should follow the American and British example by labeling ambiguously presented advertising material or instituting informal guidelines for truth in advertising was met with skepticism. In short, the efforts by advertising professionals to change the way the press handled publicity were so routinely unsuccessful that advertising remained entirely unregulated in France until after the war.

The fact that reform took place only after the First World War was not merely coincidental, for the war allowed the French to understand for the first time what was at stake for them as a nation in the organization of their information industry. Prior to 1914, the Agence Havas dominated the news and information business and set the terms for commercial and financial advertising contracts in a way that made it very easy for the press to resist pressures to abandon the old system and simply continue to cooperate with Havas instead. The agency existed as a kind of invisible monopoly, for although its presence as a controlling force in French journalism was very clear, it remained invisible in the sense that almost no one in the press seemed to recognize it as a dangerous impediment to journalistic freedom. Similarly, it was never clearly apparent to the press or to the French government until after the war that the centralized, monopolistic structure of the news and advertising business in France made it remarkably vulnerable to infiltration by foreign or domestic agents who sought to destabilize public opinion or manipulate the market. Thus, the experience of war and wartime journalism produced a shift in perceptions of the press that allowed both the French public and members of the press corps to view the structure of the newspaper industry in a new and more critical way.

Oddly enough, one of the principal catalysts for this shift in perceptions was the aggressive investigative (but more often accusational) style popularized by nationalist journalists writing during the war. The usual strategy in this kind of reporting was to create a sensation by investigating an apparently innocent commercial organization and eventually unmasking it as a front for German or Austrian espionage or as a center of enemy attempts to interfere with the French war effort. Admittedly, this kind of reporting did not originate with the war, for it had been a staple of right-wing journalism from the Dreyfus Affair onward, when Jews, rather than Germans and Austrians, were its principal targets. What did change after July 1914 was the audience for this kind of story, which had now broadened, in tandem with the increased circulation of *L'Action française,* to include most of the French reading public, regardless of the political views held by individual readers before the war.

In the books and articles on commercial conflict between France and Germany produced during the war, journalists harped on several basic themes as they uncovered ever more thrilling evidence of German commercial perfidy for their readers. These themes derived primarily from two classic prewar texts on the subject, Marcel Schwob's *Le danger allemand* (1896) and Léon Daudet's *L'avant-guerre, études et documents sur l'espionnage juif-allemand en France depuis l'affaire Dreyfus* (1913). Schwob's account is most remarkable for its insistence on the militaristic and conspiratorial aspects of German commercial and industrial organization. In a chapter on German advertising and marketing, he comments that unlike their French counterparts, German commercial representatives in foreign countries were a disciplined lot who generally possessed a strategic knowledge of the markets in which they operated. He also observes that they were expert at adapting their sales strategies to local customs, going out of their way to produce or procure the goods their customers wanted. Finally, he notes that unlike the noninterventionist French government, the German state had a coherent export policy backed up by competent commercial attachés at its embassies around the world. The conclusion he reaches as a result is not that France should begin to emulate Germany, but rather that German exporters have succeeded where the French failed because of their warlike approach to sales.[11]

Not surprisingly, then, Schwob viewed German marketing successes in France as a particularly insidious form of cultural aggression. This emerges most clearly in an anecdote he provides about the way German beer manufacturers advertise their products in France. Schwob's description of the German technique suggests that German commercial aggression could sometimes take the form of a cleverly planned assault on the French arts of living. The German strategy for deceiving the French public, he writes,

> is based on a system of large modern "brasseries." As soon as an attractive storefront or some other well-situated spot opens up on one of the boulevards, they take it over and set up a gorgeous tavern which, of course, sells nothing but their beer, with plenty of advertising. A café isn't a good enough place to sell this beer, it has to be a palace; nothing is expensive enough to introduce a German product. The gullible public sees the decor, admires and trusts its owners, drinks the liquid and naturally finds it superior because everyone there thinks it is. . . .
> If some enterprising café owner sets up his own luxurious establishment, the Germans will be there in a minute to make a deal with him. They will provide the beer at cost, or even at a loss, as long as he promises to serve only their products and advertise for them.
> The benefits here are quite apparent. Any sensible German knows that a beer served in a boulevard café is worth ten, twenty, even thirty sold in the provinces. He also knows that it will make a name for his product and create a taste for it.[12]

For Schwob then, not even something as distinctively Parisian as a boulevard cafe was safe from the machinations of German commercial imperialism. When Schwob's book first appeared, it was widely criticized for exaggerating the extent to which German products had infiltrated the French and foreign markets and for making German marketing activities appear as an organized threat to French commercial interests. However, once the war had started, Schwob's work was welcomed by economic commentators as a prescient account of Germany's commercial war aims.

Léon Daudet's *L'avant-guerre*, the second journalistic classic on Franco-German economic competition, also made much of the systematic and conspiratorial quality of German business schemes in France. As a longtime collaborator of *L'Action française*, Daudet was expert in the genre of conspiracy tales, and *L'avant-guerre* served as a kind of prototype for the paranoid narratives of wartime. It provided a wealth of detailed information on a variety of German enterprises in France and engaged in a series of anxious speculations about their strategic importance for Germany's commercial war with France, describing, among other things, a messenger service which concealed a spy ring, a mining concern in Brittany which threatened to rob France of precious mineral resources, and an electrical manufacturing concern, the Allgemeine Electricitäts Gesellschaft (known in France as the Société Française d'Electricité AEG), whose aim, according to Daudet, was to dominate the French market and make France dependent on German electrical products.[13]

However, for Daudet and many of his successors, the most insidious form of German activity in France involved the gathering of commercial information. *L'avant-guerre* begins with a discussion of the Agence Schimmelpfeng, a German concern which supplied its clients with credit information about French businesses and businessmen, as well as details about the organization of a given business, who worked there, what was produced and how, how much was sold and to whom, the financial situation of the company, and so on.[14] Daudet found the activities of the Agence Schimmelpfeng particularly disturbing because the German agency was in control of a large body of commercial data that had become essential in day-to-day business activity. Even a major

French bank like the Société Générale depended on Schimmelpfeng for the credit information it needed to evaluate potential borrowers. In his view, this left the foreign enterprise with limitless opportunities to sabotage the regular conduct of business in France by generating and disseminating false information about French companies in need of money for expansion. The systematic, centralized character of the organization made him suspicious, too, for it suggested that the agency would be a ready source of up-to-date strategic information on key industrial and commercial targets in case of war.[15] The French state apparently shared Daudet's fears, for the Agence Schimmelpfeng was closed by government orders shortly after war was declared.[16]

Like Schwob's *Le danger allemand,* then, *L'avant-guerre* pointed to several crucial (and not always merely imagined) strengths of German commercial and industrial practice that would draw considerable attention from the French press and the French government during the war. First, unlike French manufacturing, German industrial production was organized into cartels, which allowed manufacturers of a given item to produce more efficiently and to market their goods according to a cooperative plan. Second, the Germans possessed a scientific understanding of advertising and marketing techniques that had so far eluded the French, and they were capable of making their products sell by addressing consumers where they were vulnerable and overwhelming them with publicity. Third, the Germans were expert at creating huge banks of commercial information, and they had learned to make themselves indispensable in France, Italy, Switzerland, and elsewhere in Europe as the sources of sensitive information about the solvency and creditworthiness of private companies. This latter attribute was particularly threatening to the French, for it left the Germans in control of French businesses' access to credit, even from French banks. Finally, because of German state support for commercial development, Germany appeared to the noninterventionist French as a nation permanently mobilized to wreak economic havoc on the rest of the world, even in times of peace.

Thus, when the economist Henri Hauser set out to compare the state of economic affairs in France with those in Germany after a year of war, the account he produced, *Les méthodes allemandes d'expansion économique* (1916), fell squarely into the pattern of analysis outlined by

Schwob and Daudet. He begins his essay on German commercial techniques with a discussion of cartels, which he compares with trusts, noting that "while the trust is the absorption of a whole series of enterprises by the strongest undertaking, a brutal application of the struggle for existence, the cartel is a federative organization which allows the individual enterprises to exist. These enterprises . . . simply renounce a determined part of their industrial or commercial autonomy."[17] While cartels increase sales and marketing efficiency by making the sale of merchandise cooperative, they also engender a variety of regulations to ensure that all members of the cartel are in compliance with the group agreement. As a result, says Hauser, "there arises a complete system of surveillance which we in France would term inquisitorial, a whole army of inspectors . . . who act independently of and by the side of State inspectors, who arrive unexpectedly, who verify everything, the books, correspondence, warehouses. 'The manufacturer is no longer his own master,' and the secrecy of business vanishes."[18] One of the central reasons for the success of German commerce, then, lies in the willingness of German industrialists to submit to the discipline of the state and a collective organization, and to surrender their power to act independently as though they had been quite literally conscripted to do battle in the service of the national economy.

Elsewhere, Hauser invokes the systematic character of German commercial activity as a way of explaining why the effects of its dumping have been so disastrous in France.

> German dumping is a coherent system. It first kills the preparative industries in the country in which it installs itself. Thanks to the system of bonuses, it can then challenge the transformation industries.
>
> German industry thus shatters all the forces which can compete with it, in such a way as to reign over the ruins. Once again, German dumping is not a procedure of economic action; it is, in times of unclouded peace and under deceptively peaceful aspects, a measure of war. It carries agitation into the internal life of the competitors of Germany, it puts out of tune the normal play of their Customs system; it absolutely falsifies every formula of commercial liberty, of equality of treatment, or of reciprocity inscribed in treaties.[19]

The dumping of unwanted merchandise onto the French market, then, is warlike and outside the realm of ordinary economic actions inasmuch as it is organized, strategically planned so as to eliminate domestic competitors, and then carried out in concert by a united front of German manufacturers.

For Hauser, monopolistic organization and concerted action are consistently the factors that can explain German success. In his account, the Germans are able to pinpoint key French industries as targets for destruction because of their impressive centralized system of commercial and industrial information. Worse still, they are able to pass off their products on unsuspecting French consumers because of their command of scientific advertising techniques, their expertise in disguising their merchandise as the local product, and their extensive network of connections to the press through international advertising placement organizations.[20] Ultimately, Hauser argues that German commerce has evolved into a belligerent power almost in its own right and that France would do well to begin designing a defensive strategy for the economic battle that would only continue once an armistice had been signed.

> The economic battle rages every day. Every day the General Staff of the banks, cartels, and shipping companies elaborates its plans of conquest, and with marvellous flexibility adapts them to circumstances. The execution on this ground immediately follows the strategic conception. Espionage, which in matters military is only a preparation for war, is already in matters economic a form of conquest. Not content with besieging, with attempting to surmount the frontiers of the enemy, German industry plants itself, during open peace, in the very heart of the countries which she wishes to enslave, in the positions whose importance the economic strategy has revealed to her.[21]

Hauser's book, which had already run into three editions by 1917, when it was translated into English, was one of the more moderate statements in a flood of popular books and articles on the subject of German commercial warfare and espionage which became available in the second and third years of the war. Other entries into the field, among them Norbert Lallié's *La guerre au commerce allemand, l'organisation allemande, et ses résultats* (1918), Daniel Bellet's *Le commerce allemand, apparences et réalités* (1916), and Marius Vachon's *La guerre artistique avec l'Allemagne* (1916), reproduced Daudet's discoveries regarding Schimmelpfeng, the mines in Brittany, and disguised German weapons production plants located in France, and added to the lore of commercial paranoia such remarkable (not to mention improbable) tales of espionage as the one appearing in Vachon's essay on Franco-German style wars. Vachon reported on German attempts to steal the latest French styles, describing a band of state-commissioned German photographers who would check into chic Parisian hotels and promptly begin photographing everything in sight, from chairs and lamps to china and tableware, only to return home as advisers to German industrialists who hoped to flood the world market with copies of French-designed household items.[22]

For the most part, these rapidly produced and repetitive accounts of German commercial aggression were simply examples of high-level wartime propaganda of the sort many readers had come to mistrust after a year or two of war. However, despite their exaggerations and their persistent paranoia, the anxieties they expressed about cartels and monopolistic organizations in Germany had begun to make the power and the vulnerability of monopolies in France much more apparent. In at least one instance, this newly heightened sensitivity to monopolies combined with the effects of incessant campaigns of state propaganda and foreign disinformation to focus critical attention on the structure of the French press itself. This critical transformation of nationalist paranoia began in a brief collection of articles entitled *Les capitalistes français contre la France,* written by a muckraking reporter for Clemenceau's *L'homme libre,* Eugène Letailleur, better known to his readers as Lysis.[23]

In an argument not unlike those of Daudet, Schwob, or even Hauser, Lysis claimed that France was losing out to Germany as a commercial power because French capital was inadequately organized to promote its national interests, much less to protect itself from the depredations of clever German financiers.[24] Moreover, the blame for this state of affairs fell neither to the French state nor to the capitalists themselves, who, from Lysis's perspective as a radical journalist, were no worse or less competent than capitalists anywhere else. Instead, the blame could be placed almost entirely on what Arthur Raffalovitch called "the abominable venality of the [French] press."[25] The press, Lysis complained, was entirely in the thrall of the French banks and had thus compromised the French economy by failing to report that, for years, the better part of French savings were flowing out of the country into Russian or Turkish bonds and German investment schemes instead of remaining in French banks to be lent out to French entrepreneurs.[26] Lysis's complaints about the irresponsibility of the French press and its willingness not to think too hard about the implications of its financial dealings developed into rather more trenchant criticism shortly thereafter, when Lysis discovered that the Agence Havas had signed a contract with a German advertising company which left it in control of the advertising for several major dailies in Paris and the provinces (among them *Le Matin, Le Petit Parisien, Le Petit Journal, L'Echo de Paris, La Dépêche de Toulouse, La France de Bordeaux,* and *Le Progrès de Lyon*) during the first two years of the war.[27]

The Agence Havas had, of course, signed the accords unwittingly, for it made the initial contact with the Société Générale d'Annonces, a Genevan affiliate of the Berlin advertising placement agency Haasenstein and Vogler, through its own British affiliate, John Jones and Company. Besides, the restrictions included in the agreement signed were standard for the period. Still, the terms of the agreement between the Agence Havas and the SGA/Haasenstein and Vogler were potentially damaging to French commerce because they gave the SGA exclusive control over the advertisements that could be placed in the newspapers whose advertising it managed, which meant that German products disguised as French, British, or Swiss commodities could receive preferential publicity in the French press. Moreover, they endangered the integrity of French news reporting, for the contract stipulated that the SGA reserved the right to forbid publication of any kind of news that might be prejudicial to the interests of its advertisers and to refuse ads from their competitors.[28]

The revelations by Lysis, first published in a series of articles during the winter and spring of 1916–17, produced an immediate effect, for the Société Générale d'Annonces was closed and its offices placed under government jurisdiction early in 1917. Moreover, Lysis's investigation into the real dangers posed both by the corrupt organization of the French press and its monopolistic structure was the catalyst for a round of serious efforts to reform the French press after the war. His critique of deceptive commercial practices also helped to lay the groundwork for a movement among advertisers and industrialists during the 1920's to eliminate fraudulent advertising, protect trademarks, and make it easier for consumers to distinguish between French and foreign products.[29]

Lysis himself continued his career as a political gadfly, founding his own reformist newspaper, *La Démocratie nouvelle,* which served as a platform for his ideas about how the republican political system might be reorganized and French financial practices reformed.[30] Lysis's deep mistrust of politicians and the French political system as a whole made him typical of postwar reformers on the left and right who sought to eliminate irrationality from the process of governance. His analysis of contemporary institutions focused on the corruption and cynicism of the press and the power-hungry maneuvering of those who ran what he called "l'industrie politicienne."[31] Although he had been a fierce opponent of censorship during the war, Lysis was also sharply critical of the laissez-faire liberalism that prevailed in newspaper publishing circles before the war. He believed that market manipulation, fraud, and unreliable financial bulletins had flourished precisely because the press was underregulated and because publishers had never been held sufficiently accountable by the state or a professional regulatory organization for the accuracy of the information they printed.

He charged the French press with pandering to the worst tastes of its public, and lowering the tone of public debate by attempting to entertain its readers rather than providing them with the information they needed to function in a democratic society. In his view, the way news was presented in the popular press was an enormous insult to the French population.

> It would seem that we think [the electorate] is incapable of understanding anything at all serious when in fact it is neither dull nor narrow-minded; this is clear to anyone who has tried to interest the public in the great problems that will determine the future of our country. These problems are not transcendental, particularly when they are not phrased in Latin: when translated into plain language, they engage our common

sense and can be understood by anyone, especially in France where the people are intelligent.[32]

For the future, he envisioned a press that would report in depth on issues of national significance and provide a critical perspective on the vagaries of Third Republican politics, rather than the merely interested viewpoints that had been the staple of prewar journalism.

For Lysis, the long-term effects of wartime censorship and unreliable reporting had combined to produce a full-scale crisis of the public sphere, which he conceived of as an issue of public hygiene, both literally and metaphorically. The French government, he complained, had demonstrated little or no respect for the liberty of the press during the war. It had also abdicated its responsibilities as a regulatory force, leaving newspaper publishers to abuse their freedom. Moreover, it had completely neglected what he saw as its duty to create the conditions that would foster a truly democratic public life. Among other things, Lysis believed that the government of the Third Republic had failed its citizens politically by neglecting to regulate alcohol consumption more carefully.

> We have universal suffrage, and here the people are sovereign. They direct our politics, yet we allow them to drink! There are nearly 500,000 places where liquor is served in France, while there were only 50,000 thirty years ago. In Paris there is a bar or a café for every four buildings on the average. In the poorer neighborhoods and near factories, there is often one bar or two for every building. This has a stupefying effect on the population and results in the derailment of social life. Sincerely, what good can come of elections, what can we expect from the people under these conditions?[33]

Worse yet were the intellectual contagions produced by the inaccurate and sensationalist reporting and the fraudulent advertising of a degenerate press. Following Gustave Le Bon (whom he greatly admired), Lysis argued that the health of the polity was genuinely endangered by the lack of objectivity or scruples that characterized the world of newspaper publishing.[34] He suggested that governmental authorities owed it to the public to regulate the press more carefully, fighting fraud and misrepresentation and loosening ties between newspapers and individual politicians as a measure of public hygiene.[35]

Lysis's *dirigiste* proposals for resolving the problem of the French public sphere were not at all uncommon among postwar reformers. Like many of his contemporaries, Lysis associated progress with the imposition of scientific rationality, and he shared with the advertising community (among others) the hope that the public life of postwar France might be reformed through the rational reorganization of the government and its functions as well as a more scientific approach to the management of public opinion.

In his 1917 manifesto, *Vers la démocratie nouvelle,* Lysis called for an end to the literary politics that had dominated parliamentary life in France during the Third Republic and under previous regimes. He maintained that under the current electoral system, it was next to impossible for the government to formulate sound economic and social policies because those with practical experience in science, industry, and finance would remain chronically underrepresented while members of the liberal professions and career politicians held the floor. Thus, Lysis proposed that the old electoral process be abandoned altogether in favor of a system organized on corporatist and productivist lines: all those who worked in a single industry, whether workers or management, would be grouped within a single voting unit and asked to select candidates who would represent their industry or profession. In this way, he gloated, "the number of lawyers, doctors, professors and journalists who are now our masters would be reduced from three hundred to thirteen, while the number of deputies representing agriculture, industry, commerce and transportation, owners and workers alike, would increase from one hundred and twenty to four hundred and fifty!"[36] From this perspective, the public sphere could only be reformed if the press were held to a higher standard of disinterestedness and politics were made "rational" through the election of legislators from the technical and productive sectors.

For Lysis and the numerous reformers and technocrats who would follow in his wake, one of the crucial lessons of the war was that France had been careless in safeguarding her own best economic and strategic interests because of a misguided faith in laissez-faire practices of governance. Although nationalist propaganda during the war was designed to ensure compliance, its tone of ever-suspicious investigation had, in at least one instance, proved enabling as the critical tool that helped to expose the corruption of the French press monopoly. Once the war was over, those who had deplored the failure of the press as a source of information and the incompetence of the wartime regime turned their reformist energies to the restructuring of the French economy and French political life. However, their zeal for social change was often accompanied by disdain for democratic forms of government, despite the concerns of Lysis and others who valued participatory politics. The final legacy of propaganda, at least at the level of journalistic debate, was a new politics of efficiency promoted by reformers of every ideological stripe, from socialist humanists and corporatist social Catholics to the technocratic engineers and planners of X-Crise and the Taylor-inspired Comité National de l'Organisation Française (CNOF).

Sadly, the practical results of Lysis's crusade in the realm of advertising placement and newspaper production were rather less impressive. In 1923, a consortium of advertising and newspaper publishers founded the Office de Justification des Tirages, an organization designed to provide neutral verification of the dailies' circulation figures and thus a more reliable estimate of their worth to potential advertisers. For the most part, though, French newspaper publishers were hesitant to consent to circulation audits, and the organization failed in 1939.

There were similar efforts by advertisers to clean up the pages of the French press. Octave-Jacques Gérin, director of *La Publicité*, attempted to promote American methods once again by encouraging French ad men and newspapers to adopt the American advertising profession's policy of truth in advertising by agreeing not to place or publish deceptive advertisements. Also in 1923, the Communist daily, *L'Humanité*, and the Radical newspapers *L'Oeuvre* and *Le Quotidien* launched a short-lived campaign to eliminate advertising passed off as news in the French financial press. Finally, with the arrival of the Cartel des Gauches to power in 1925, the minister of labor and hygiene, Justin Godard, made an abortive attempt to stamp out ads for patent medicines. However, most of these efforts were inconclusive, for the only initiative that resulted in a lasting institution was the journal *Vendre*'s effort to create a professional committee to judge the trustworthiness of ads placed by reputable agencies. An office for the verification of advertising claims came into being in 1935, and was succeeded after 1945 by an organization that still exists today, France's Bureau de Vérification de la Publicité.[37]

The "abominable venality of the French press," then, was just one of many obstacles to professional progress faced by the advertising community of the 1920's, and its relative failure to produce lasting institutional change speaks volumes about the resistance of the majority of advertisers and publishers to change of any sort.[38] However, the debate that grew up in the wake of the Havas scandal was one that would continue to resonate in the imagination of technocratic reformers like Lysis who were disillusioned with liberal politics and sought new solutions to France's problems.

The Culture of Business

In interwar France, advertising had a cultural significance that extended well beyond the commercial domain. While the plans of advertisers to increase productivity, reorganize distribution, and introduce mass marketing promised to revolutionize the French market for consumer goods, there was considerably more at stake than profitability in the growth of the advertising profession during the 1920's and 1930's. Advertising had come of age at a time when French elites in politics, business, and journalism had begun to rethink the relationship between culture, commerce, and government. Many among them cherished the hope that the rise of scientific techniques in business and industry, embodied by advertising and the new scientific management movement, would lead to the discovery of some ideologically neutral technique for resolving the social conflicts and political crises that had plagued the Third Republic. At the same time, they were deeply suspicious of the new methods and feared that advertising and scientific management were only the beginning of a wholesale dismantling of time-honored French cultural traditions.[1]

The history of modern advertising and that of scientific management techniques followed a roughly parallel course in the France of the 1920's and early 1930's. In the minds of their advocates, as in the eyes of the public, the two movements were all of a piece. Those who sought to introduce scientific methods in advertising were primarily technicians and industrialists who, like their counterparts in the scientific management movement, saw the streamlining of communications techniques as an essential part of a much larger project aimed at the development of a rationally ordered society.[2] For French social commentators and critics, then, and even for some of the business people who promoted them, modern advertising techniques amounted to a kind of Taylorization of the public sphere; they stood as a symbol of all that was most appealing and disturbing about modernity.

The spread of scientific techniques for communication in industry and the mass media raised a series of larger questions for the French about their identity as a nation and as a culture and about what modernization and rationalization might mean for French social traditions and standards of living. Despite a long history of technical innovation and engineering successes, despite a national educational system designed to encourage the development of scientific and technical prowess, the French were profoundly ambivalent about the potential impact of industrial modernity on their culture.

This ambivalence expressed itself in a constant demand for the integration of tradition and modernity. In order for modern innovations in publicity and management to win acceptance by small businessmen or the general public, they had to be camouflaged so as to appear commonsensical and in keeping with long-established commercial practices. As a result, it was not uncommon for a professional advertiser to present his or her ideas about advertising design and mass communications as an attempt to improve scientific methods (especially those based on foreign examples) by infusing them with traditional French business sense. The discourse and practices of industrial modernity often served, too, as a means for revitalizing older ideas about management and hierarchy without substantially changing them.

Richard Kuisel has argued that despite the enthusiasm for planning, renovation, and reorganization that swept France after the war, the planning movements of the 1920's and 1930's accomplished relatively little and served to mask economic stagnation. Ultimately, he dismisses them as another example of the French tendency simply to theorize about social change rather than taking more practical steps to make it happen.[3] However, one might also argue that this very tendency offers a key to understanding the ways in which the French attempted to come to terms with industrial modernity. For French social commentators, as for the more visionary members of the business community, business, culture, and the social order were all inextricably entwined. The debate over the dangers of scientific management or advertising techniques offers evidence that for modernizers and their antagonists, it was impossible to think about the reorganization of industrial life without considering its potential effects on French cultural traditions.

Several generations of economic historians have identified the French as a people whose culture made them resolutely opposed to modernization. While they did ultimately adopt modern techniques and strategies in industrial production, management, and communications, the impetus to modernize in France frequently grew out of its opposite: the wish to preserve what they idealized as "traditional" relations between the social classes and to protect the artisanal traditions of the past. Modernity was palatable only when it could be presented as a renovation of time-honored customs.

In the literature on European economic development since 1750, the French economy is most often represented as a truly anomalous case. The economic historians and development economists of the 1950's and early 1960's were generally at a loss when it came to France, for its history never quite fit any of the models they had developed to describe the various stages of economic growth in industrializing societies. In the light of Walter Rostow's schema, France presented a puzzle, for its economy never "took off" with the sudden spurt of manufacturing growth that he believed had characterized industrialization in late eighteenth-century Britain and late nineteenth-century Germany. Moreover, despite the relatively steady growth of the French economy and the strength of France as a military and diplomatic power in the nineteenth century, the French never managed to gain the upper hand in the economic struggles between the western industrial powers. Thus Alexander Gerschenkron dismissed the French economy as "backward," noting that the French had come late to industrialization and developed too slowly ever to overtake their main competitors. Even French entrepreneurial culture proved unsatisfactory to the new generation of economic historians, prompting David Landes to suggest that the French possessed none of the values and attitudes that predisposed a nation to commercial and industrial success.[4]

During the mid- and late 1960's, the French path to industrial modernity was rehabilitated slightly as economic historians refined their statistical techniques and economists grew less sanguine about the benefits of unrestricted industrial growth. In the late 1960's, both Rondo Cameron and François Crouzet suggested that while the French experience of gradual industrialization was atypical, it was certainly not a history of failed capitalism.[5] Crouzet believed that French economic history could provide an alternative model for economic growth that took place in a more measured and less socially disruptive fashion than what had occurred in late eighteenth-century Britain.[6] In a similar vein, Patrick O'Brien and Caglar Keyder claimed that when such factors as the quality of life and the culturally conditioned nature of economic expectations were taken into account, nineteenth-century France emerged as a more useful model for a kind of economic development that took into account human needs and values.[7] Most recently, Jean Bouvier, Patrick Fridenson, and others have attempted to argue that although various episodes in French economic history defy liberal expectations for rational economic behavior,[8] they also possess an economic and cultural rationality that demands explanation in less rigidly growth-oriented terms.

Regardless of the position one takes on the nature and significance of French economic development in the modern era, it is clear that cultural concerns have an effect on the forms that economic activity takes. Until quite recently, though, cultural treatments of economic development have mainly been used to explain economic failure and deviations from economically rational behavior. Only rarely, as in the work of O'Brien and Keyder, has culture been invoked as a means of broadening the spectrum of possibilities for "rational" economic and social decision making. David Landes's classic (and still influential) account of the peculiarities of French commercial culture is a case in point.

In the United States, Landes has been one of the most eloquent and influential exponents of the view that French cultural attitudes consistently contributed to the retardation of French economic growth throughout the nineteenth and twentieth centuries. He has argued that French businessmen were hindered in their attempts to compete economically by a guild mentality characteristic of the *ancien régime* and by an ingrained belief that a business of any size could be successfully managed in the same cautious manner one might adopt for a small family enterprise. For Landes, the conservatism of French businessmen posed serious obstacles to the commercial exploitation of technical innovations. It also emerged as an economic impediment in investment and long-term development strategies, for the French frequently displayed great unwillingness to take such risks as investing in new equipment, developing new products, or testing different production techniques. Moreover, their fears of specialization, economic interdependence, and long- or even short-term indebtedness made them vulnerable to the more audacious economic ploys of their German and Anglo-Saxon competitors.

His critical assessment of French economic culture encompasses not only entrepreneurship but also commercial practices and consumer attitudes. For example, in his essay on the economy of postwar France, he takes the French business community to task for its poor marketing strategies and its unwillingness to work at cultivating the domestic market. For the French merchant, he writes, "Each transaction is considered a unique opportunity to make money. Take while the taking is good. The customer is not there to be served, cultivated, courted, persuaded to buy what he needs, and even more, what he should need or does not need. He is there on his own initiative to satisfy self-felt wants and should pay for this satisfaction as dearly as possible. He is simply a walking purse." The notion of customer service is nonexistent in France, he claims, and "in case of dispute, the customer is always wrong."[9] However, he places some of the blame for the slow recovery of the French economy on the fact that the French are woefully inadequate as consumers. Among other things, they spend excessive amounts of money on domestic help, entertainment, vacations, and café life, and fail to understand the value of acquiring consumer durables. They are deeply resistant to installment buying and cannot learn to throw things away. "Indeed," Landes remarks, "the waste characteristic of American life is by French standards almost immoral. No Frenchman will ever understand how an American can trade in last year's car simply to have a later model."[10] The French are a people ill-equipped to confront the revolution in consumer durables; in short, they are a Keynesian nightmare.

For all that Landes's observations may describe commercial realities that have persisted late into the twentieth century, the larger conclusions he draws about the implications of French resistance to American-style industrial modernity are more problematic, especially when one considers the relative success of the French advertising business today or the triumphs of French transportation and communications engineering since the Second World War. Often, the seeming resistance of the French to modernity disguised an attempt to come to terms with the problems of mass production, mass communication, and mass society in ways that took into account conservative social and cultural values they nostalgically identified as traditional.

In his book on the Vichy regime, Robert O. Paxton has noted that traditionalist rhetoric often masked the government's determination to modernize the French economy and introduce the rule of the technocrat.[11] In fact, this strategy was not new to Vichy and had been in use within the French business community for most of the interwar period. Any perceived persistence of *ancien régime* practices in the France of the 1920's and 1930's was only apparent and never real. Both the battles that accompanied the introduction of Taylorism and the debate that raged over the threat of Americanization demonstrate that traditionalist and preservationist rhetoric generally served to cloak modernist designs. Time and time again, the French would reject foreign conceptions of modernity only to welcome them once they had been revised into a form more compatible with French culture.

For the businessmen, politicians, and social commentators in interwar France who took up the subject of the American economy, the United States was an object of tremendous envy and admiration, at least in certain respects. Until the Great Depression and even well into the 1930's, as France began to experience its own difficulties with stagnating wages and prices, the United States appeared in French accounts as a laboratory for social and economic experimentation and a model of modern economic organization. Americans were deemed to be expert at finding new ways to improve the equilibrium between production and distribution, increase organizational efficiency, stimulate consumer desire, and spur economic growth. However, when it came to applying American methods at home, the French tended to regard *américanisme* with a more jaundiced eye. In most French accounts, the United States emerged as a dystopia of mechanical standardization and cultural homogeneity in which the various European nationalities that composed its population were denatured and culturally neutralized by the demands of their lives as workers and consumers.

One common criticism of the American system, which surfaced in the writings of Catholic moralists and socialist reformers alike, was that the efforts of American industrialists to increase productivity and promote greater consumption had made soulless materialists of the American population. Traditionalists claimed that Americans were people of shallow culture who lacked taste and were easily fascinated by gimmicks, gadgets, and glittery spectacles, while socialist critics complained that high standards of living among American workers had made them into willing accomplices of the capitalist system. Worse still, Americans were thought to have lost much of their individuality as a result of strongly assimilationist pressures in everyday life, the introduction of scientific management techniques in the workplace, and the increasing standardization of consumer goods.

One of the most insistent and influential popularizers of these views in France was the novelist and journalist Georges Duhamel. One of his best-known works, *Scènes de la vie future,* details his experiences during his extensive travels through the industrial centers of the Northeast and the Midwest. For Duhamel, social activity in the United States is so well organized that its human vitality has been lost altogether. "Between myself and the citizens of America lies a monstrous phantom barrier made of laws, institutions, prejudices and myths, a social apparatus without equal in the world and incomparable in history. Rather than a people, I see a system. Men . . . here appear to me as pure ideograms, signs of an abstract, algebraic and yet fantastic civilization."[12] This account of the abstract, almost symbolic character of American public life situates

Duhamel within a long French (and western) tradition of touristic an-
thropology in which the foreignness of an indigenous population's behavior is generally marked by its formulaic, mechanical, or overly conventional quality. It also suggests that Americans, whose social system
here takes on mythic proportions, are somehow not altogether human,
at least in the French sense.

Duhamel's anxieties about the standardized rituals of American life
bespeak more specific fears about the potential dangers inherent in
American scientific and industrial practices. Perhaps the most telling example of this appears in an episode where Duhamel engages in a conversation with a fictional American scientist, Parker P. Pitkin, about
eugenics. Duhamel hints to Pitkin that given American scientific prowess, it ought to be possible to create a system for identifying the genetic
legacy of stored sperm. In this way, potential mothers could have their
choice of genetic "design features," rather as though they were making
decisions about the style and color of a deluxe automobile to be custom
manufactured in Detroit. He is enumerating the various male types that
might prove attractive to American women when Pitkin interrupts him:

> "Not too many types if you want to keep the price down," said
> Parker, suddenly growing serious.
> "Fine! Two types at most, like with apples and oranges. But for the
> sake of certain natural requirements, we still need to think about the deli-
> cate question of pleasure. Perhaps some clever mechanism . . ."
> "Oh," he said, "there's no problem if it's something mechanical!"
> And with that, he began to draw a sketch.[13]

Duhamel's fear, then, was that American technological know-how
would supplant French artistry in every sphere, replacing time-honored
productive (and in this case, reproductive) techniques with more mechanical procedures. However, the anecdote also served to reassure his
readers that while Americans were indeed expert at cost-cutting innovations and ingenious technical designs, not all aspects of everyday life
were suited to the triumph of American engineering. For the time being, anyway, Duhamel's French audience could rest secure in the
thought that, despite the inhuman modernity of American society, individuality and craftsmanship retained their status as cherished cultural

values in France and that they, the French, remained the undisputed masters of artisanal attention to detail.

Ultimately, concern for detail and particularity took on a certain moral quality in Duhamel's essay, for he was convinced that Americans had sacrificed their individuality for the sake of collective material success. He complained that American dress was overly standardized, diminishing the individuality of its wearers to such an extent that most American women appeared to him to have been mass-produced. The American woman, he reported, had become a commodity: "a modern goddess, reproduced by the millions through the efforts of a vigilant industry to be the pride and joy of the American [male] citizen."[14] He faulted Americans for leaving their most important personal and social decisions to experts, and found their faith in science to be naive and unquestioning. He was also dismayed by Americans' relative lack of concern for privacy and their failure to resist the intrusive counsel of an army of moralists, hygienists, and advertisers.[15]

Duhamel also felt that independent critical thinking in the United States had been deeply compromised by advertising, which he saw as the ultimate insult of American culture to the French sensibility. In his attack on publicity he resumed his high moral tone, claiming that advertising constitutes an inhuman assault on the senses and an affront to dignity. However, his frequent references to the crowdlike, whorish, and savage aspects of advertising suggest that, in his view, the aesthetic threat posed by American mass culture had a political dimension as well. In American cities, "Pleasures are offered to the public like the worst mercenary embrace, without requiring anything more of it than a vague and unbinding attachment. . . . Everything is arranged to prevent boredom above all else! There is no room for intelligent action, discussion, reaction, or participation of any sort."[16] In America, then, advertising, like prostitution, threatened to undermine civic virtue (and perhaps *virtus* as well) by encouraging passivity and obsession with the pursuit of pleasure.

Elsewhere, he interpreted brightly flashing signs as a typically American means of intimidating and indoctrinating the passerby. Similarly, the neon and blinking lights of Broadway indicated rampant aesthetic disorder, while the appallingly carnivalesque quality of the street scene suggested incipient social disorder as well. In fact, Duhamel's discussion of street advertising bears a close resemblance to the writings of Gustave Le Bon or Hippolyte Taine on crowd behavior. Its chaotic energy reminded him of an undisciplined popular movement, while its competitive display recalled the savagery of wild animals caught in the evolutionary struggle for survival:

> It's a charivari of light, a riot, a *mélée*. The triumph of discord and disorder. Discipline is minimal, barely enough for the raging mob. In the shadows, the only law is the survival of the fittest. [This is] the bush country, with all the accompanying savagery.[17]

Thus Duhamel discovered the Wild West in central Manhattan.

It would be easy to dismiss these reflections on the desperate state of American culture as little more than the irascible scribblings of a cranky Parisian native in temporary exile from his favorite café. However, numerous French politicians and businessmen in the years between the wars shared Duhamel's views on the social and cultural effects of American industrial progress, insisting that France could only progress by finding her own peculiarly French solution to the problem of industrial modernization. Moreover, anti-Americanism was not always the province of those who were opposed to modernity; often, the most virulent criticisms of the United States came from those who saw themselves as industrial and commercial innovators committed to reworking American techniques into forms suitable for European applications.

The advertising community was a perfect example of this, for French advertisers were engaged in a constant struggle to translate American techniques from one culture to another. This was not always simple, and in some cases it proved to be patently impossible, as in the case of the Middieshade suit campaign. In 1931, the Middieshade Suit Company began an advertising campaign in the United States for suits that were all of the same cut and color. Their advertisements emphasized the savings in production costs that could be achieved by eliminating different styles and a wide choice of fabrics, and argued that all men look their best in blue. While the stylistic appeal of the campaign is dubious, the suits were something of a marketing success during the Depression because they were relatively inexpensive and well made. However, French advertisers singled out the Middieshade campaign as a prime example of an American sales success that could never be duplicated in France. In *La Publicité,* Andre Sédillot commented that although the French believe that variations in cut, color, and fabric texture are all essential to the making of one's personal style, "it cannot be the same on the other side of the Atlantic, because factories have standardized the colors of suits whose cut already reveals their origin, which only accentuates the resemblances among them even more. . . . Americans look like a crowd of workers in their Sunday best."[18] He further noted that despite the influence of Anglo-American techniques on French commerce, the Middieshade campaign served as proof that the psychology of the American consuming public was completely different from that of French shoppers.

In the advertising journals of the late 1920's and early 1930's, references to the straightforward, unsophisticated tone of much American advertising abounded, as did paeans to the cultivation and discrimination of the French public. In the words of Marcel Hercat, newly named editor of *La Publicité,* "The refinement and restlessness of our ancient civilization unconsciously urge us to exercise our critical spirit . . . and demand more subtle, thoughtful techniques of persuasion."[19]

Paule de Gironde, an ad designer with Dam-Publicité and a columnist for the trade journal *Vendre,* seconded these opinions, noting that in the United States, ads were designed in accordance with corporate sales policies; they were meant to draw attention to themselves and be read, while the visual impression they created was of little importance. The American advertisement "does not need to be aesthetically pleasing, as it would in France, in order to be noticed." For an American reader today, it might seem obvious that successful advertising design aims to sell products and make money. However, such concerns were often foreign to the French advertising profession. Thus, when American ads came up for evaluation in the French trade press, they were routinely criticized for their unattractive commerciality, their obsessively detailed depiction of the objects they were meant to sell, and the standardized quality of their appeals to consumers. Worse yet, the French found that American advertisers lacked any sense of the differences between social classes.

American advertisements were addressed to a public that bore almost no similarity to its French counterpart, for Americans had no common cultural heritage, no ingrained sense of class distinctions, and no sense of what constituted truly elevated taste. In Mme. de Gironde's view, American ads were created for a poorly educated audience of *nouveaux riches* who were incapable of appreciating simplicity or stylization and who could only be reached through ads that featured realistic representation and kitschy wallowing in detail. Ads that, in France, would be most suitable for workers could also be used in the United States to appeal to those who were in charge of factories, because as she put it, "In America, everything is standard: people and things. Everything is standardized and according to formula: taste, habits, and sensibilities. This standardization is intentional, the result of thought and organization and is a source of pleasure for Americans, just as originality is a source of pride for us in France."[20]

These recurrent references to Americans as a standardized, undifferentiated, and eminently egalitarian mob, "a crowd of workers in their Sunday best," suggest that the threat posed by American methods of production and marketing was more than simply economic, for above all else, Americanization meant the end of what were generally viewed as "traditional" relations between the classes in French society. Jean Renoir's *La grande illusion* attests to the contemporary perception that aristocratic values were on the wane in France and that the manners of the prewar world were on the verge of disappearing altogether. In fact, in the years between the wars, the French had every reason to believe that their culture was about to be overtaken by the brave new world of the mass societies: America, the Soviet Union, and after 1933 Germany. International competition had forced the French to recognize their weakened position as an economic and military power, and increasingly businessmen, politicians, and cultural figures found themselves struggling to defend their cultural *patrimoine* by finding an alternative route to modernity that would preserve the values of an earlier age in both their liberal and pseudo-aristocratic variants.

Part of this task of defense involved identifying the contributions that French civilization could make in areas already claimed by more dynamic nations, such as industrial psychology and management technique. As Anson Rabinbach has shown,[21] the French had made a serious and distinctive contribution to the study of the human role within the automated factory. It differed on many counts with the work of American experts in the field of motion study precisely because of a conjuncture of scientific and political concerns specific to continental Europe, if not exclusively to France.

When the French translation of Frederick Winslow Taylor's *Principles of Scientific Management* first appeared in 1911, it was greeted with moderate enthusiasm by all interested sectors of French capitalism: industrialists, industrial scientists, and even the leaders of the Confédération Générale du Travail were eager to learn about this powerful American production technique. Taylorism would enable the French to reproduce the miracle of American productivity, with consequent rises in real wages, through means that could be more or less mechanically adopted in French enterprises. But the story of Taylor's reception in France is also a parable of the fraught relationship between Gallic capitalism and its apparently hegemonic and increasingly intrusive American version. Eventually, owners, technicians, and workers alike came to see in this foreign scheme of scientific management a threat to French efforts at achieving industrial prosperity without abandoning traditional social and cultural values.

By 1911, Taylor's writings were no longer a complete novelty to the engineers and other technical specialists within industry. Original versions of his technical papers[22] had been in circulation for several years, and since 1909 the French engineer Henri Le Châtelier had published translations of these and other works, as well as research notes on experiments in scientific management at home and abroad in his newly founded journal, the *Revue de métallurgie*. However, the publication of his major work in France coincided with a wave of excitement within the business and scientific communities over the potential of the latest American methods to rationalize French industry and improve its overall productivity.

Taylor's work on motion study promised to increase profitability for manufacturers by applying a series of relatively simple techniques designed to increase the productivity of individual workers. By studying and perfecting the movement patterns of workers on the job, Taylor hoped to establish normative procedures for different tasks and ensure that the energy expended as they were performed was not dissipated in unnecessary movements but always channeled to a productive end.

Initially at least, the great majority of French industrialists were hesitant to adopt Taylorist techniques in the factories they owned, for they were loath to relinquish control over any aspect of their businesses to experts whose consultations were likely to be expensive and of uncertain value. Perhaps even more significantly, though, many industrialists, already accustomed to more paternalistic relations in the workplace, were concerned that the introduction of scientific management techniques would erode their authority by making workers' performance on the job something that could be evaluated with reference to (relatively) neutral scientific standards rather than more personal judgments. In both respects, then, Taylorism encountered some of the same obstacles to full implementation that American advertising techniques did when they were first introduced in France.

Even so, Taylorism, like advertising, had a number of well-known and influential advocates in the years before the war. Often, these individuals had backgrounds in engineering, or they manufactured items (such as automobiles) that were dependent on cutting-edge technologies, and it may be that such factors made them especially receptive to schemes for rationalizing industry along purely scientific lines. Henri Le Châtelier, Taylor's translator and popularizer (to whom Emile Pouget referred as "Taylor's French Barnum"),[23] was widely recognized in both business and academic circles for his work in metallurgy and his path-breaking research on high-temperature measurement. Charles de Fréminville, another ardent promoter of Taylorism, worked as an engineer and technical director in the automobile industry and served for a time as the chief engineer of the Paris-Orléans Railway. Louis Renault took an immediate interest in Taylor's ideas and began to experiment with them as early as 1907, when he introduced a motion study expert into his automobile plant in order to evaluate the efficiency of current production techniques and to propose a new plan that would rationalize production. The Michelin brothers, André and Edouard, were also avid supporters of motion study and rationalization, and they made a concerted effort to implement Taylorist policies in their factories during the

First World War in order to increase their output of defense materials.[24]

Moreover, manufacturers were not the only members of the business community in France to be inspired by Taylor's writings. The Ravisse brothers, who edited *Mon Bureau*, were enthusiastic publicists on the subject of scientific management from the moment their journal was founded in 1909. In their view, the potential applications of scientific management in the world of business were endless, for Taylor's ideas about reducing mechanical tasks to their simplest components and establishing the "one best way" for efficiently performing those tasks could readily be put to use in any kind of industrial or commercial enterprise, from a factory or a workshop to a store or an office. Thus they presented their own advice about rational office management, orderly systems for filing business documents, and techniques for exacting optimal levels of productivity from one's office staff as a kind of Taylorization of the white-collar workplace.

In the French context, Taylorism was so closely tied to the project of rationalization *à l'américaine* that one enterprising advertising agency tried to capitalize on the association by comparing its services to those of a Taylorite consultant imported from the United States. The agency, run by the founder of *La Publicité*, Octave-Jacques Gérin, published an announcement of its services featuring twin photographs of Gérin and Taylor. It read:

> Taylorize your sales. Thanks to the rational organization of labor, Taylor has managed to increase the productivity of manual laborers by a ratio of 3:1. As you know, advertising is to sales what labor is to production, and Gérin is, in France, a specialist in the organization of advertising, just as Taylor, in the United States, is the great organizer of factories.[25]

Presumably, by invoking Taylor's successes in American industry, Gérin hoped to suggest that a professional ad agency in France, inspired by American techniques, would be able to rationalize the unpredictable business of advertising and sales, rendering it efficient by introducing systematic techniques for presenting new products to the French public. The ad provides some evidence, too, of the widespread hope among businessmen and technicians before the war that in the new era of industrial efficiency, all aspects of productive life could be made more rational.

Finally, the announcement hints at the possibility that the process of communication itself might be Taylorized, stripped to its essentials and carried out in as streamlined and effective a manner as possible.

Initially, the response of labor to scientific management closely resembled that of engineers, industrialists, and advertisers. In the years before the war, and even well into the 1920's, many labor organizers were quite sanguine about Taylorism, for they saw in it the prospect of better working conditions, increased earning power for workers, and expanded availability of consumer goods. CGT representative Hyacinthe Dubreuil claimed that workers generally approached the subject of scientific management without prejudice, for they were able to recognize how Taylor's methods might advance their own economic interests. "With remarkable foresight," he wrote, "[some] declared that they would agree to the application of the system if they were assured that the general public would benefit by the reduction effected in the cost of production, explaining that they would be satisfied with the profits which would accrue to them in their capacity as consumers."[26]

In fact, early efforts to introduce scientific management techniques into French factories were relatively successful, for researchers often welcomed the input of employees. The fatigue researchers Jean-Marie Lahy and Armand Imbert both believed that workers should play a role in determining how rationalization would be put into practice on the job. Imbert even invited the CGT to participate in scientific debates about workplace safety.[27] At the outset, then, both Taylorite motion study experts and French fatigue researchers usually enjoyed the cooperation of factory workers in their experiments with new techniques for reducing fatigue and increasing output.

However, contemporary reports[28] suggest that despite the enthusiasm of labor organizers, workers tended to share their employers' reservations about the new methods, albeit for rather different reasons. For factory workers, the substitution of scientific management for paternalism could also mean the dehumanization of the workplace, the devaluation of craftsmanship, and the disruption of familiar daily routines. Despite labor's initial acceptance of Taylorism, the new methods grew increasingly unpopular once they were put into practice on a regular basis. By 1912, Renault employees demanded that the motion study experts who came to evaluate them be required to spend a full shift working at each job they were to study before they set new standards for the performance of workers. In the years directly before the war, then, Taylorism and motion study were routinely criticized for making factory work less remunerative and more exhausting, more mechanical and less creative. Emile Pouget, an anarcho-syndicalist leader who had written a book on industrial sabotage, argued in *L'organisation du surménage* (1913) that motion studies turned workers into machines by overemphasizing the value of strength and dexterity and diminishing the value of their intelligence and inventiveness. Similarly, in *La vie ouvrière*, Alphonse Merrheim complained that Taylorism reduced the worker to "an automaton ruled by the automatic movements of the machine" and contributed to the general de-skilling of the workforce.[29] Ultimately, French industrialists' experiments with motion study were brought to an abrupt halt in 1913 when workers at Renault, the Berliet truck factory in Lyon, the Compagnie Générale d'Electricité in Ivry, and (Établissements) Arbel in Douai struck against Taylorism on the grounds that the introduction of motion study had simply been a pretext for management to increase the workload without adequately compensating the workers for their increased levels of productivity.[30]

Taylor's theories received an equally mixed reception from French researchers who had studied movement and fatigue. Motion study and fatigue science had long been established as legitimate fields of inquiry in France, but for the most part, the French experts in these areas were marginal figures with relatively little influence within the business community. Thus, when Taylor's ideas first began to spread among industrialists, French scientists welcomed this development as an opportunity for them to gain increased recognition and support for their own work. There were enormous differences, however, between the basic theoretical grounding and underlying aims of French fatigue science and those of Taylorism. In his works on scientific management, Taylor had one essential goal: to increase the profitability of the manufacturing enterprises where he consulted by training their employees to perform their assigned tasks with greater economy of motion. Apart from that, he had relatively little to say about management issues, and he was not especially interested in workplace concerns not directly related to profits, such as the creation of healthy, safe working conditions or the reduction of conflicts between employers and employees.

By contrast, as Anson Rabinbach has argued,[31] Taylor's French counterparts were scientists with a utopian vision who saw work in a considerably less instrumental light than did Taylor and his disciples. French research on fatigue had grown out of Hermann von Helmholtz's writings from the 1850's and 1860's on the conservation of energy and corporal physics. Helmholtz suggested that all different forms of energy, whether human, animal, mechanical, or chemical, could be understood as equivalent. One immediate result of this was that European scientists abandoned the idea that human and animal movements were governed by laws peculiar to them as living beings, and they began to think about human exertion as another kind of mechanical problem susceptible to study as such.[32]

The spread of Helmholtz's ideas in France was largely due to Etienne-Jules Marey, a physiologist who pioneered the photographic (and cinematic) study of movement in France. Marey, who held a chair at the Collège de France from the 1860's until his death in 1904, was particularly fascinated by the problem of representing motion. He first gained notoriety by arguing against his colleague Claude Bernard that physiological processes could be understood in mechanical terms. "The animal organism," he wrote, "is no different from our machines except by its more advantageous efficiency."[33] This new view of the body made possible a more sophisticated understanding of muscles and the way they functioned, for once he began to consider the body in mechanistic terms, Marey soon recognized that muscles excelled in managing energy. Muscles could absorb, store, and release energy at varying rates and remain elastic in the face of shock, while machines were much less flexible when it came to using different kinds of energy and converting rapidly from one form to another. Marey's insights into the physiology of movement soon led to more detailed studies on the storage and conversion of energy in muscles and muscle fatigue.

Around the turn of the century, the Italian researcher Angelo Mosso of Turin began to study fatigue in the hope of demonstrating its objective existence as a physical and chemical phenomenon rather than as a mere subjective state. He took Marey's work one step further by designing the ergograph, a machine which allowed him to measure and record the decline in muscular force that occurs as a task is repeated and fatigue sets in. Ultimately Mosso and Marey paved the way for a generation of industrial researchers whose work on fatigue was less theoretical and more concerned with working conditions and the performance of actual tasks on the job. Their writings also affected contemporary debates about labor and the social question by recasting work as a physiological problem rather than a moral one. From the 1870's onward, it became increasingly common for scientists to stop insisting on the laziness and intractability of the working classes, and instead to see labor demands for shorter hours, more frequent breaks, and healthier working environments as expressions of real physical needs. The studies carried out by fatigue specialists at the turn of the century provided some legitimation for workers' complaints about factory conditions and suggested to both labor and management that their conflicts might be resolved by appeal to the relatively neutral standard of scientific evaluation.

By the time Taylorism was first introduced in France, then, the second generation of fatigue researchers in the French tradition had come to see their work as science with a social purpose. Ernest Solvay, a Belgian disciple of Marey and Mosso, founded an institute in Brussels that would be devoted to the development of scientific schemes for social improvement. Solvay hoped to unite physiology and psychology into a single program for increasing "social efficiency"[34] by bringing together Helmholtzian theory with Alfred Binet's work on attention and intellectual fatigue. In France, scientists were equally optimistic about the larger applicability of their work to social problems. Thus Jules Amar, an experimentalist noted for his work on respiration and fatigue, began to advocate shorter working days whose length would be determined so as to ensure optimal performance by workers of different ages, sexes, and physical capacities.[35] He and his colleagues Jean-Marie Lahy and Armand Imbert also supported the institution of regular rest breaks in factories at scientifically determined intervals.[36]

For the French research community, then, Taylor's approach to scientific management was anomalous and somewhat threatening with its insistence on profitability at all costs and its limited interest in the larger social implications of motion study. Not surprisingly, Taylor became the target for a series of sustained attacks as his ideas were implemented in the years directly before and during the First World War. He was frequently criticized by French scientists for focusing too narrowly on the specific parts of the body that performed a useful task and neglecting the overall effects of fatigue on the activity of his experimental subjects. Many French researchers complained, too, that his approach to motion study was unscientific. Their work on respiration and heart rates during physical and mental work was designed to address larger questions about the mechanism of fatigue, while Taylor approached his motion study projects like an engineer with a discrete problem to be solved. Finally, Taylor was faulted for having no coherent views on hierarchy, the exercise of authority, or the resolution of disputes between labor and management. His critics charged that he simply ignored such problems, assuming that they would disappear in the face of wage increases and the other material benefits attendant upon increased productivity.

Perhaps the most trenchant criticisms of the Taylor system in France came from two management experts, the fatigue scientist Jean-Marie Lahy and the mining engineer Henri Fayol, who were concerned by the lack of social vision in Taylor's work. In their respective writings on the subject, both Lahy and Fayol observed that, although Taylor had been tremendously innovative in his emphasis on the abilities and performance of individuals, this narrow analytic focus was also the source of his system's greatest weaknesses.

By concentrating exclusively on individual behavior, they claimed, Taylor had blinded himself to the various social factors that might contribute not only to optimal productivity but to the overall health of the economy and to the amelioration of social conditions. Lahy worried that this excessive individualism would lead to increasingly exploitative working conditions in factories, which would, in turn, make it even more difficult for exhausted workers to function as citizens under a democratic political regime. In a rather different vein, Fayol feared that by reorganizing the workplace in terms of functions rather than according to hierarchy, Taylorism would disrupt the paternalistic relations, deemed traditional, that obtained between workers and management in most medium-sized and even large enterprises. Despite their dissimilar views on the ultimate aims of social organization, though, Lahy and Fayol did share a common purpose in opposing Taylorism and American methods more generally. In their subsequent writings on scientific management, both men attempted to construct alternatives to Taylorism that incorporated rationalization techniques proven in the United States while reworking them so that they would mesh more precisely with French social institutions.

Jean-Marie Lahy, a physiologist and research supervisor in experimental psychology at the Ecole Pratique des Hautes Etudes, was probably Taylor's harshest French critic. As an affiliate of the Ecole Pratique and, later, the Institut Psychologique de l'Université de Paris, Lahy was part of an elite group of academic researchers whose work in applied psychology was supported by the French state. He was also well connected in business and industrial circles, however, and he spent significant amounts of time and energy attempting to facilitate contacts between the business and academic worlds and encouraging private sponsorship of research in applied psychology. From the mid-1920's onward he consulted with the Société des Transports en Commun de la Région Parisienne in order to create a battery of psychological tests for potential streetcar drivers and to establish a laboratory for psychological testing (under the administration of an in-house Service de Prophylaxie Mentale). As a researcher for the public transit company he was deeply concerned with safety issues and did extensive work on driver reaction times, night vision, and the conditions that make for optimum visibility. He also wrote numerous articles for business journals on scientific techniques for professional selection and founded his own journal of industrial psychology, *Le travail humain,* in 1933.

Lahy attacked the scientific management movement on the grounds that it treated workers as though their lives simply began and ended in the workplace without any significant social or intellectual components. In the years between the Renault strike and the outbreak of the First World War, Lahy wrote a series of articles on Taylor's methods for *La Revue socialiste, L'Action nationale,* and other publications that were finally collected in *Le système Taylor et la physiologie du travail professionel* (1916). Here he complained that in practice Taylorism was nothing more than "the net result of a system that has evolved to the point where nothing matters but productivity on the job. The American engineer has simplified the movements and work methods *not* to protect workers but only to ensure that everyone will overproduce."[37] For Lahy, a sensible and humane practitioner of scientific management would begin restructuring the workplace by considering the worker (especially the *male* worker) as a social individual with many responsibilities outside of the factory. In general, he noted, workers made their most important contributions to French society not as producers of goods in industry but in the various roles they played as parents, spouses, citizens, upholders of French standards of taste, or community leaders.[38]

Lahy began his essays by calling attention to the social costs of exploitative management, arguing that men cannot be expected to perform as though they were machines.

> Man differs from other living beings and that automatic entity which is the machine in the diversity of his mental imagery and his movements, and in the relationship he has established between his ideas and his actions in order to perfect the latter.
>
> However, once a man goes to work, his [mental] imagery and his movements are reduced to the necessities of his occupation; the field of his consciousness is restricted. The modern inclination to limit human activity in order to increase the precision of its movements leads to gains and losses. We must find the point of equilibrium between the excessive human automatism of modern labor and the lack of focus that results from too few constraints.[39]

In Lahy's view, then, truly scientific management would recognize human intellectual energy as a valuable social resource. While a disciple of Taylor might tend to discount the importance of workers' mental lives and seek to harness their mental and physical powers to productive ends alone, a properly trained psycho-physiologist would adopt a more utopian and technocratic approach, focusing instead on techniques for husbanding the energy of the working classes and apportioning it rationally amid the competing demands of work, the home, and public life. As Lahy concludes, "For the benefit of owners, workers, and the race, it is the duty of the psycho-physiologist to insist on human concerns in the scientific organization of labor."[40]

For all his cavils with the Taylor system, Lahy was willing to grant that the new method had certain advantages. Its success in the United States and the spectacle of American productivity in general had helped to frighten sluggish French capitalists into thinking more seriously about modernizing their production plants. The real problem lay in the fact that relatively few French industrialists had been willing to face the challenge of devising a plan for rationalizing their factories that was suited to the specific needs of their enterprise. Instead, they were content to adopt fashionable, ready-made American solutions to problems of management and motivation that were specifically French. In order to modernize the French economy, writes Lahy, "it would have meant hiring engineers and biologists, and helping them to achieve their goals effectively; it would have meant utterly transforming outdated methods, breaking with routine, investing capital, and in short, taking risks. But French industrialists are not eager to make such an effort. They have preferred to welcome innovations from the New World and to adjust them, for better or for worse, to things as they stand."[41]

From Marey and Frémont to Amar, Imbert, and Lahy, the indigenous tradition of fatigue science had proved itself more than equal to the task of renovating French industrial practices. French motion study experts and psycho-physiologists had invented new techniques for streamlining production and improving working conditions, and had devised strategies to ease the tensions between labor and management. Lahy believed that the greatest strengths of French fatigue science lay in its respect for the humanity of workers, its willingness to accommodate social demands, and its ability to rationalize tasks requiring complex skills and judgments. Ultimately, he blamed Taylorism for interfering with the development of French research programs in applied psychology. In his view, Taylor's methods offered an easy and somewhat formulaic remedy for industrial sluggishness that appealed to owners and managers of factories precisely because of its failings: its lack of concern for the safety, health, and well-being of workers and its single-minded, almost obsessive insistence on profitability.

However, the roots of Lahy's suspicions about Taylorism emerge most clearly in an essay that he published in 1911, *La morale de Jésus, sa part d'influence dans la morale actuelle.* Here, Lahy attempted to argue that the solution to contemporary social problems lay in the development and propagation of a scientific ethics. While he recognized that Christian teachings contain many valuable ethical insights, Lahy felt that Christianity had lost its validity as a basis for social solidarity. Despite its appeal as a complete system for understanding the world, its moral prescriptions no longer corresponded to the day-to-day reality of the average man or woman. He believed, for example, that in modern society the notion of community could only make sense when it was expressed in scientific terms. In a comparison of the Christian and modern worldviews, he wrote:

> Jesus believed that all men should love one another in God, for they were all brothers through the mythical parenthood of their heavenly Father. Our ideal of solidarity rests on different foundations. The positivist notions that have come to us from physiology, political economy, and so forth have changed this formula to the point where Christianity is no more than a symbol which evokes progressive ideas and emotions. This is why it persists, despite the decay of the religious system. If Jesus had possessed the science of a Karl Marx in addition to his emotional appeal, he might have ensured the continuation of his work by founding it on experiments rather than on vague beliefs. Even his dream of brotherly love cannot be superimposed on a society where solidarity is organized; only the poetic formulas remain, empty of any content.[42]

In contemporary France, then, the mythic community of believers could no longer serve as a point of reference for social judgments. Instead, social policy was to be formulated by experts on the basis of scientific demonstrations and hard evidence, and science would become the new religion of the people.

However, Lahy's hope for applied psychology and other social sciences in the French context was not that they evolve into a soulless technology for social management. Ideally, a French science of society would develop as a kind of updated religion that retained the social and spiritual vision of religious teachings while reworking them in materialist terms. Thus, when Lahy criticized Taylor, it was with his own utopian goals in mind. In his view, Taylor's work was less advanced than French fatigue science because he had failed to adequately conceptualize human activity in scientific terms and because Taylor resolutely refused the utopian possibilities of scientific management. For Lahy, then,

Taylor was at fault for attempting to establish a science of social management without taking into account the social and moral dimensions of work and leisure.

In many ways, Lahy's utopian vision made him a worthy successor to the Saint-Simonians and a precursor to the French technocrats of the late 1920's and 1930's, who hoped to end the political strife and social inequities of Third Republic France through the judicious application of science. While his early research focused on recognizing the physiological symptoms of mental and physical fatigue, much of Lahy's later work was devoted to identifying the emotional and neurological attributes that would best suit an individual to a particular career. In his ideal society, each person would be assigned the professional task that best corresponded to his or her neurophysiological constitution.

Lahy also shared with later technocratic planners a fascination with the problem of how information was disseminated in society. Throughout the interwar period, he was affiliated with various progressive groups that saw communications psychology as a key to social and economic progress. During the early 1920's, he maintained a loose tie with the group of artists, aesthetes, and technophiles who contributed to Le Corbusier's journal *L'Esprit nouveau* through his wife, Marie Lahy-Hollebecque, an educational psychologist who wrote literary criticism for the journal. He wrote the introduction for Paul Dermée and Eugène Courmont's influential book on advertising and psychology of perception, *Les affaires et l'affiche,* using it as an opportunity to call for increased support of French research in applied psychology. He was also a great advocate of scientific popularization, for he believed that if the public was kept informed of recent developments in the natural and social sciences and their relevance for the quality of life, a more scientific attitude would prevail among the population at large and social peace would ensue. Finally, in the 1930's, he was one of the founding members of Jean Coutrot's Centre d'Etudes des Problèmes Humains, a study group of technocratic humanists, largely from industry, who sought scientific solutions to contemporary social problems.

In some ways, Lahy's prewar critique of Taylorism was ahead of its times, for it raised concerns that would only be addressed seriously again in the late 1920's and early 1930's, after the second wave of enthusiasm for scientific management had died down. However, by the time Lahy's essays appeared in book form, in 1916, the situation in French factories was already quite different from the one Lahy had described. Despite the anti-Taylor strikes of 1912–13, French industrialists turned to Taylorism with renewed hope and enthusiasm once hostilities broke out between France and Germany in July 1914. The war years, then, represented a temporary interruption in French attempts to find a separate and culturally appropriate path to industrial modernity. For the time being, the pragmatic consensus among industrialists, management experts, and labor seemed to be that sectarian quarrels about competing management methods should be set aside while all interested parties joined in a kind of *union sacrée* to support the rapid implementation of Taylorism in French munitions factories.

Judith Merkle has argued that mass conscription and the conversion of major industrial plants for military purposes created the ideal circumstances for the adoption of Taylor's methods in France.[43] Before the war, the workshops in French factories had been dominated by highly skilled laborers who were accustomed to a great deal of autonomy in deciding how to do their job. As a rule, these workers were reluctant to allow motion study engineers to interfere with their work habits or to give their employers greater authority over them by relinquishing effective control over the technical information they needed to do their jobs.[44] Once mobilization began, however, these conditions changed dramatically. Industrialists were under greater pressure from the state to standardize their production techniques and reorganize their facilities for the manufacture of armaments. Moreover, their labor force had changed almost overnight, for their employees were now predominantly unskilled women with little or no heavy industrial experience. These new employees had fewer ingrained work habits to overcome, and perhaps as a consequence they were less resistant to the interventions of motion study engineers. Even so, most employers tended to describe their experiments with Taylor's theories with the more neutral term *scientific management,* shying away from any more overt mention of Taylorism for fear of offending their employees and reawakening collective memories of the anti-Taylor strikes in the years before the war.[45]

Still, Taylor's principles of functional organization offered a ready solution to the dilemma of restructuring production, while motion study made the job of training inexperienced workers manageable by simplifying tasks and spelling out every step of their execution. In one form or another, Taylorism affected nearly every aspect of French munitions production during the war, from the manufacture of gunpowder to shipbuilding, shell production, and the aircraft industry.[46] Ultimately, the state itself became an advocate of the Taylor system when Georges Clemenceau sent out a circular, dated February 26, 1918, that encouraged all armaments manufacturers to inform themselves about scientific management and established departments for the implementation of Taylorist planning in every factory that produced for the military.

Once the peace was restored, however, the debate over the use of American or more properly Latin methods in French factories started up again with renewed vigor. Just after the war, the mining engineer and organizational theorist Henri Fayol presented his work on public and private administration as a Gallic alternative to Taylorism.[47] Unlike many of the French fatigue scientists, whose background was in psychology, Fayol was initially trained in engineering and spent his entire career in industry, working as an engineer and manager for the Compagnie Commentry-Fourchambault et Décazeville, one of the largest coal mining enterprises in France. In his writings on administration, Fayol tended to deify management, likening corporate heads to heads of state and suggesting that French industry would be best off under the autocratic rule of a well-trained managerial *classe dirigeante*. His criticisms of Taylor were based less on the unscientific character of Taylor's ideas than on the differing social roles played by engineers and administrators in the United States and France.

As a theorist, Fayol was best known for a series of books and articles[48] in which he described the techniques he had used in his own company to increase the efficiency of his administrative staff and ease tensions between employees and management. In fact, Fayol's reputation as an administrative expert was based largely on his successes as the general manager of Commentry-Fourchambault between 1888 and 1918. When he took over, the mining company was in the midst of a financial crisis, but he found a way to make the business profitable once again. Over the next three decades, Fayol reorganized the company from the top down with special attention to administration and finances, leaving it in a strong financial position when he retired.

Unlike Taylor, whose management techniques might best be described as authoritarian, Fayol believed in what he would have described as paternalism—that is, the capacity of an enlightened capitalist class to build substantial profits, a healthy labor force, and a stable social order. He felt that every kind of business problem could be solved by reforming the attitudes and practices of management. His most influential work, *L'administration industrielle et générale* (1916), emphasized the importance of leadership in the creation of a disciplined working environment. Fayol observed that while most business leaders would agree that discipline was essential to the successful functioning of their enterprise, very few of them were able to think about discipline as anything other than a reflection of the moral qualities of their employees. His approach to the problem was to focus on the role of management in setting a moral tone for a business, commenting that discipline might best be defined as "what leaders produce."

Fayol was also a firm believer in the value of centralized leadership, and he used this belief to bolster his conviction that the success or failure of a business depended almost entirely on the strength of its management.

> Centralisation, like the division of labour, is one of the laws of nature; in every organism, whether it is animal or social, sensations converge towards the brain, or management, and from this brain, or management, are sent out the orders which set in motion all parts of the organism. Centralisation is not a system of administration, which . . . can be adopted or discarded at will; it is always present to some extent, so that the question of centralisation or decentralisation is simply one of degree.[49]

Thus, in Fayol's administrative science, the impulse to create centralized, hierarchical systems of social relations was construed as natural and somehow inevitable.

This view enabled Fayol to draw a clear distinction between his own methods and those of his American rival. Fayol's main quarrel with Taylor concerned one of the central innovations of scientific management, the concept of functional organization. In the functionally organized workshop, employees were supervised according to the kinds of tasks they performed, rather than by virtue of their place in a hierarchy. Under this system, it was more than likely that a single worker would receive instructions from two or more supervisors. In Fayol's opinion, this was a formula for low morale and disorganization, since employees would have no coherent sense of authority on the job. "I think it is dangerous," wrote Fayol, "to allow the idea to get about that the principle of unity of command is unimportant and can be violated with impunity. We ought to retain the old scheme of organisation, in which unity of command is respected, until a new order arises."[50] In other words, Taylorism would only work in France if the hierarchical nature of social relations were suddenly to change.

Although Fayol and Taylor did differ somewhat in their views on authority in the workplace, the allocation of specific tasks, and the importance of leadership, their systems were essentially complementary. Taylor focused on increased efficiency in the performance of specific tasks and measured the capacities of individual workers, while Fayol was much more concerned with rationalization on an elite level. However, Fayol had a real interest in presenting his work as a French alternative to Taylorism, and he went out of his way to create the impression that their ideas opposed one another. In conjunction with his own remarks on centralization, he quoted Taylor at length on the evils of "military" (i.e., hierarchical) organization so as to suggest a serious divergence in their views. In 1919, he also founded a competing institute for scientific management, the Centre d'études administratives, in order to promote his own organizational theories.

Fayol was also known as an advocate of more practical psychologically oriented training for future managers. He opposed the highly theoretical instruction in advanced mathematics that they received at the Ecole Polytechnique and the Ecole des Mines, complaining that the typical graduate of these prestigious state engineering schools was skilled only in solving technical problems and had no idea how to win the confidence and loyalty of the people he was called upon to lead and no sense of the psychological and social issues involved in working with employees. Fayol developed management training programs that became tremendously popular[51] and were employed by the state to train future businessmen, military officers, and state officials in a diverse array of institutions, among them the Ecole des Hautes Etudes Commerciales in Paris, the Ecole de Guerre, the Ecole de l'Intendance, and the Ecole du Commissariat de la Marine.

Fayol's popularity can partially be explained by the fact that he offered a version of scientific management that was readily assimilable by the French business community. The French generally preferred Fayol to Taylor and read him as an introduction to the subject because, as Paul Devinat put it in a report for the International Labor Office, Fayol's work was "easier to read and more attractively expounded from the point of view of the Latin mind."[52] Fayol spoke to French sensibilities precisely because he had succeeded in striking a balance between individualism and social concern in his account of the administrative function. By insisting on the crucial role of leaders in industry, Fayol restored to contemporary industrial managers some of the vanished romance of the nineteenth-century entrepreneur. The old-style capitalist, whose personal intervention influenced every aspect of his company's development, had gradually become outmoded in the face of modern management techniques. However, Fayol's paternalist administrators retained their power as individuals capable of making wise policy decisions, exerting a moral influence over their employees, and triumphing over economic obstacles of every kind by virtue of their personal qualities as leaders.[53] At the same time, though, his managers were expert technicians whose extensive training in applied psychology and organizational science allowed them to further both their social and commercial aims. Ultimately, Fayol's writings were more readily accepted in France than Taylor's because they made it possible to believe that administrative modernity was not incompatible with the continued existence of fundamentally corporatist relations between employers and employees.

Although Fayol strove to distinguish himself from his American counterpart, both Fayolistes and Taylorites shared common aims and worked in mutually reinforcing directions. After the war, Fayol used his Centre d'Etudes Administratives as a base from which to spread his ideas on scientific management beyond the business community and into the military and state bureaucracy. As a consultant, he presided over the reorganization of the French postal service and even proposed to rationalize the executive branch of French government with a plan for the establishment of an Office of the Prime Minister, which would coordinate the activities of various cabinet members in their respective ministries. Although Fayol presented his ideas on management as a set of theories both separate from and competitive with those of Taylor, one of the main effects of his work was to arouse the interest of industrialists and administrators in scientific management and lead them to read Taylor.

Given this state of affairs, it became increasingly difficult for Fayol and his followers to insist on the difference between their ideas and those of the more mainstream scientific management movement. Finally, at the third International Management Congress held in Brussels in 1925, Fayol gave a speech in which he claimed that, contrary to what many people believed, there was no real contradiction between his ideas and Taylor's, upon which Fayol's group merged with the French Taylorist society to form a new organization, the Comité de l'organisation française. However, despite the apparent institutional triumph of Taylorism, Fayol proved to be too powerful a presence to simply be subsumed into the canon of Taylorian doctrine.

Fayol's work on management, with its emphasis on hierarchy and leadership, was better suited to the kinds of workers and administrators already at work in French factories. In Taylor's scheme, the engineer was someone with a great deal of practical knowledge who had risen from the ranks and emerged as a particularly skilled worker with some technical training. Thus the relationship between engineers and men was relatively unproblematic, since the engineers were clearly the superiors of the workers where technical knowledge was concerned.[54] In France, as Judith Merkle has pointed out, both educational and artisanal traditions helped to create a rather different situation. Engineers were not necessarily men with any particular practical knowledge of the jobs they were hired to oversee, because their training had been primarily theoretical, while workers often possessed a kind of monopoly over the practical knowledge regarding the work they had to do. What made Taylorism so difficult to apply in its American formulation was the almost insuperable class barrier between workers and engineers and the suspicions on both sides that resulted. By contrast, Fayolism dealt with the more global problem in rationalizing production, at least in the French case, which was how to inspire trust and get past class antagonisms.

Fayolism met with enormous success in France and, after 1945, in other industrial nations as well. As late as 1964, *Business Week* suggested that Fayol had been the first to outline the principles of modern management and that most managers were fundamentally Fayolists, whether or not they were familiar with his writings.[55] In the battle against Americanization, then, Fayolism was a clear and lasting victory for the French way of doing things.

The development of scientific management in France amounted to a complete rethinking of the American approach to efficiency. For Taylor and his American disciples, the best way to increase the efficiency of a system was to break it down into its component parts and subsystems, analyzing isolated movements and determining how wasteful motions might be eliminated at the level of individual workers. The French tended to approach the problem in a more sociological fashion, examining the way the productive system functioned as a whole and proposing more broadly conceived solutions. For Fayol, as for the French fatigue scientists, the physical and psychological well-being of the workers was at least as important for increased efficiency as innovations in work methods or improved equipment.

The movement to rationalize industry and modernize commercial practices in France belonged to a different intellectual and cultural tradition than similar movements in the United States, England, or Germany. The French industrialists and engineers who promoted scientific management both before and after the war were the heirs of the utopian socialists of the 1830's and 1840's and the syndicalist organizers of the 1860's and 1870's. They were keenly attuned to the social, cultural, and even hygienic implications of their industrial and commercial projects, to the point where their discussions of working conditions in factories would routinely consider the effects of exhausting, repetitive labor on the ability of workers to perform their duties as citizens. By the same logic, essays on modern advertising techniques tended to evolve into disquisitions on the sources of French taste and the future of French traditions in the decorative arts.[56]

The utopian impulses behind industrial rationalization in interwar France bore something of a family resemblance to the forces that motivated the aesthetic projects of certain modernist artists, at least in the visual arts. Modernists and modernizers alike shared a taste for totalizing enterprises, projects such as filmmaking, urban planning, mass communications, or scientific management that involved the mobilization of vast numbers of people and resources to achieve a carefully orchestrated effect, whether it was economic, social, political, or aesthetic. Both groups were also powerfully attracted to scientific techniques as a means of legitimizing their activities. The appeal to science lent engineers and managers a kind of rational moral authority, while it offered artists the prospect of greater aesthetic control over their material and, at times, over their audiences as well.

A number of historians have cited the French obsession with planning, the intellectualism of their approach to scientific management, and their abiding concern over the effects of modernization as evidence of a peculiarly French inability to make real economic progress without being hindered by cultural concerns.[57] Instead, this chapter has argued that the only way French industrialists and engineers could successfully achieve rational reforms was by presenting them as part of an effort to preserve what they nostalgically identified as tradition while bringing it up to date, or by insisting on the higher aesthetic, philosophical, or spiritual goals they would ultimately serve. In interwar France, then, the path to industrial development lead directly through the realm of high culture.

CHAPTER 4

Catholicism and Modernity

In the minds of the French intellectuals and industrialists of the 1920's, the notion of modernity began to take on definite form as a complex of interrelated developments, none of which could be understood in isolation from the others. Advertising, scientific management, economic planning, and even modernist aesthetics had all become part of a single system in which the founding ideas that informed one sort of endeavor could be brought to bear usefully in another. Modernity thus conceived produced a startling array of projects and plans for transforming French society in a unified manner, bypassing politics in order to use science as a means of reintegrating social, spiritual, and economic concerns.

Of these progressive schemes and attempts at systematic social critique, some of the most influential were those generated by the social Catholic movement. Within the world of business, the social Catholics were the direct heirs of Henri Fayol. Many of the lay members were engineers and industrialists who occupied leading positions in the scientific management movement, while others were generally reform-minded members of the liberal professions. As managers, they tended to approach labor relations in a way that placed workers and workplace conflicts within a larger social and spiritual context. During the battles over Taylorism in the 1920's, social Catholic intellectuals came to the defense of human values, arguing for the right of workers to varied and engaging work and opposing the heartlessly mechanistic views of rationalization *à l'américaine.* Nonetheless, they advocated a modified version of scientific management techniques on the grounds that factory employees, and the public at large, were likely to benefit both morally and materially from increased productivity.

The social Catholics were corporatists and communitarians who saw their ideas as an alternative to liberalism and socialism that depended on science, rather than politics, as a means to moral progress. Their strong affinity for social engineering projects placed them in the forefront of the technocratic avant-garde in France during the 1930's and made them relatively influential in the movement to rationalize and modernize the economy. However, their grounding in the Catholic faith committed them to the defense of traditional social values.

The story of the social Catholic movement, from its roots in the founding days of the Third Republic to its heyday amidst the technocratic experiments of the 1930's, provides us with a glimpse into the ways that elites from those traditional strongholds of French Catholicism, the aristocracy and the military and later the haute bourgeoisie, confronted the challenge of modernity by carving out for themselves a new leadership role in a republic defined henceforward as militantly secular and democratic. Moreover, the tensions that emerged between tradition and technocracy in the writings and speeches of social Catholic planners foreshadowed many of the contradictions of ideology and image that would later plague the Vichy government.

Social Catholicism first emerged as a coherent body of thought in the crucible of war and insurrection, as the French army went down in defeat before the Prussians in 1870 and then returned home to face the urban insurrection of the Paris Commune in the spring of 1871. The earliest social Catholics were a group of young aristocrats led by René de La Tour du Pin and his friend Albert de Mun, who met during their military service after both were captured and held prisoner by Bismarck's soldiers.[1] Their time in captivity provided an opportunity for the two youthful noblemen to discuss their hopes and fears for

France's future. What grew out of their conversations was a vision of a nation splintered by class hatred, struggling to maintain its identity in the absence of true leadership.

In the early 1870's, the Catholic Church had barely begun to consider social questions let alone organize around them. Pope Pius IX was noted for his resistance to modernity and his spirited defense of established social hierarchies. Moreover, the French Church remained a deeply entrenched bastion of conservatism. As good Catholics, then, and members of the nobility, de Mun and La Tour du Pin looked first to France's revolutionary heritage as the root of the country's current crisis. As they saw it, at least initially, social reconciliation could come only with the abandonment of the revolution's insistence on the rights and liberties of individuals and a new attention to the reconstitution of community. However, de Mun's thinking would soon undergo a dramatic transformation as a result of his encounters during the Paris Commune.

After his release by the Germans, de Mun returned to Paris where he was soon called upon to join in the French army's efforts to suppress the uprising of the Paris Communards in the spring of 1871. What he saw in Paris would prove decisive: he admired the bravery and determination of the Communards, and was shocked to discover just how deep ran their hatred and contempt for the bourgeoisie and its government. He was also appalled at the utter disregard he observed among his peers for the wretched living and working conditions of the Communards and their families.

He emerged from this experience determined to build a social movement that would help to bridge the enormous divide of consciousness and sympathy between the classes, bringing together workers, bourgeois, and aristocrats in a setting where some conversation could begin on "la question sociale." So it was that in 1871, along with his brother and La Tour du Pin, he founded the Oeuvre des Cercles Catholiques d'Ouvriers, an organization whose aim was to provide workers with both moral and material assistance. The Oeuvre des Cercles sponsored religious study groups, moral recreations, and a limited loan program, among other things. However, for de Mun, the group's larger social purpose was to help neutralize class hatreds by reinstating patterns of sociability based on the model of artisanal corporations, where journeymen and masters formed a single community, but the hierarchical distinctions between them remained clear.

The Oeuvre des Cercles had limited success with workers, no doubt in large part because of the hierarchical structure of the study groups and the reluctance of their aristocratic leaders to institute more democratic procedures within them.[2] Membership in the groups increased steadily through the 1870's, but dropped off after 1880, dwindling to almost nothing by the turn of the century. This first social Catholic experiment in building trust between the classes ultimately foundered on its leaders' failure to find a way of reconciling the demands of individualism (and increasingly a burgeoning class consciousness) with the promised benefits of reintegration into a paternalistic community.

Still, de Mun, La Tour du Pin, and their collaborators had stumbled upon the basic elements of analysis of French society that would evolve, by the 1930's, into a potent formula for social criticism. First, they sought to redefine the French nation as a unified community in which all social classes shared a common interest. Second, they insisted upon the role of educated elites as leaders who were responsible for the moral welfare of society at large. Third, they recognized that the Catholic Church could no longer close its eyes to the realities of industrial modernity and working-class politics. And finally, the social Catholics placed a new emphasis on finding practical solutions to contemporary social problems. Later generations of Catholic thinkers and activists would turn this concern for concrete action into a fascination for technocratic solutions to social ills, among them corporatist techniques for ensuring the social peace. For Albert de Mun and his cohort, though, the central aim of Catholic social action was to improve relations between the classes by reinstating Catholic elites as France's natural moral leaders.[3]

Leadership remained a consistent theme of social Catholic commentary even as the Church's official position on social issues evolved. With the accession of Leo XIII to the papacy in 1878, the social Catholics found themselves for the first time much more closely in line with official Church teachings. This shift in perspective took shape most noticeably with the papal encyclical *De Rerum Novarum* issued by Leo XIII in 1891. In the encyclical, the pope criticized liberal economic doctrine for reducing human beings to the status of machines whose needs were merely material rather than spiritual. Leo's predecessor, Pius IX, had fiercely opposed the idea that the Church should intervene to alleviate the sufferings of the working poor on the ground that such intervention would disrupt divine plans for their salvation and divert the attention of Catholic organizers from spiritual matters to more temporal concerns. Thus the new pope's concern for social activism served to encourage a resurgence of Catholic activities designed to improve the lot of the least privileged members of French society.

More than that, the new pope's attitude encouraged many elite Catholics to begin thinking about their own roles as lay leaders in a different way. For most of the nineteenth century, Catholic social interventions were intended to moralize the lower classes, whether through religious instruction or charitable work aimed at creating greater order and thrift in working-class households. While these preoccupations persisted well into the interwar period, the promulgation of *De Rerum Novarum* marked the beginning of a subtle shift toward a new ethic of engagement, rooted in the notion of what Paul Rabinow has termed "pastoral care."[4] In this new schema, lay elites were called upon to attend to members of the lower classes not so much within the context of the family but as individuals with complex psychological, social, physical, and economic needs. Rather than dispensing advice, instruction, or even material assistance, the new role of the social Catholic militant was to serve as a kind of social engineer or expert manager, bringing leadership and technical expertise to the project of reestablishing social harmony in France.

Hubert Lyautey's intellectual evolution provides one of the clearest examples of this new managerial sensibility in social Catholic thought. Lyautey, who would later become a Maréchal de France and governor of France's colonial possessions in North Africa, was one of de Mun's earliest converts to the social Catholic cause in the 1870's. Over the years, though, he grew disillusioned with de Mun and his projects, discarding his ideas as backward-looking and fundamentally unsuited to the challenges of the modern era. Eventually, Lyautey came under the intellectual influence of Count Melchior de Vogüé, a Catholic aristocrat of pro-modern sentiments who wrote regularly for the *Revue des deux mondes*. The count introduced his young protégé into the most respectable circles of Parisian society, what historian Christophe Prochasson describes as "that official, honorific, and dominant milieu where conservative Republicans crossed paths with monarchists only partly won over to the cause of the Republic."[5]

Despite the conservative circles in which he moved, de Vogüé was an outspoken advocate of modernity who stressed the importance of practical social interventions that would bring together France's Catholic and aristocratic heritage with the increasingly secular orientation of its newer bourgeois elites. Under de Vogüé's tutelage, then, Lyautey learned, as he would later put it, "to seek out the ties between tradition and progress"[6] and to translate his moral impulses into innovative social policy. Ultimately, it was at de Vogüé's request and with his sponsorship that Lyautey published his pathbreaking essay, "Du rôle social de l'officier," in the *Revue des deux mondes* in March 1891. The essay first appeared anonymously because of a proscription on publishing for military officers who were on active duty.

Lyautey's essay, while concerned primarily with conditions inside the French army, laid out a new path for paternalist social reform programs of all sorts and in some ways provides a vision of what social Catholicism would become in the twentieth century. It begins with the observation that with the advent of the Third Republic, the face of the French army had changed rather dramatically. With the shortening of a tour of duty from seven years to two, and the imposition of a universal military service requirement, military service had become democratic in a way it had never been before. Men of all social classes were now forced into proximity for long periods in a setting that brought out their similarities as much as their differences and compelled them toward the common goal of national defense. In consequence, he noted, those called upon to command would need to recognize their new role as agents of mass socialization who were preparing their men not only as soldiers but as future citizens in a democracy.

The task of the new military officer was as much psychological as it was strategic, Lyautey argued, and the successful officer would be the one who took an active and personal interest in his men. French officers of the old style were notorious for their indifference to their charges as individuals. The average French officer, Lyautey claimed, was often better acquainted with the quirks and peculiarities of his horses than he was with the human qualities of the man under his command. The net result of this was a soulless and directionless army in which officers and men no longer shared a common vision or purpose.

The remedies Lyautey proposed for this state of affairs were simple but radical in their aims and scope. First, he recommended that officers make a point of systematically gathering information about their troops, including details regarding the family background, education, physical and mental health, and personal histories of the men in their battalion. In this way, he suggested, "even before he has spoken to a single one of them, [the officer] will have an initial idea of their moral physiognomy."[7] Moreover, he actively cast officers as a new kind of social pedagogue, noting that in times of peace, those in leadership roles became "social agents" whose primary task was that of education for life after the army.

Equally essential to Lyautey's vision was that officers develop a more personal rapport with their men, both as individuals and as a group. Lyautey counseled an open and friendly demeanor since, in his experience, "these men . . . are often shy and mistrustful; they open up to cordial treatment, but turn in on themselves when treated brusquely. They will love those who care about them." At the same time, he insisted on the importance of the officer as disciplinarian and father figure. By virtue of his position, Lyautey observed, the military officer had a kind of built-in moral authority that leaders in the civilian world could never command. Precisely because he was bound by the same rules as his men, the officer could be seen as both moral exemplar and comrade, rather than as a distant and unconcerned authority figure. In addition, he became the ideal judge and arbitrator of disputes, since his own actions were constrained by law and military discipline. In fact, the entire system "brings out his personal independence and the disinterested nature of his actions." The modern officer, then, became for Lyautey the agent of pastoral care and therapeutic social discipline *par excellence:* his job was to care for his men by seeking out information about them, and to apply a set of rules for discipline in as neutral and fair-minded a way as possible, in part because he was subject to the same constraints.[8]

While this vision of the military officer is certainly utopian, it is also significant for the vision it provides of the officer as a unique "social agent" who could straddle the boundary between therapeutic care and paternalistic control of the individuals in his charge. Lyautey's essay represents nothing less than the earliest form of a technocratic vision of social management organized around the complementary goals of care and containment of those who had not been called to lead in French society.

In his history of colonial urban planning, *French Modern,* Paul Rabinow has used Lyautey as an example of the shift in elite thinking about social issues from an ethic of social compassion and a concern for the moralization of the masses to a new interest in gathering information about the lower classes and regulating their behavior through an appeal to science and impersonal social norms. Lyautey's writings certainly belong to the latter category, and Rabinow notes quite rightly that the future colonizer's turn from the moralizing projects of his early years to the management strategies of his later life is marked by his abandonment of all ties to the social Catholic movement. However, it is interesting to note that even though Lyautey's Catholic collaborators continued to insist on the moral and spiritual import of their work, they, too, became increasingly interested in grounding their social projects on a firmer and more empirical basis. They simply followed Lyautey into the realm of science and the norm without ever truly considering the implications of this move for their own moral vision. The literature of social Catholicism, even in the hands of its most intellectually astute practitioners, is characterized by a kind of schizophrenic insistence on joining social science perspectives with Catholic morality. This chapter will explore some of the contradictions that emerge from the efforts of social Catholics to use Catholic teachings as the basis for a modern moral science.

The secular roots of social Catholic thought lay in nineteenth-century utopianism, most notably in the works of the social engineer Frédéric Le Play and the anarcho-syndicalist thinker P.-J. Proudhon.[9] Like the later social Catholics, both Le Play and Proudhon were concerned with the problem of coordinating production in a rational manner, and both believed that French economic and social life could only be materially improved through the development of a more scientific understanding of production techniques and social relations. As Catholics, members of the movement were also inclined to share their views on the foundations of social order, emphasizing the family, rather than the individual, as the basic social and economic unit. Le Play's vision of the rationally ordered society was much more carefully planned and regimented than Proudhon's, which, in true anarcho-syndicalist fashion, was built around organized associations of independent small producers who had agreed to cooperate. However, for all that their views were essentially collectivist, both placed great importance on the role of individuals as social beings and members of various intermediate social bodies such as the family, professional organizations, associations of neighbors, consumer groups, or unions based on some common economic and political interest.

Probably the most important thing the social Catholics derived from their utopian predecessors, though, was a fascination with sociology. This was particularly true of the writers and organizers to be discussed here, a group of moderate to left-leaning Catholic intellectuals, clerics, and community leaders who met each year at the Semaine Sociale de France. The Semaines Sociales, which began in Lyon in 1904, usually consisted of a weeklong conference devoted to the discussion of Catholic perspectives on contemporary social problems. For the most part, those who participated in the meetings were not to the far left of the French Church either theologically or socially. They were outflanked on the social left by such populist organizations as Marc Sangnier's Le Sillon and Father Desbuquois's rural movement, l'Action Populaire, and on the theological left by the liberal movement within the Church, which tended to take a more libertarian approach to social issues. However, the openness of the Semaines Sociales to recent scientific developments and modernity in general was enough to provoke virulent attacks on their efforts from the more traditionalist wing of the Church that still held to the teachings of Pius IX.[10] In the years before the war, sessions were called on themes of general social and theological concern, such as the role of the family or the meaning of work in Christian life, the notion of responsibility, or the problem of economic inequities in society. During the interwar period, however, conference organizers tended to focus discussions on more specific problems, and the list of issues chosen reads as a kind of barometer of current social concerns. Topics for the meetings included the economic role of the state (1922), the crisis of authority in France (1925), the role of women in society (1927), Christian morality and business (1931), education and the social order (1934), corporatism (1935), and even class conflict (1939).[11]

Marius Gonin, the Lyonnais lay organizer who founded the meetings, saw them as a forum in which social debate might move beyond the antagonisms between religion and science that had dominated public discussion during the Third Republic. Instead, he hoped to create an atmosphere in which recent scientific insights into contemporary social problems could be infused with or incorporated into Catholic teachings. In fact, the motto he adopted for the early meetings was "Science for Action." Although the association between Catholicism and applied science was never practically developed until after the First World War, those who participated in the Semaines Sociales were from the outset thoroughly serious about the prospect of developing a Christian form of social science.

For one early keynote speaker, Henri Lorin, it was imperative that Catholic thought become more scientific and, equally, that contemporary science begin to incorporate Christian perspectives. He established the general position of the Semaines Sociales with regard to the social sciences when he wrote:

> As active members of the legitimate Church, we seek to collect and coordinate the social facts of our times and to interpret them. . . .
>
> Thus, our method consists of observing social facts scientifically, so that we can interpret, correct, and improve [those facts], placing ourselves within a Catholic atmosphere and clarifying the rules of thought and action which derive from Catholicism.

> [Our method] is both scientific and inspired by the Catholic faith. But how is it scientific?
>
> We gather and organize social information. Our scrupulous attention in choosing observation procedures, our awareness of contingencies and circumstances, our research in history, geography, law and psychophysiology, our polls, our statistics, and our monographs, all through scientific means ... are the rigorous requirement for our success.[12]

Lorin argued that in their forays into the social sciences, Catholics needed to learn how to develop the normative dimensions of social interpretation. In his view, the most important task of the Catholic researcher or activist was not to gather information and provide a neutral interpretation of it as a secular sociologist would, but instead to make moral judgments about social facts and use them as the basis for a plan of social activism.

Monseigneur Deploige, a speaker at the 1913 Semaine, further developed the notion that scientific and religious aims should be brought into harmony with one another in a paper entitled "L'idée de responsabilité dans la sociologie contemporaine," where he analyzed a series of articles from *L'Année sociologique* and Emile Durkheim's *Les règles de la méthode sociologique*. Durkheim came in for criticism from Deploige on several counts, for the bishop complained that he refused to employ moral judgment as a principle of analysis, diminishing the role of individual psychology in moral decision making, and overemphasizing the importance of the collectivity in determining the kinds of moral choices that individuals make. However, Deploige was most deeply disturbed by Durkheim's insistence that "our method is independent of any philosophy. . . . Sociology ought not to take sides [in the debate] that divides metaphysicians," and his further contention that sociology "has no more business affirming [human] liberty than it does [in espousing] determinism."[13] Ultimately, he objected to Durkheim's belief that society is subject to the same kinds of mechanistic laws that govern the physical world. He concluded that more Catholics should engage in sociological research in order to demonstrate, first, that sociology and metaphysics were not necessarily incompatible and, second, that the science of sociology need not be dedicated to the advancement of a positivist or determinist world-view.[14]

However, debates at these meetings were hardly limited to theoretical concerns. The interest of social Catholic commentators in sociological theory was generally mediated by a set of more practical concerns about the state of French economic life, and the Semaines Sociales developed a complex and wide-ranging critique of various aspects of contemporary economic activity. Prior to the First World War, this economic critique developed primarily in the form of consumer activism and more theoretical debates over the structural problems posed by unregulated mass production and consumption. Institutionally, the social Catholics were known for their promotion of consumer cooperatives and their sponsorship of such groups as Mme. Brunhes's Ligue sociale des acheteurs, which advocated morally responsible consumerism. The Ligue sociale was a women's organization which mounted periodic campaigns to keep department stores closed on Sundays so that both employees and female shoppers could benefit from a Sabbath day. The group also encouraged members to consider how their own patterns of consumption might affect working conditions in the garment industry and retail trades and to shop in a more socially responsible way.

Although their work with cooperatives and consumer groups suggested a gradualist, meliorative approach to the problems of consumer society, the social Catholic critique of consumerism was actually far more radical in its aims than appearances would indicate. For the most part, the directors of these organizations and their membership envisioned a future in which capitalism had been fundamentally transformed from a system based on unregulated self-interest to one in which most economic activities were regulated in keeping with moral and communitarian interests. What distinguished the social Catholics from socialists, syndicalists, and other groups critical of capitalism, though, was that their writings included no substantial critique of private property. In the social Catholic formulation, then, economic regulation would serve neither to redistribute property nor to equalize access to resources. Instead, it would ensure that the basic needs of various groups in French society were met in order to preserve social harmony within a hierarchical system.

The writings of Maurice Deslandres, a consumer organizer who taught law at the University of Lyon, provide a case in point. Deslandres opposed fashion on the grounds that it was an essentially bourgeois convention which, when it reached the lower classes, spread discontent and produced irrational and even harmful economic behavior. The increasingly uncontrollable desire of consumers of all classes for fashionable objects was, he felt, liable to destroy the equilibrium of the French economy by making it more and more difficult for manufacturers to anticipate the demands of their customers.

At the 1911 Semaine Sociale, he presented an extensive critique of the fashion system, claiming that for the sake of French economic health and stability, fashion must either be eliminated altogether or organized so that consumer demand would match the productive capacities of the fashion industry.[15] Fashion, he believed, was inherently destructive because it produced rapid and unpredictable changes in styles from season to season which ultimately resulted in chaotic patterns of production. In the French fashion industry, long periods of depressed demand for certain items would typically be followed by periods when producers could not make enough of the same previously spurned commodity to satisfy consumers. These wild market fluctuations were almost impossible to predict or prepare for, and they decreased the efficiency and profitability of most enterprises by forcing manufacturers to invest in new equipment and retrain their employees to produce articles for which there would be no reliable demand once they went out of fashion again. Moreover, he argued, this production system had deleterious effects on the lives of the workers, mostly women, who were employed in garment manufacturing by subjecting them to periodic unemployment, followed by weeks of overtime work that lasted far into the night. Finally, this combination of unpredictable hours and boom or bust cycles of work availability posed a serious moral threat to these female workers, for it placed them in what contemporary social hygienists might have described as an unstable or precarious domestic situation and discouraged them from managing their finances with any semblance of regularity.

Most of all, though, Deslandres disapproved of fashion because he believed that it was fundamentally demoralizing for female consumers.[16] Constantly changing styles encouraged them to purchase cheap, poorly made merchandise that would last no more than a season and to discard more solid and serviceable articles of clothing well before they were worn out because their cut was too obviously outmoded. Deslandres also felt that fashion had already begun to disrupt the social order, complaining bitterly of "the mobility, . . . the generalization, . . . the suddenness, the domination, the excessiveness and the democratization" that characterized the contemporary fashion system. He was particularly disturbed by the fact that, as he put it, "fashion knows no social bounds; it originates in a certain class, but spreads to all of them. Expensive designs, which start a fashion, are soon made up into cheap copies."[17] Although in his view fashion led all women to indecency and frivolity, bourgeois women's styles were especially dangerous to working-class women, who would abandon all thought of their children, husbands, or domestic duties in order to ape their social betters.

True to his heritage as a utopian who envisioned a coming era of economic rationality, Deslandres proposed that if French society were to be reorganized so as to bring supply and demand into greater harmony, fashion would cease to exist because its social function would have disappeared. Under the new economic order, the classes would live at peace with one another and social envy would dissipate. Women, now reined in by the dictates of economic reason, would come to resemble men. "If women had a less futile understanding of life," wrote Deslandres, "if their social function were not to be pleasing and to draw attention to themselves, in short, if women became more virile and men ceased to regard them as elegant objects of pleasure and amusement, fashion would soon go out of fashion."[18] Deslandres's criticisms of the fashion system, then, were founded on a more fundamental moral critique concerning the deterioration of relations between the sexes and between the classes.

Throughout the 1920's and particularly in the immediate aftermath of the war, debates in the Semaines Sociales continued to focus on the social and moral dimensions of commercial activity. Directly after the war, Catholic writers and activists noted that years of deprivation had suddenly swept the nation into a frenzy of consumerism. Etienne Martin-Saint-Léon, who headed the library and archives of the social Catholics' Musée Social, complained that rampant overconsumption was driving up prices and producing a dangerously high rate of inflation. The root cause of this, in his view, was a sudden promiscuous mixing of the trades and the professions: too many people had abandoned their habitual occupations in order to engage in speculation and illicit commerce. Speculation on the prices of staple commodities had gotten out of hand because there were too many middlemen, most of them commercial novices who cared only about profits. Such individuals lacked the corporate interests and sense of responsibility to their trade that would keep more established businessmen honest and force them to keep their prices under control. In this new climate of speculation, then, the rules and conventions that ordinarily governed social and commercial relations had broken down altogether, for as Martin-Saint-Léon observed:

> We have seen journalists, actresses, and concierges buy and resell coal or sugar, while members of high society, even in its most exclusive circles, have invented new careers for themselves as car salesmen and purveyors of a curious array of goods from warehouses in America and elsewhere, all without paying any commercial taxes. This example has been contagious to the point where a large number of individuals have entered the market, adding to an already lengthy list of those engaged in suspicious transactions, while reviving and spreading the custom of mysterious payoffs, percentage commissions, and to call things by their right name, bribery.[19]

For Martin-Saint-Léon, an enormous part of the blame for contemporary economic problems could be placed on excessive individualism and the collapse of corporate discipline. He suggested that in their thirst for luxury, modern Frenchmen and women had forgotten the social implications of their actions as consumers and needed some sort of institutional reminder in order to control their excessive behavior. Thus, his remedy for the economic upheavals of the postwar period was to reorganize both merchants and consumers into corporate bodies founded on solidarity and mutual responsibility. These would effectively replace the individualistic chaos of a market economy by mediating the conflicting interests of the two groups.

In the period immediately following the war, Maurice Deslandres proposed a similar solution to the ills of free-market capitalism, suggesting that the new economic order be structured to take into account the fact that in modern society, most individuals participated in social life primarily in their role as consumers. He complained that the predominance of liberal economic theory in France had made economists and social reformers alike regard consumers as independent individuals concerned only with the pursuit of their own personal interest. This had blinded them to the possibility that consumers, too, might constitute a distinct social group with common interests and goals and a specific place within a corporatist economic scheme. By redefining consumers as a group founded upon natural bonds of interest, Deslandres hoped to demonstrate that even within contemporary mass society, where liberals saw nothing but isolation and incipient anomie, there might still be some basis for associational life. As he observed at the 1922 meeting of the Semaines Sociales:

> Before, we represented society to ourselves as an inorganic multitude. Men appeared as abstract beings who were all alike, simple units within a vast whole.
>
> Today, . . . we see men in terms of their occupations, their social roles, and their concrete social functions. In this light, they appear to us above all as consumers and users, the future recipients of all the goods and services exchanged in society.[20]

This attempt to rethink consumer society in organicist terms was a common project among social Catholics in the decade after the war. Eugène Duthoit, the president of the Semaines Sociales and a member of the law faculty at the Catholic University in Lille, devoted a series of opening lectures to the topic during the 1920's. A founding member of the group that organized the Semaines Sociales, Duthoit had long advocated the reintroduction of moral principles into business practices, arguing that ownership of commercial or industrial property brought with it specific social responsibilities. He was publicly censured for his views on this subject in 1909, when the ex-Jesuit Abbé Fontaine published a tract, "Le modernisme sociologique," denouncing the Semaines Sociales for aiding in the process of secularization by demonstrating too little respect for property and too much sympathy for democratic and collectivist ideas. In 1913, he was warned by the rector of his university, Monseigneur Margerin, that he and his collaborator, Henri Lorin, had been singled out for criticism by Cardinal Merry du Val on the grounds that they had confused justice with charity. They had, in fact, enraged Church authorities by suggesting that property owners who did not respect their social obligations had no real rights of ownership.[21] Ultimately, Duthoit and Lorin recanted some of their more radical statements in order to maintain Church support for the Semaines Sociales, but despite this, Duthoit remained true to his convictions as an advocate of a moral economy.

For Eugène Duthoit, then, the most pressing problem of the postwar era was the material and spiritual disorganization of economic life brought about by the experiences of the First World War. In key defense industries, he argued, wartime production pressures had resulted in a transformation of managers' attitudes and policies regarding the men and women they employed. Efficient production was now the sole priority in modern factories, while attention to working conditions and the psychological effects of labor had all but disappeared. The war had enabled industrial leaders to neglect their social obligations as employers and encouraged them instead to think about their enterprise only in terms of efficiency, productivity, and profitability.[22]

This disorganization was apparent in other sectors of the economy as well, for the privations of the war years had produced a thriving black market, adulteration and false labeling of goods, and a real decline in the spirit of professionalism and guild solidarity among the makers and sellers of everyday commodities. Duthoit complained that wartime uncertainties had resulted in a new economy, based on speculation and short-term goals, that was inimical to the traditions of French commerce. Among other things, rationing and the scarcity of goods had produced a proliferation of useless middlemen who "have committed no capital, taken no risks, and have hardly worked. . . . [In addition, they] are usually unfamiliar with the trade specialty they have chosen to invade or even with commercial activity."[23] Duthoit feared that the hoarding and artificially high prices of commercial speculators could only harm more traditional merchants by drastically reducing overall sales. The economy would simply contract as French consumers grew frustrated with the vagaries of the market and learned to do without various commodities.

In Duthoit's eyes, however, the greatest failures of postwar capitalism lay in the realm of investment. Increasingly, French investors had lost their sense of connection to, and responsibility for, the companies in which they invested. Part of this was the heritage of the investment scandals of the late nineteenth and early twentieth centuries, but the speculative climate that grew out of the war had also played its part in keeping French investors from any sustained contact with the realities of capitalist activity. Duthoit blamed the fluidity of market relations, observing:

> The facility with which stock market transactions can allow one to become or cease to be a shareholder; the powerlessness of individual shareholders in meetings, where they can only form voting blocs with others if their material interests are threatened; their lack of familiarity [with the business] have all made the investor into an amorphous entity, both socially and morally. The modern corporation has all the appearances of a Republic because its plenary assembly of shareholders has the right to freely appoint the management. But this Republic is only a façade. By virtue of the fact that many companies have the same administrators and shared interests and are subject to the same financial influences, their organization is much more feudal than democratic. The existence of a plutocracy which influences national and international politics is one of the facts that dominates and helps to explain the history of our time.[24]

Implicit in this critique of financial democracy is the suggestion that the economic disorder engendered by liberal capitalism had helped to bring about moral and political chaos as well. The effects of laissez-faire liberalism in the marketplace were anything but democratic, for the impersonality of market relations and the utter lack of regulation by the state or professional organizations made it all too easy for those with money and power to impose their best interests on the rest of society. For Duthoit, then, the task of Catholic reformers was to remoralize both economy and society by reaffirming the personal responsibility of both merchants and investors for their commercial activities, and by insisting that economic decisions could never be separated from their social and moral consequences.

Duthoit's program for reintroducing moral concerns into economic activity in many ways typified the social Catholic approach to the problem of industrial modernity. Duthoit sought to steer a clear path between liberalism and socialism, criticizing both for heightening class conflict rather than seeking to resolve it by bringing owners and labor into a more cooperative relationship. The economic solution he envisioned would be based on strong professional organizations, modeled on *ancien régime* corporations, which would ensure against fraud by setting strict and collectively enforced standards of quality for products. These groups would also raise standards for professionalism among merchants and help to calm the overly competitive atmosphere of modern-day capitalism by making producers realize that they had interests in common. Finally, Duthoit hoped that if industrialists and workers were to reorganize themselves along corporate lines, this would enable them to adopt a less conflictual approach in their dealings with one another. For Duthoit, as for the social Catholic movement more generally, the modernization of industry could succeed in France only to the extent that it managed to combine technological innovation in the productive sphere with respect for traditional patterns of economic behavior.

Under Duthoit's presidency, the Semaines Sociales produced a wide-ranging critique of what the French referred to as *rationalization*—the new techniques of scientific management (and especially Taylorism) imported from the United States—and its larger implications for French society.[25] Duthoit himself had set the tone for this critique in his lecture from 1920, "La crise de la production et la sociologie catholique," by suggesting that the postwar drive to build up the economy and stimulate production was little more than a continuation of hostilities in economic form.[26] The result of this ongoing battle was the mindless pursuit of increased productivity, regardless of the human costs. Throughout the 1920's, then, discussions of industrial and commercial issues during the Semaines Sociales frequently centered on the problem of overproduction and the concomitant dehumanization of the workforce in a system that was geared primarily toward increased output and improved mechanical efficiency.

In the earlier part of the decade, Catholic critics of rationalization tended to focus on the most immediate effects of scientific management methods in the workplace. As a result, they joined in the debate that was raging in business circles between those who advocated Taylorism (and American methods of scientific management more generally) and those who favored Fayolism, an indigenous theory of management that stressed organization from above. The social Catholics tended to prefer Fayol, in part because he was French and thus understood the French workplace better, but also because they felt he had successfully integrated scientific concerns with respect for human needs and the variations in individual psychology. By contrast, Taylorism came under heavy attack at the Semaines Sociales, but more for its symbolic function than as an actual set of practices.

G. Perrin-Pelletier, addressing the annual meeting at Rennes in 1924, suggested that there was no real conflict between the two techniques since they were fundamentally incomparable and, in fact, complementary: Taylorism proposed a model of organization that grew from the bottom up, while Fayolism concentrated on the role of leaders in creating corporate unity, bolstering morale, and establishing a clear chain of command. Perrin-Pelletier's real complaint about Taylorism, at least as it had been implemented in France, was that while it made great claims for itself as a scientific approach to labor management, its utter exclusion of the human factor made it "antiscientific."[27]

The science exemplified by Taylorism, then, was for Perrin-Pelletier an alien discipline and one inimical to French traditions in every respect. "The fact that we do a timed study of every movement," he wrote:

> cataloguing them into productive and useless movements, does not mean that some parts of "useless" motions are not still important. Man is not a machine and cannot be reduced to the state of an automaton. In an ancient civilization such as ours, much more than in America, we must recognize that in order for tasks to be properly executed [by workers], a certain application and taste are required. This taste can only be stimu-

lated by a varied [employment] which the automatic and mechanical uniformity of repetitious movements does not permit.[28]

The American model of scientific management would have to be modified in significant ways before it could be usefully implemented in French workshops, for French craftsmanship resided precisely in the individual human gestures that made each piece of work unique and in the varied work experiences that helped to produce distinct and well-formed tastes. Ultimately, Perrin-Pelletier argued that scientific methods would have to be radically reworked before they could be usefully employed in French industry. A truly French science of management would take into account the spiritual aspects of production and make a serious effort to integrate traditional production techniques with more mechanistic modern approaches.

Despite his fulminations against Taylorist methods, Perrin-Pelletier was certainly no backward-looking opponent of science—or of modernity, for that matter. His approach to the issue of industrial modernization was more preservationist, for he was convinced that there could be no real innovation in production methods that was not firmly grounded in tradition. Tradition and science were perfectly compatible, for as he observed,

> Tradition is not routine, because in truth it cannot be definitively fixed and rendered unchangeable. It preserves those parts of ancient methods and customs that secular experience has shown to be effective and excellent, while still remaining open to the progressive penetration of science, taking from it with prudence and reserve useful modifications and even outlandish novelties after testing and proving them.
>
> Thus understood, tradition is not an obstacle or a chain; it is a link, and a form of continuity. . . .
>
> If it is to retain this benevolent character, it must not approach science with fear or defiance; for that reason it must come to know and respect science. Otherwise, [tradition] is likely to freeze and fall into the slumber that leads to death.[29]

Ideally, industrial science would benefit from the psychological and spiritual insights of French cultural tradition while the tradition itself would become more flexible, more self-critical, and ultimately stronger as a result of its contact with new ideas. For Perrin-Pelletier, of course, Catholic teachings were an essential part of French tradition and one that had become increasingly embattled with the imposition of a more secular worldview by the state educational system.[30] Thus, he concluded his remarks with the vision of a future in which the central conflict of Third Republic politics had been resolved once and for all: he imagined a world in which the scientific community had abandoned its materialist presuppositions and accepted the limits of science, learning instead to embrace the higher human (and divine) truths of Catholicism. True social progress, then, would develop from the synthesis of technical know-how and a divinely inspired vision of social order.

Later commentators at the Semaines Sociales took Perrin-Pelletier's discussion of industrial rationalization as a starting point for their analyses of the ways in which modern business techniques were likely to change the shape of social life. For the Abbé Danset, a member of the grassroots organization L'Action Populaire, rationalization had ceased to be an issue that concerned only industrial leaders and government officials. In his 1927 address, he described it instead as a matter of popular concern, a fashionable *phénomène de grand public,* "the item that has won the day, the word on everyone's lips, the great success of the season, the latest creation from the Grand Bazaar of economic novelties."[31] From the perspective of labor, the movement among industrialists to rationalize production was an exciting development, for scientific management techniques promised to end cyclical unemployment by introducing an element of predictability into the productive process.

Although Danset was a firm advocate of Fayol's management techniques, his evaluation of Taylorism was surprisingly positive: he praised Taylor's attempts to understand work in a scientific manner and faulted him only for paying too little attention to the initiative and creativity of workers. Danset admitted that he had been skeptical about scientific management until he saw it in operation among artillerymen in the trenches during the First World War: the methodical and disciplined training they had received in the operation of machine guns gave them the courage, he claimed, to continue to follow orders and fight rationally even during a bombing attack. However, like many of his contemporaries, Danset concluded that Taylor's methods would be useless in France, "a country known . . . for its artisanal traditions and the pride of its craftsmen."[32] Nonetheless, he felt that American business had an important lesson to teach the French about the social responsibilities of capitalists. Citing Taylor and two other eminent American businessmen, Henry Ford and Edward Filene, on the idea of service, Danset concluded that a business deserved to be profitable only after it had performed some real service to society. Taylor, Ford, and Filene had almost certainly described the American conception of service, in which a merchant's close attention to the needs and desires of customers and the consuming public at large grew out of a well-developed sense of commercial self-interest. However, what captured Danset's imagination in their accounts was the idea that commercial activity might be rationally organized around the interests of consumers. For Danset, then, whatever the shortcomings of American methods, they offered the French business community a model of a coherent social and economic vision. Thus he called on technically trained Catholic elites to offer their services as "intellectuals for productivity" who would restore order to the French economic system by providing it with a vision, long since lost, of the common good.[33]

Some commentators shared Danset's faith in the power of rationality to moralize contemporary French society. At the 1929 meeting of the Semaines Sociales, Paul Devinat, who had prepared a report on the progress of scientific management in Europe for the International Labor Office two years earlier,[34] predicted that if psychological research could be successfully integrated into scientific management techniques, the resulting *psychotechnique* would probably bring about the end of class conflict. "Scientific management," he wrote,

> was not designed to be a moral or philanthropic activity. Nor was it meant as goods politics. Its inspiration derives not from philosophical or religious doctrines, but from the best interests of the factory. In a word, it sees respect for justice as a means, and not an end. . . .
>
> With this as a given, . . . scientific organization must remain within the technical role it has allotted for itself. However, in acknowledging

that good returns are impossible in the absence of respect for justice, it does provide us with a certain [moral] comfort.

If it is possible to accommodate the spiritual and moral aspirations of workers to the demands of production, why should we remain burdened by Marx's gloomy prophecies? Why should we tremble at the dreadful prospect of eternal class conflict, when we can progress with easier spirits toward a future of peace and industrial brotherhood? [35]

While technology by itself was morally neutral, it might still serve as a powerful tool for the elimination of social conflict when combined with a more comprehensive social and moral vision.

However, the possibility still loomed large in the minds of many social Catholics that increased industrial efficiency and the growth of a consumerist mentality might well have a demoralizing influence on French society. At the 1929 meeting in Besançon where Devinat presented his views, the social benefits of economic reform were still open to question from a variety of perspectives. Eugène Duthoit opened the meeting with an address on the rationalization movement that explicitly criticized the excessive faith of some of his colleagues in material solutions to the social problem. He began by observing that the notion of rationalization was alien to the French sensibility, for as he put it, "The very word conflicts with our French habits."[36] He went on to note that even the progressive industrialist Ernest Mercier described rationalization as "a German word and a European idea which has emerged through the study of the methods and spirit of American industry."[37] Rationalization could not be explained as part of any specific national tradition, and by the same token, it was almost impossible to situate within any particular moral tradition. For Duthoit, as long as productivist techniques remained morally neutral and unmarked by the character and traditions of a single nation, they would continue to pose a serious threat to French social and economic stability.

Duthoit feared that the spiral of ever-increasing production proposed by the advocates of industrial reform would soon lead to market saturation, production surpluses, and eventually a dramatic economic collapse. As he saw it, advertising and international marketing might provide a solution to this predicament, but only in the short term. Marketing goods to less-developed nations could only work for as long as they remained in a state of economic dependence on those countries which had industrialized first. Once these markets were exhausted, there would be nothing left but to exhort satiated domestic consumers to new excesses of materialism and suffer the social consequences.

> It will be argued that the countries with the oldest industrial plants will soon find a market for their excess production as a result of the increasingly refined needs of their populations. This is unclear, because in societies where all material desires have been satisfied while moral progress has lagged, there is a punishment: declining birth rates and eventually reduced consumer buying power.[38]

Whatever the flaws of Duthoit's economic analysis, his vision of the future was clear: unless the growing power of industry was constrained by moral concerns, the new prosperity brought on by industrial reform would lead to materialism, the dehumanization of work, and ultimately the decline of national vitality in the form of continuing denatality.[39]

Similar concerns surfaced over and over again in the Semaines Sociales held immediately before and during the onset of the Great Depression. Although France was slow to feel the effects of the crisis, events in other countries gave French economic analysts material for reflection on the mechanism underlying the depression. The analysis that emerged from the Semaines was highly critical of rationalization and the growth of consumer society, for Catholic thinkers believed that both the mechanization of industry and an increase in unregulated mass consumption had played key roles in creating a lasting depression.

In 1932, Joseph Daniel argued that the current economic crisis was the direct result of postwar pressures to strengthen and stimulate the economy. Daniel believed that during the postwar reconstruction period, industrial leaders everywhere had been so determined to build up their production facilities and make their nations economically independent that they had wildly overspent, investing vast sums of money to acquire the latest production technologies, regardless of the cost or the likelihood that this new, expensive equipment would soon be outdated.[40] European business leaders had also failed to take into account the capacity of their markets to absorb new goods, and they engaged in heedless overproduction, counting on their ability to persuade consumers to buy things they neither needed nor could afford.

"We already know the process," wrote Daniel. "Producers must stay ahead of consumer demand, provoking and speculating on the desire, rather than true need, for luxury items, cars, radios and so on. ... They must provide their customers with the means to acquire these items by lending them the necessary sums and allowing them to repay them in weekly or monthly installments. This leads consumers to purchase things in the present which should have been bought in the future."[41]

He concluded that producers exhausted market capacity in advance and continued to overproduce because they had failed to realize that these new markets, created by credit, were not stable and could not be counted on in the future.[42] The problem with consumer credit, then, was that it allowed industry to tap into its potential markets prematurely, rather than suffering the consequences of overproduction more immediately. Moreover, Daniel suggested, credit might even be held responsible for the failure of businesses that produced things consumers genuinely needed by diverting their buying power to more desirable and less necessary objects.

Both Daniel and Duthoit expressed an ambivalence about rationalization and the development of consumer society in France that surfaced repeatedly in social Catholic discussions of the economy from the prewar period well into the 1930's. The tension within the social Catholic analysis between the modernizing impulse and the desire to preserve traditional patterns of social relations emerges most clearly in the addresses on advertising and its social effects that were presented over the years at the Semaines Sociales. Advertising, and more generally, the shaping of public opinion by the press, had become a topic of interest for the Semaines as early as 1910, when Henri Moysset spoke on the irrationality of public opinion and the dangers of literary politics.

As a young man, Henri Moysset was something of an anomaly at the Semaines, for he was both a social Catholic and a socialist sympathizer. He was also well connected to the world of sociology, and he prepared his own study of German public opinion, *L'esprit public en Allemagne dans les vingt ans depuis Bismarck,* in 1911. In addition, he collaborated with Marcel Déat, who was at that time a young militant of the SFIO, on an edition of the collected works of Proudhon.[43] Within the context of the Semaines Sociales, then, Moysset represented a leftist and remarkably secular point of view. He was well read in contemporary crowd theory, and provided a description of the formation of public opinion in his talk that was strongly reminiscent of the work of Gustave Le Bon and Gabriel Tarde, or for that matter, Emile Durkheim.[44] "Public opinion is first of all, but not exclusively, the sum of individual opinions," he wrote.

> Thus, it is a sort of general judgment of men and things. . . . [Public opinion] is the sum of forces accumulated, in circulation and in formation within the soul of the crowd, whether that crowd is an anonymous mass of men, an assembly, a people, or many peoples. . . . These forces bear witness to the race, the traditions, the institutions, the social state, the logic, and the political passions of a people, and to everything else that helps to create the character of an age. . . . At times these ideas are clear and simple, although more often they are complex and obscure, for opinion, like the conscious mind, has a subconscious, a "subliminal" area whose emanations cross the threshold [of consciousness], penetrating the zone where reason projects its light onto the structure of things.[45]

Moysset went on to argue that in recent years the intellectual elite had lost its primary role in the creation of public opinion. Instead, public opinion came into being through journalistic affirmation and repetition, readers' tendencies toward imitation, and what he described as "emotional contagion,"[46] a condition that resulted from the technological fact that news could now be released simultaneously all over the world, joining the various audiences that received it into a single intellectual community.

However, unlike Le Bon, Tarde, and other contemporary theorists of crowd behavior and collective mental states, Moysset did not immediately leap to dire conclusions about the political irrationality and irresponsibility of the collective popular mind itself. In fact, quite the contrary: in his view, crowds and other collectivities could be impulsive and credulous, but they were also gifted with "a Homeric imagination"[47] and capable of heroic behavior inspired by conservative or revolutionary impulses. Thus, Moysset was less alarmed by the disorderly tendencies of crowds than he was by the deceptive strategies of those who managed to capture their attention. Public opinion had become a political problem in contemporary France because the press was organized as a commercial operation and because journalists, rather than disinterested intellectuals, had the greatest influence on the public imagination.

Ultimately, Moysset proposed that the literary politics of journalists be supplanted by a more scientific politics that would originate in the teachings of social scientists. He invoked the traditions of the Enlightenment and the Revolution to make his case, observing, "It was a few ideas, expressed in a taut, muscular language, as supple as a linen garment, and a few books written by an oligarchy of intellectuals that came to the attention of the logically minded population that made the French Revolution." These influential books were utterly different from the "industrial literature" cobbled together for profit by contemporary presses, for they were deeply personal works that grew out of the intellectual passions of great minds. For Moysset, then, the public sphere would remain in danger until the commercial republic of letters, represented here by the shallow literary hacks who dominated the French press, had been supplanted by a rationalist aristocracy of scientists. As he concluded,

> Condorcet believed that popularizations were the greatest accomplishment of the eighteenth century. However, we should be careful not to forget, as Taine remarked, that Voltaire had a laboratory, while Montesquieu dissected frogs and wrote [scientific] essays on echoes and kidney stones. Diderot taught mathematics and learned about industrial techniques, while Rousseau was a botanist. In short, "the leaders of public opinion" were all versed in the physical and natural sciences, at least to some degree; they had a passion for it, just as today's leaders . . . have a passion for the social sciences.[48]

Moysset's account of the Enlightenment was a technocratic one, and in this respect his views on the management of public opinion placed him firmly within the social Catholic tradition. Like Duthoit, Devinat, Daniel, and others who commented on industrial rationalization in the 1920's, Moysset believed that scientific methods of organization could pave the way to real social progress in a wide variety of areas. For many of them, a well-managed, orderly society was a moral one. Thus, the task of Catholic elites in contemporary French society as elaborated by the Semaines Sociales was to advocate science in a critical fashion and to serve as "moral engineers"[49] who would ensure that rationalist organizational methods were imbued with psychological insights and spiritual values.

Moralization and modernization were linked again in social Catholic discussion during the final months of the First World War in the business journal *Vouloir*. The editors of *Vouloir* had subtitled their publication "Journal d'action economique et sociale" and described it as a social Catholic and Saint-Simonian journal.[50] Although there were no direct links between the Semaines Sociales and the journal, *Vouloir* shared the preoccupation of other social Catholic intellectuals with the problem of reorganizing and rationalizing the French economy and introducing modernizing techniques from abroad. As early as 1917, the journal had begun to print articles criticizing government policies toward advertising, arguing that the new taxes it proposed on catalogs, posters, billboards, and neon signs raised relatively little money for the state treasury because collection mechanisms had been so poorly specified by law. Moreover, the taxes made advertising prohibitively expensive even for large concerns and utterly out of reach for smaller companies with limited budgets. *Vouloir* maintained (as did the larger trade journals) that the state had drastically limited not only the potential development of the French advertising business but the growth potential of the French economy as a whole by restricting the expansion of advertising for a wide variety of consumer products.[51]

Despite its social Catholic and Saint-Simonian leanings, *Vouloir* was almost indistinguishable from the modernizing business journals such as *Mon Bureau* and *La Publicité* that had appeared before the war.

Like both of these publications, *Vouloir* made itself an outspoken advocate of scientific advertising techniques and favored the introduction of modern rationalization strategies in both commerce and industry. Its editors also insisted, as did their secular counterparts, that false advertising, adulteration, *contrefaçon,* and other forms of fraudulent commercial activity were rampant within French manufacturing, distribution, and sales and that they could only be eliminated through the development of strong professional organizations with clearly defined standards for the ethical conduct of business.

During the war, when most business publications had suspended their activities altogether, *Vouloir* became the organ for many ideas about rationalization that later became staples of secular professional discussion. Throughout 1918, the journal ran a series of essays by Raymond Clémang on the psychology of advertising which were remarkably similar to articles on the psychology of memory and attention that had begun to appear in *La Publicité* on the eve of the war.[52] Like his predecessors and a number of authors from the 1920's, Clémang favored the theories of perception and attention developed by Hippolyte Bernheim and the Ecole de Nancy in the late nineteenth century, and believed that it might soon be possible for advertisers to use psychology to predict and control the effects of their campaigns.

What made *Vouloir* unique during the war years was the readiness of its editors to identify the quest for commercial modernization with the social Catholic project of remoralizing French society. In November 1918, shortly after the armistice, *Vouloir* published a small announcement for a meeting of a new association of advertising professionals, the Conférence des Chefs de Publicité du Commerce et de l'Industrie (CCP), entitled "La publicité, arme d'après-guerre," which ran:

> In the economic battle of tomorrow, advertising will be an all-powerful weapon. In the United States, it has become the most formidable force behind commercial activity in modern times. It can and must become equally influential in France. But in order to achieve this result, producers and retailers must *abandon* the old formulas of unsystematic advertising and turn resolutely in the direction of *scientific and moral advertising.*[53]

For this group of social Catholic technocrats, then, scientific techniques would be essential to the task of moralizing commercial activity. Their enthusiasm for science soon spread, however, and within a few years after the war, social Catholic ideas about organization and the relationship between economic activity and moral issues had become an important part of public discussion about French commercial reconstruction, even among convinced secularists.[54]

Henri Moysset, Raymond Clémang, René Castelneaux, and others who collaborated on *Vouloir* represent the modernist moment in social Catholic thought. With their training in sociology and psychology, they believed that the social sciences might provide some new techniques for solving contemporary social problems, especially those problems which arose from the specific conditions of modern life. Hence Moysset's idea that scientists should become the legislators of contemporary public opinion, which was otherwise uncontrollable, and *Vouloir*'s advocacy of scientific advertising techniques as a means of moralizing both the advertising business and consumerism. However, there was a side to social Catholic thinking that was deeply suspicious of both social scientists and technocratic visionaries, whether or not they claimed to be inspired by Catholicism, on the grounds that they had lost their spiritual perspective by focusing too intently on man's material existence.

Deslandres, Martin-Saint-Léon, and many of the other early organizers of the Catholic cooperative movement were ambivalent about consumerism in just this way. They knew that if Catholicism was to triumph over socialism in winning the hearts and minds of working people, Catholic organizers would have to pay serious attention to their material needs. However, they still tended to approach the subject in a rather otherworldly fashion, denying the real pleasures of acquiring objects and hoping to persuade working-class consumers that spending for material luxuries was an immoral diversion of funds that might otherwise be used to provide a Christian education for their children, and a distraction from spiritual goals.

The commentaries of Marius Gonin and André Roullet from the early 1930's on advertising and consumerism form part of this latter tradition and provide a critical counterpoint to the chorus of enthusiasm for technocracy from earlier meetings of the Semaines Sociales. In his 1931 essay, "L'aspect moral du problème de la publicité," Gonin, one of the founders of the Semaines and director of the *Chronique sociale de France,* argued that advertising, and scientific advertising in particular, posed a serious threat to the consumer's ability to determine his or her economic actions freely. The messages of advertising, he said, had become inescapable in contemporary society. Even worse, they were so successful as a scientifically designed form of manipulation that, as he put it, "We watch and listen, completely taken in, yet convinced that we are still free to decide on our own. In spite of ourselves, though, we are penetrated by impersonal voices and suggestive images which fix in our memory the name of a firm or the qualities of a product."[55]

Even though advertising had established itself more slowly in France than in the United States or England, its effects on consumer behavior had been all the more insidious since "it was less a matter of conquering a new set of clients than of changing the habits of customers who were already accustomed to buying things."[56] The critical spirit of the French, as well as their attachment to traditional ways of doing things, held back the spread of scientific advertising techniques for a while, but since the war, the advertising industry had blossomed as a result of new external pressures to boost French export sales and increase domestic consumption of goods.

For Gonin, the social effects of advertising had been disastrous in several respects. First of all, advertising was responsible for giving the working classes a taste for novelty and luxury and encouraging them to spend money on inessential items. It had also introduced credit sales as a promotional scheme, encouraging buyers to break the time-honored French taboo against indebtedness in order to gratify their immediate desires. Its worst effect on contemporary social life, though, had nothing to do with buying and selling. Advertising had done real damage to public debate in France, both by imposing limits on the freedom of the press to report negative information about its advertisers and by underestimating the intelligence of the consuming public and attempting to undermine consumers' liberty of thought.[57]

Gonin took issue with modern advertising techniques for precisely the same reasons that *Vouloir*'s editors had advocated them. The problem with contemporary advertising, as he saw it, was that it was based on a set of scientific presuppositions about the nature of human perceptual processes that made human beings into manipulable automata, incapable of exercising rational judgment once they were in the thrall of a captivating image. He noted with displeasure that advertisers had devised their techniques on the basis of cursory readings in the work of William James and Bernheim and Liébault of the Ecole de Nancy. Their central aim, he said, was to find a way of "manipulating human nature." For all their scientific pretensions, advertising experts succeeded only in demonstrating that "in advertising, the scientific method means using habits deeply inscribed in the brain for commercial ends, knowing how to play off the intellectual and imaginative reflexes engendered by the associative process, and understanding how to employ factual demonstration and rational argumentation in one's own interest."[58] In order to illustrate the problem, Gonin selected a passage from Octave-Jacques Gérin's popular advertising manual, *La publicité suggestive* (1927), in which Gérin argued, following Gabriel Tarde, that most human opinions were not original to those who held them, but composite ideas created by the psyche out of the various competing influences that clamored for its attention. Such a view of human mental processes, Gonin observed bitterly, was tantamount to a proclamation of "the nonexistence of human freedom."[59] In their theories and in their practices, then, advertising professionals displayed the utmost disrespect for human free will.

Gonin also claimed that the French practitioners of scientific advertising had been both naive and self-serving in their adoption of American views about advertising as a public service.

It never seems to occur to those who have popularized these methods that they might provide occasions for abuses of various sorts. For them, *advertising is dominated by the idea of service.* This conviction grows out of an idea that appears throughout the writings of American businessmen today: [they seem to believe] that all men are honest, that if you work for them, they will simply pay you, and that Publicity, like sales, is part of an educational system for familiarizing people with the advantages of whatever service is being offered them. Thus, advertising should be truthful and only make offers that are rigorously guaranteed.[60]

For Gonin, then, all talk of rationalization and progress through scientific advertising was so much nonsense, for deception was the very essence of advertising. In fact, his discussion here recalls Eugène Duthoit's remarks from ten years earlier about the disengagement and irresponsibility of investors in the current marketplace. Advertising was dangerous for French commerce because it could operate independently of any human agent. While the proper task of sales was to build a relationship with one's clientele and educate customers about their purchasing decisions, advertising sold in a way that implied no human contact, no personal relationship between the buyer and the seller, and no reliable presentation of the qualities of the items for sale.

Ultimately, Gonin argued that if scientific advertising were to become moral, advertisers would have to forgo most of their insights into human psychology, relying primarily on rational argumentation as a means of persuasion. Moreover, they would have to develop a greater regard for the liberty and human dignity of their customers, since in the current scheme of things, advertisements served only to confuse the consuming public, arousing its irrational desires and destroying its critical capacities. Otherwise, he concluded, scientific advertising was liable to produce an economic and cultural catastrophe:

> Pushed to its extreme limits, the system makes Publicity a sovereign to whom everything belongs. Ultimately, it creates a consumerist morality whose fundamental principles are immoral, placing materialism above spirituality and condemning the ancient virtue of moderation as a flaw. Who could fail to see that such an understanding of Publicity can only increase current economic instability and at the same time make us lose sight of justice and the common good?
>
> Freed of all moral attachments and dedicated to serving as the indispensably powerful aid of the press, Publicity will become a formidable instrument for misguiding and perverting the public spirit. Those who control it will be able to set their price for determining the beliefs of entire populations and thus destroy the sources of morality and public life.[61]

Gonin's analysis of advertising took him several steps beyond Deslandres, Martin-Saint-Léon, and other earlier critics of consumerism who participated in the Semaines Sociales. Like the technocrats, Gonin saw advertising as part of a larger movement toward economic and cultural modernization which had the potential to supplant traditional French values, substituting profligacy and speculative investing for thrift, charity, and economic stability. And even though he reached markedly different conclusions than they had about the possible benefits of scientific advertising and other rationalization techniques, he shared one important aspect of their thinking about the role of Catholic intellectuals in the world of business. Both Gonin and the technocrats believed that the Church had a place as an influence on secular activity and that it was the responsibility of educated Catholics to develop a unifying spiritual vision of French society and culture at a time when industrial modernity threatened to alter irrevocably the customs and practices of labor and exchange in everyday life.

Despite the broad range of opinions represented in the Semaines Sociales, there was a certain coherence to the social Catholic vision of contemporary French society. The social Catholic critique grew out of a fundamental belief in the importance of the individual as a psychological and spiritual entity and as a being rooted within a social tradition and within spiritual and temporal communities.[62] The relentless fear that surfaced in the papers presented at the Semaines Sociales was that the forms of modern life imposed by industrial capitalism militated against both individuality and community. In their place, the modern system offered a social organization based on an impersonal and mechanical egalitarianism that identified individuals solely in terms of their productive function and their value as consumers.

Consequently, the social Catholics sought to imagine a new social order that placed greater emphasis on the individual, whose worth transcended the realm of economics. At the core of their proposed transformation of modern industrial society, the Catholics placed the values of order (which could mean anything from hierarchical organization to corporatism or even collective bargaining) and responsibility. The social Catholics used the term *order* strategically, invoking it as the remedy for the economic and social disorder brought on by years of liberal unwillingness to regulate the economy and years of Republican insistence that no single social or spiritual doctrine should occupy a predominant place in an egalitarian and secular polity. True social and economic order, claimed the Catholics, could only be achieved by those who began with a well-developed vision of a transcendent moral order.

Paradoxically enough, this insistence on order and the responsibility of French elites for contemporary social problems pushed the social Catholics toward scientific management and technocratic schemes for the elimination of social conflict. While they were quick to criticize secular industrialists and managers for their thoughtless and at times inhuman misapplication of scientific principles, the social Catholics were also convinced that scientific techniques for management and communications, when informed by spiritual aims, could serve as powerful tools for the reestablishment of social order. Thus the social Catholics became great advocates of modernity in spite of themselves, justifying their modernizing efforts as an attempt to defend and renovate tradition.

As a practical influence in business, social Catholicism was a force for modernization and reform in a wide variety of areas. Within industry, engineers of social Catholic convictions helped to set up rationalization programs, while business owners frequently experimented with new management methods that would provide an example of how to run an enterprise in a humane fashion and without class conflict. Catholics played an important role in X-Crise, the organization of reformist *polytechniciens,* and instituted the first professional organization of engineers, the Union sociale des ingénieurs catholiques.[63] The Institut Catholique in Paris and the Catholic universities in Lille and Louvain were also the first to make courses in advertising and marketing a part of their curriculum, and several of those who wrote for and edited *La Publicité* and *Vendre* were hired to teach them. However, the most important effects of social Catholic thinking emerged in the writings and organizational activities of two men, Lucien Romier, an organizational consultant and economic journalist, and

Jean Coutrot, the editor of *L'Humanisme économique* and the founder of the Centre d'Etude des Problèmes Humains, whose activities are discussed in detail in the final chapter.

Lucien Romier, an historian by training, was best known as a *porte parole* for a variety of industrial organizations in the 1920's and 1930's. He was also the editor of *La Journée industrielle*[64] and the chief political editor for *Le Figaro*. He spoke frequently at the Semaines Sociales and gained considerable notoriety in intellectual and business circles with a series of books on economic reform in France. Probably the most successful of them was his now-classic 1927 essay on the dangers of American methods, *Qui sera le maître, Europe ou Amérique?* Romier became especially influential during the Vichy régime, when he was one of Marshal Pétain's two *secretaires d'état,* along with another former colleague from the Semaines Sociales, Henri Moysset, who had gone on to become a professor at the Ecole d'Etudes Navales.[65]

In his first address at the Semaines Sociales, "La Solidarité Européenne" (1926), Romier argued that European culture had a specific contribution to make to the international debate over how best to organize an economy in the postwar world. His central point was that Europeans had a common heritage which they could invoke as an alternative to the consumerist and communist visions from abroad of the ideal society that threatened to impose themselves in Europe. Romier faulted contemporary European intellectuals for being either too nationalist in their concerns or too internationalist, without considering the possibility that they might gain something from speaking as members of an intermediate community of Europeans. As he saw it, then, the European response to the challenge of modernization would be a collaborative effort to coordinate economic and social life with political and spiritual issues which would transcend nationality while still respecting the local cultural differences that gave each nation its character.[66]

Romier's second address at the Semaines Sociales, "La Déprolétarisation des Masses," raised the issue of social solidarity once again. He began by arguing that both contemporary socialists and liberals had misunderstood capitalism for, as he put it, "Capitalism based on the circulation of wealth does not necessarily lead to either the isola-

tion of individuals from society, nor [does it lead] to class warfare."
Rather, he wrote,

> It implies solidarity, and not just de facto solidarity, but one based on prin-
> ciples and imposed by the overall condition of the economic system. In-
> dividuals . . . are in solidarity with others who belong to the same economic
> bloc. Demands for collective progress have made everyone an "employee"
> or a "salaried worker" engaged in a common effort to increase the overall
> social "return." Similarly, everyone has become a "bourgeois" because each
> individual profits from the general well-being [of society].[67]

By this reasoning, then, the deep divisions in contemporary French
(and European) society might be eliminated if only workers and owners could be taught to see that they had interests in common that
might serve as the basis for increased cooperation between them.

Romier complained that so far, France had inherited the worst of
both the American and the Soviet systems, for on one hand, class conflict was rampant, and on the other, the pleasures of everyday life were
becoming increasingly mechanical and commodified. Moreover, despite the fact that economic growth had brought nearly everyone (at
least in Romier's estimation) to a general level of material well-being,
that same growth had produced a society in which everyone who
worked, from owners and professionals to workers and salaried employees, was enslaved by "a pitiless formula based on economic return." Thus France had allowed itself to become a nation of proletarians, rendered passive by the demands of materialism and a mechanistic system of production.[68] Traditional habits, tastes and ideas were
losing out to the imperatives of mass culture, for as Romier observed:

> For hundreds of millions of people today, possessing electric lighting,
> driving a car and going to the movies have become our uniform model of
> happiness. The sentimental pleasures have given way to mechanical ones.
>   But as it grows more uniform, the field of pleasures has also become
> more restricted, and seems more sterile to the degree that the mechanical
> arts are involved. . . . The uniformity of tastes and the growing obsession
> with the mechanical have brought us back to a childish, passive notion of
> happiness, an essentially "proletarian" happiness.[69]

As a corrective to this state of affairs, Romier proposed a program
in the workplace and in the schools, designed to deepen the scientific

and moral culture of the French population. Workers, he argued, needed to learn something about science if they were to spend their time in an environment full of machinery. Some exposure to the basic operating principles of the machines they worked with might help to eliminate class conflict by increasing their sense of control and mastery, and thereby building up their sense of dignity on the job. It might also persuade them that they were not simply passive drones enslaved by a mechanistic production system, and that they still retained some degree of self-determination in their work.

Romier's greatest hope was that such "cultivation" would transform a nation of proletarians into a society in which everyone subscribed to middle-class values. He felt that proper education would provide workers and managers alike with a new sense of purpose on the job, inspiring them to abandon materialism and return to more traditional values. Commercial occupations and commodified pleasures could never achieve this, for the commercial mentality encouraged individuals to see one another as competitors for the same material benefits. "Commerce," he wrote, "has always supported material progress. But in itself, it is neither educational nor moralizing. . . . Commerce, which sets men against one another, is in this respect far inferior to the professions, which set man against nature. Hence the difference in 'mentality' between an engineer and a shopkeeper."[70]

Thus, Romier invited the working classes, and the managerial classes as well, to aspire to the condition of the engineer, who possessed an integrated vision of the world, both moral and mechanical, and the technical abilities that would enable him to master it. Such mastery, said Romier, held the only true potential for happiness that remained in modern industrial society, for as he trenchantly observed, "The deepest and most lasting happiness does not come from enjoyment. It derives from strength, invention, construction, fertility, mastering matter, the conscious direction of one's own activities or those of others, and understanding and teaching the superiority of human character."[71]

In both of his interventions at the Semaines Sociales, Romier held out for the French a vision of themselves as Europeans whose mission it was to be the guarantors of culture and civilization in a world where mechanistic values had come to predominate. The cultural solidarity he saw as natural among Europeans bore a strong resemblance to the corporate economic solidarity he hoped to foster among French workers and management. In each case, Romier made an argument for the restorative power of cultural tradition and the cultivation of the intellect, invoking science as a means to the restoration of traditional values, and a scientific approach to culture (and acculturation) as a means of resisting, and refashioning industrial modernity.[72]

Romier's views on the use of science as a means of strengthening French cultural traditions place him within a tradition of social Catholic thought that extends back to the founders of the movement, Henri Lorin, with his call for a constant renovation of tradition, and Marius Gonin, who invented the slogan "Science for Action." Like many of his predecessors at the Semaines Sociales, Romier was critical of industrial modernity, but enthusiastic about modern management and mass communications techniques as promising new ways of promoting social harmony and economic equilibrium. Romier's rejection of conventional political paradigms, too, was typical of the social Catholic movement as a whole, as was his quest to engineer a solution to contemporary social problems that would bypass socialist and capitalist analyses altogether.

Romier's typicality makes it tempting to argue that his later activities as a member of the Vichy government and an economic adviser to Pétain were simply the logical outcome of his social Catholic convictions. After all, a number of Romier's colleagues went on to collaborate, seeing their participation in the Vichy régime as a chance to test their social theories with a free hand. Robert Paxton has described the economic policies of Vichy as a series of determined efforts at modernization which were presented to the public as a reinforcement of traditional values,[73] and in fact, Lucien Romier's career exemplifies the tensions inherent in this combination of seemingly contradictory aims. He advocated economic planning and other technocratic management methods as a means of ensuring the social stability required to preserve French culture and traditions and transmit them from generation to generation. However, despite the similarities between social Catholic ideals and the vision that animated the social and economic programs of the Vichy régime, Romier's intellectual development was only one of several paths followed by those who had participated in the social Catholic movement. The career of Jean Coutrot, which is analyzed in detail in chapter 5, provides another excellent example of social Catholicism in action, and shows how the movement's ideas about technocracy, hierarchy, and human worth might be taken in a slightly more secular and technocratic direction.

From its inception, the social Catholic movement was geared toward the accomplishment of a series of concrete aims: the elimination of class conflict through education and cooperation, the provision of social services on the basis of a new science of society, and, from the early twentieth century onward, preservation of France's cultural traditions in the face of increasing pressures toward a greater standardization of cultures within the industrialized world. Perhaps less evident as a persistent theme in social Catholic discussion is the role of leadership in a modern democracy. From Hubert Lyautey's early efforts in the direction of a new science of management to Lucien Romier's reflections on the "deproletarization" of French workers, the movement placed a strong emphasis on the continuing role of elites as social engineers whose scientific expertise made them uniquely suited to lead. Finally, social Catholicism played a crucial part in defining what it might mean to be European, and French, in a world increasingly dominated by powerful and aggressive nationalist states.

For the French social Catholics, what made European culture distinctive (and French culture above all others) was its attention to traditional social relations and all that they implied in education, in aesthetics, in industry, and in politics. In the European setting, then, democracy could never be permitted to devolve into the rule of the masses. Instead, democracy could succeed in Europe only as a form of mass participation in public life for which the tone and terms were set by scientifically educated elites.

CHAPTER 5

The Modernist Enterprise: Jean Coutrot and the Art of Social Engineering

Our investigation into elite encounters with the culture of modernity has led us to explore a broad cross-section of commercial, cultural, managerial, and journalistic activities during the interwar years. As we draw nearer to a conclusion, several consistent patterns of behavior emerge. Whether they were joined by their desire to reform the journalistic profession, reinvent commercial advertising, reorganize French factories, or infuse new life into Catholic social programs, the reformers and modernizers of the 1920's and 1930's were all engaged in a struggle to preserve France's cultural identity, despite enormous pressure to embrace modernity in the form of international mass culture. In addition, most of the figures discussed here were eager to ensure that their role as social and cultural leaders would remain secure, even if old social hierarchies would have to be fundamentally recast.

At the same time, the modernizing elites of France were consistently fascinated by the promise of science as a panacea for all manner of social ills. From the social Catholics' embrace of "science for action" to the advertising community's confidence in the fundamental laws of human perception and the scientific management movement's "human motor,"[1] a new and more mechanistic view of the individual and of social interactions more generally was helping to pave the way for an increasingly technocratic vision of society. Perhaps most important of all, though, were the changes brought about during this period in the way elites thought about the relationship between technical knowledge and social life.

Historian Christophe Prochasson has characterized the years between 1880 and 1910 as "les années électriques," a period in which the number of scholarly and intellectual publications grew at an unprecedented rate, in tandem with an explosion of international scientific meetings designed to promote the rapid dissemination of knowledge across both national and disciplinary boundaries.[2] If the years preceding our own period of inquiry, then, were known for the expansion of scientific activity and communication, the years between the wars served to confirm that phenomenon and carry it in a new direction. During the 1920's and 1930's, scientific and technical knowledge continued to grow, as did its potential field of applicability. Communication began to increase between the disciplines as well as between the scientific community and those artists, intellectuals, engineers, and industrialists who saw themselves as advocates of modernity, not only in theory but also in application.

The interwar period saw the formation of various elite reformist groups, usually with a strong practical orientation and a profound faith in the benefits of a rationalistic, scientific approach to the management of social affairs.[3] As a rule, these groups sought to use technical knowledge as a means of fundamentally rethinking the way Frenchmen worked, consumed, and spent their leisure hours. While often eclectic in their recruitment, these organizations had as their common aim the generation of concrete proposals that would transform some aspect of French economic or social life. A random sampling of a few such groups might give us Le Corbusier and his collaborators at *L'Esprit nouveau*,[4] or perhaps the consortium of modernizing architects, engineers, and planners around the journal *Plans,* or even more probably the group of Polytechnique-educated industrialists and engineers who founded X-Crise in hopes of awakening French industry to the perils of international competition.[5] Regardless of their individual orientations, these interwar organizations all envisioned technology as the optimal medium for the transformation of society. In that sense, they might best be described as the beginnings of a French technocratic avant-garde.

Admittedly, the appearance of a new group of small, forward-looking organizations busily issuing manifestos that detailed their revolutionary, or at least modernizing, intentions was hardly a novel phenomenon within the context of Parisian intellectual life in the 1920's and 1930's. However, these technocratic reformist groups were unusual, and even innovative, in their insistence on bringing together individuals with a variety of technical competencies and areas of expertise, and providing them with a forum in which they might meet to exchange ideas and discuss contemporary social problems. In their quest to rethink France's future, then, the activities of these modernizing technocrats helped to break down the boundaries that separated the domains of art, academe, and engineering from the world inhabited by politicians and industrialists. If the early years of the twentieth century had helped to usher in a new era in the dissemination of scientific knowledge, the interwar period saw that knowledge variegate and recombine in a startling array of new forms as the circulation of ideas increased.

The 1920's and early 1930's also witnessed an increase in the number of ideas that were exchanged across cultural boundaries, often with thoroughly unpredictable results. The interwar technocrats were not infrequently inspired by techniques and models drawn from the United States, Germany, England, and occasionally even the Soviet Union. However, as they processed these various influences from abroad, the French recast them in more familiar forms and made them their own. Technocratic modernity took on a very particular character in France. Our aim here will be to provide one detailed example of the way a member of the modernizing elite tried to reconcile his most deeply held ideas about culture and society with the innovative possibilities he saw in modern science and technology.

This chapter examines the activities of a single French industrialist and technocrat, Jean Coutrot, in relation to the various elite groups and individuals with whom he worked over the course of his life. In many ways, his career exemplifies the kinds of conflicts and challenges faced by traditionally educated elites during the interwar years. Like so many of his contemporaries, Coutrot possessed a level of technical training that effectively propelled him into the world of modernity. At the same time, though, that training left him with a strong attachment to certain aspects of the aristocratic past and a penchant for asking questions and framing debates in ways that bore the recognizable stamp of Parisian literary and intellectual culture.[6]

By retracing Coutrot's career in some detail, I hope to show how one man struggled, not always successfully, to achieve some kind of synthesis between his own serious devotion to the concerns and conventions of French high culture and his equally strong commitment to the language and methods of modern science. In many ways, the polymathic reach of Coutrot's intellectual projects is a testimony to the brilliance of the interwar French elite, while the contradictions that plague his social vision speak volumes about that elite's fears and shortsightedness.

Jean Coutrot was a noted engineer and industrialist who graduated from the Ecole Polytechnique, the prestigious national engineering academy founded during the Napoleonic era, along with the Ecole des Ponts et Chaussées and the Ecole des Mines, as a training ground for the military engineers who would become France's future officers. As a member of the entering class of 1913, Coutrot attended classes only briefly before his education was cut short by the outbreak of the First World War. Once a star athlete, Coutrot was seriously wounded in battle, and he returned to the Ecole Polytechnique in 1919 as a scarred veteran whose movements were hampered by an artificial limb. With his marriage to Annette Blancan in 1917, he became an engineering consultant and, later, associate director at her family's paper products factory in the Paris region, Gaut-Blancan and Company, thus entering the world of French industry and gaining, by proximity, access to Parisian intellectual life as well.[7]

Coutrot came of age as an engineer and a manager during the 1920's, when France was still deeply engaged in the struggle to overcome the material devastation of the First World War. As a result, his own ideas about national regeneration took shape in an intellectual environment that introduced him to a broad range of views about the role of scientific management and other new organizational strategies in the coming renewal and restructuring of French social and industrial life.[8] He himself was closely associated with the rise of Taylorism and standardization in French manufacturing circles during the period of reconstruction. He regularly attended meetings of the Groupement pour le Commerce et l'Industrie, which brought together owners and directors of major industries to discuss the problems facing management in the current economic climate,[9] and he later became a key participant in the reformist activities of the Comité National d'Organisation Française, or CNOF.

As a member of the CNOF, Coutrot first came into contact with several individuals who would later become his associates at his Center for the Study of Human Problems in the late 1930's.[10] His affiliation with the CNOF allowed him to become familiar with most of the established figures of the scientific management movement, including Hyacinthe Dubreuil, Henri Fayol, and André Michelin, and to gain an initial entrée into the world of politics via André Tardieu, the Radical politician and promoter of technocratic policies who briefly presided over a Center-Right pro-industry government in 1929 and 1930.[11] He also encountered several management experts who had long been associated with the social Catholic Semaines Sociales, notably Joseph Wilbois, the founder and director of the innovative Ecole d'administration et d'affaires, and Maurice Ponthière, publisher of *Mon Bureau*.[12]

Coutrot made regular contributions on a variety of technical subjects to the Ecole Polytechnique's alumni newsletter, *X-Information*. More importantly for his burgeoning network of contacts, he became, in 1931, a founding member of X-Crise, a group of Polytechnique graduates that included Jacques Branger, Gérard Bardet, Robert Gibrat, Alfred Sauvy, and Jean Ullmo. The members of X-Crise were, for the most part, neo-liberals who were increasingly disturbed by the Third Republic's inability to propose effective solutions to the growing social and political unrest that had grown up in the wake of "la crise," France's ever-deepening economic downturn.[13] While the members of X-Crise hotly debated the merits of state *dirigisme* over a more laissez-faire approach to economic policy, Coutrot stood firmly on the side of planning and state intervention, a view that allowed him to fit comfortably as an appointed official of both the Popular Front government and the Vichy regime.

As with many of the economic and social visionaries of the early

1930's, Coutrot's politics were ill-defined and at times somewhat op-
portunistic. As a member of X-Crise and the CNOF, he frequented
neo-liberals and Socialists, Radicals and Catholics with equal aplomb,
casting his own views as in some sense above the partisan quarrels of
day-to-day politics. In consequence, his intellectual friendships spanned
the spectrum of contemporary French politics, from the Socialist
deputy Charles Spinasse to the anarcho-syndicalist and sometime
fascist Georges Valois. While Coutrot's relationship to Valois was
intermittent, tumultuous, and characterized by highly public disputes,
it also played an essential role in the development of his thinking
about economic planning and finely tuned management techniques as
desirable substitutes for the conflicting ideologies of the political
sphere.

Coutrot and Valois first became acquainted in the early 1930's, after
Coutrot had begun to publicize his ideas regarding the importance of
economic planning and the need for technocratic solutions to contemporary political problems. Valois's political evolution is far too complex
to be fully described here, but his ideas had evolved from the Proudhonian anarcho-syndicalism (and briefly, Catholicism) of his youth to a
royalist position in the early 1920's, when he was affiliated with the Action Française. With the banning of the Action Française in 1925, Valois
created Le Faisceau des Combattants et Producteurs, France's first
openly fascist organization, which had entirely collapsed by the end of
1927. Disillusioned with the right, Valois returned to his syndicalist
roots, and for a time he became an advocate of scientific management
and economic planning as the keys to France's recovery from the effects
of the war and economic crisis.[14]

Coutrot was associated with Valois between 1932 and 1934 as a financial backer for Valois's new publication, *Chantiers collectifs,* which
advocated cooperative and corporatist arrangements in industry as a
means of furthering the advance of rationalization and scientific management. The two men shared a fondness for the theories of Hendrik de
Man, a Dutch corporatist thinker whose writings on the virtues of economic planning and the reorganization of industrial production along
corporatist lines were widely read in France in the early 1930's.[15] Their
collaboration was short-lived, though, for within no time, Valois had

sufficiently returned to his anarcho-syndicalist roots to mistrust his collaborators from the higher reaches of industrial management. By 1936, Valois was attacking Coutrot as a predatory capitalist who saw economic concentration and organization as a vehicle for the advancement of his own personal and economic interests. With the fall of France in 1940 and the establishment of the Vichy government, Valois returned to praising Coutrot, describing him approvingly as a "revolutionary capitalist" whose ideas about planning and European economic unity would pave the way toward a more prosperous future.[16]

Revolutionary or not, Coutrot can certainly be understood today as a man who, like Valois, struggled to find a comfortable place for his ideas somewhere between the ideological commitments of the Socialist or Communist left, the proto-fascist tendencies of the far right, and the increasingly authoritarian views of the mostly neo-liberal technocrats with whom he most often made common cause. What emerges in his writings and his projects, then, is the portrait of an engineer and industrialist whose vision was resolutely original in his plans for a future in which social conflict could be engineered out of existence through a clearer understanding of human capacities and limitations, and a man who was disturbingly retrograde in his uncomprehending contempt for liberal politics.

Given Coutrot's training as an engineer, much of his writing involved specific technical discussions of industrial planning.[17] However, over the years, his attention slowly shifted from the more immediate practical concerns involved in running a business to a broader interest in mass communications and the psychology of motivation, both in the workplace and, later, in French society as a whole. He took special note of advances in communications, studying the use of graphic techniques and film in the workplace. He was particularly fascinated by film's potential to make workplace communication clearer and more immediate and to provide graphic technical instruction on the job. Beyond that, he saw film as a marvelous new propaganda device that might serve French manufacturers well as a means of combating socialism by allowing the owners of large enterprises to spread a positive message about their contributions to France's industrial progress.

In the 1930's, Coutrot rose to national prominence with the publication of two books, *De quoi vivre* (1935) and *Les leçons de juin 1936—l'humanisme économique* (1936), in which he began to grapple seriously with the psychological and spiritual aspects of the social question. *De quoi vivre* laid out the theoretical foundations for Coutrot's later speculations by arguing that man,[18] like other natural phenomena, was subject to what he called the law of alternation: human happiness was basically bound to fluctuate from day to day as the human organism passed from a state of desire to one of satiation and back again. As a result, Coutrot reasoned, it might be tempting to view life as a series of meaningless oscillations and despair of ever finding any meaning in it. Ultimately, he maintained, the only thing that could motivate a human being to action was something that appealed to his or her higher spiritual nature, that is, the prospect of engaging in acts of genuine creativity. *De quoi vivre* concluded on a hopeful note, as Coutrot explained how the techniques of scientific management might help to ensure that even the least skilled factory worker derived some creative satisfaction from his or her work.

His second book, *L'humanisme économique,* was written in response to the massive strike movement of 1936 that followed on the heels of the Popular Front's election in May and continued after its accession to power in June 1936.[19] Although the new book returned to many of the issues addressed in *De quoi vivre,* this time Coutrot focused his inquiry more specifically on the events at hand, attempting to understand the underlying causes for labor unrest. Again he claimed that the promise of material well-being was not enough to motivate human beings in modern mass society and that the key to management in the future would lie in a deeper understanding of the irrational impulses that shape human behavior. These ideas won him the attention of the Popular Front prime minister Léon Blum and his minister of the economy, Charles Spinasse,[20] who appointed him to run COST, the Centre Nationale d'Organisation Scientifique du Travail, under the auspices of the Finance Ministry. He remained in this post as a member of each successive government until his death, by suicide, in the spring of 1941.

By anyone's standard, then, Jean Coutrot was well entrenched in France's industrial and technocratic elite during the interwar period. He had contacts in the highest reaches of government and among some of the most ardent modernizers in French industry. However, Coutrot was a man of many interests who took particular pride in his intellectual frequentations outside the realm of business. In particular, he was noted for his extensive network of connections in the literary and artistic world. During the late 1920's, he became friends with the Russian émigré designer Sonia Delaunay and her husband, the avant-garde painter Robert Delaunay, helping Mme. Delaunay get her start in the world of Parisian haute couture. Among other things, Coutrot provided both technical counsel and much of the financing for her earliest forays into the commercial production of her fabric designs, and later advised her on the day-to-day operations of her couture boutique. In exchange, he was able to make regular purchases of Delaunay's distinctive fabric and clothing designs at cost, dressing himself and his family in outfits that can only be described as wearable art.[21]

The Delaunays were not Coutrot's only point of access to the world of Parisian intellectual culture, for he was known in a variety of avant-garde circles as well. Coutrot managed to befriend Antonin Artaud at a critical moment in his film career and promised to help him find backers for a film project.[22] He was widely read in contemporary French literature, in all its factions and *tendances,* and he freely quoted from the works of Blaise Cendrars, Paul Claudel, and Drieu La Rochelle, among others, in his own writings. He also had numerous contacts in the worlds of publishing and academe, particularly among those who specialized in aesthetic philosophy and criticism: the writers André Lhôte, Jules Supervielle, Jules Romains, and Aldous Huxley were among Coutrot's intimates, as were the noted aesthetic philosopher Victor Basch and the art historian and critic Henri Focillon. Moreover, Coutrot himself was a contributor to the avant-garde journal *Orbes,* and was invited several times to write on topics concerning industry and the arts for the *Nouvelle revue française.*

If nothing else, Coutrot's serious involvement in the world of aesthetic activity and criticism would seem to indicate that he held the work of artists in high esteem. In examining his reading notes and his early writings, though, one comes away with the sense that his engagement with aesthetic issues ran far deeper. Coutrot identified quite strongly with artists, so much so, in fact, that he used the aesthetic as a way of thinking about his own role as an engineer and a factory manager. This is not altogether surprising: the Ecole Polytechnique, one of the grandest of France's *grandes écoles,* saw itself as a training ground for France's future leaders. Consequently, its curriculum emphasized advanced studies in high culture with a special emphasis on science,[23] rather than the purely scientific studies one might expect in an engineering school. For Coutrot, then, there was no firm boundary separating the creative endeavors of those with scientific training from other sorts of creative activity.

It is perhaps worth noting, too, that during the 1920's and early 1930's, the engineering profession itself was not yet solidly established as a legitimate elite occupation or even as a genuine profession. The Ecole Polytechnique itself only belatedly recognized its graduates as engineers, properly speaking, following the state decree of October 10, 1937, that officially granted former students the title of *ingénieur diplomé.*[24] For the young Coutrot, artistic and philosophical culture doubtless beckoned as a way for him to lend weight and significance to the various practical pursuits and projects that engaged him. Like his colleagues in advertising, Coutrot may well have discovered that he could locate himself much more readily, both intellectually and socially, in the world of aesthetic discussion than in the more fluid, unsettled realm of the emerging professions.

However, Coutrot seemed taken with aesthetic issues for other reasons as well. He was obsessed with the idea that the activity of management was in many ways comparable to that of artists. Many of his earliest writings were devoted to exploring the aesthetic side of industrial activity on the grounds that, by acting and organizing, the industrial manager could attain to the summits of human creativity in a way that placed him on a level with those who spent their lives producing works of art. Coutrot was also deeply concerned with the psychology of the creative process, and he returned repeatedly to artistic creation as a model for all human creative activity.

In an essay on industry and creativity from 1929, first published in the avant-garde journal *Orbes,* Coutrot reflected on the romance of business in the modern era, beginning with a quote from the surrealist poet Blaise Cendrars's *Le plan de l'aiguille:* "Our business activities are no longer simply business; instead, they are what we want them to be: our adventures, our love affairs, our desires, our most obscure thoughts and needs, our wildest dreams."[25] Of course, not every factory manager would have been so eager to embrace a modernist poet's vision of his industrial activities. Coutrot's point, though, was that, by neglecting the role of inspiration in entrepreneurial activity, managers were missing out on an essential fact about themselves and about their employees. Industrial work had to appeal to the emotions of the people who did it, rather than simply relying on their attention or their effort. Instinct, feeling, and habit, he observed, dictate the majority of an individual's creative acts, rather than reason. A truly insightful managerial psychology, then, would focus on the emotional and spiritual factors involved in work rather than insisting on more purely rational methods to motivate workers to improved performance.

More than that, an enlightened modern manager would be forced to recognize the strength of the irrational and unconscious motivations that helped to structure his own working life. To be sure, running a business was a serious matter, but at the same time, there was a ludic aspect to it that could tap into a director's hidden energies. As Coutrot noted, "The energy source that nourishes the businessman in his daily life is less the hope of profits to be gained at some distant point in the future, and acknowledged only in the abstract form of a balance sheet, than the unconscious appeal of a pleasure [from work] that is more on a level with [the pleasures to be found in] sports or art."[26] In other words, Coutrot meant to go one step further than any of his Fayolist colleagues in recasting Taylorism within the categories of French culture: by drawing attention to the role of inspiration in business, he hoped to alter forever the activity of industrial management by transforming it into a form of artistic creation.

Elsewhere in the essay, Coutrot rhapsodized about the ideal manager as a kind of sculptor, carefully fashioning his organizational work of art, or as a gardener, pruning and shaping the delicate organism entrusted to his care. "Selecting human wills," he wrote, "sorting these unstable and precious plants, modifying them, making grafts between them, helping them to blossom, dividing them into harmonious groups, giving to each one its own material and moral place, coordinating their activities, bringing into equilibrium the delicate interplay

of orders, production and delivery through continual adjustment—
what more noble activity could there be, what labor more intoxicat-
ing?"[27] In this scheme, then, human beings and the machines they operated became the medium in which the manager's creative vision could
be realized at last.

In a piece from 1930, "Le cinématographe et l'organisation scientifique du travail," Coutrot developed the art/industry analogy even further, arguing that cinema was the industrial art *par excellence*. Film, he
observed, was the only art form that required something approaching
industrial levels of organization in order to be produced. Moreover, because movies were so expensive to put out, their makers were forced to
be attentive to the demands of the mass public in a way that an industrialist could appreciate more easily than most artists. Finally, he wrote,
cinema was the only art that could not be cultivated by an isolated individual. Making a film meant mobilizing actors, writers, technicians, and
equipment, as well as the vast sums of money required to pay for them.[28]
In the end, Coutrot claimed, film was a hybrid of art and industry, a
truly modern form of enterprise which demanded of its practitioners
that they be equally at ease in managing images and human beings. The
filmmaker was "at once a captain of industry and the worthy successor of
the priest and the poet."[29]

Ultimately, though, it seems that Coutrot insisted on the similarities between art, industry, and, as in the preceding passage, even the
priestly function as a way of arguing that modern industry itself was
the consummate art form. Despite his serious preoccupation with literature and the plastic arts and his regard for his artistic friends,
Coutrot occasionally expressed contempt for those who were satisfied
with the less heroic forms of self-expression. In *De quoi vivre*, he cited
Freud to the effect that self-expression in itself was unremarkable,
since every neurotic makes of his life a sort of poem. He concluded
that, in the end, industry was the superior form of poetic expression,
since "like the neurotic, the warrior or the man of action lives his
poem; he tastes the same aesthetic pleasures as the clumsy or impotent
individual reduced to versification or painting; besides this, he savors
the intense joy of molding the real, or permeating it with the waves of
energy emitted by his own will."[30]

Coutrot's interest in the aesthetic, then, had at its root a desire to demonstrate that in the modern world, managers and industrial "men of action," rather than poets or priests, would become society's moral and spiritual leaders. This preoccupation became apparent in various of Coutrot's reading notes and later writings. In some notes from the late 1920's, he fastened upon a statement made by the Catholic writer (and later French ambassador) Paul Claudel: "Poetry is the effect of a certain need to act, to realize in words the idea one has of something."[31] Claudel went on to claim that in this sense the functions of poetry and prayer are one, since both aid in uncovering the divine essence of living beings and serve as evidence of divine grace. Coutrot, however, found this interpretation thoroughly objectionable on the grounds that Claudel had turned poetry into little more than a form of disinterested awareness, detached from practical concerns of any sort. "The poetry that counts," he added, "is [the poetry] of action or of scientific research that adds to knowledge."

> Poetry was always one of the most effective forms of action, as long as its rites, blended with those of religion, reached the gods or its incantations changed the course of destinies. [Whether they were] magicians, historians or high priests, [these poets] scarcely gave a thought to disinterested action. Instead, they sought to manipulate the greatest and most mysterious of powers.[32]

Coutrot's project, then, was to claim that industrialists and scientists were the true heirs of the ancient poets and seers, while contemporary artists were merely a pale imitation of their powerful and daring predecessors.

These concerns continued to inform Coutrot's thinking about aesthetic questions until the end of his life. However, by the time *De quoi vivre* appeared in 1935, he had almost entirely recast the problem. Instead of debating the merits of artistic creativity vis à vis industrial production, he had begun to re-envision the conflict as one between the excessive individualism of the modern artist and the more collectivist imagination of the industrial magnate. Coutrot maintained that contemporary artists had slipped into an unhealthy disregard for the general public, giving up their ancient role as leaders and retreating into personal fantasies. The antidote for this, in Coutrot's view, would be a new science of art that focused on such issues as the physiology of aesthetic experience and the state of public mental hygiene.[33] Henceforward, art, too, would have a role to play in the reorganization of French society.

In his writings, Coutrot collapsed the distinction between art and industry, placing engineering and industrial endeavor at the summit of elite culture in order to promote his own technocratic and moral vision of French society. Erasing the boundary between *techne*, or practical creativity, and *poesis*, or invention of a more disinterested sort, finally meant eliminating the distinctions between individual and collective needs as well. Coutrot's social vision posited a perfect overlap between the demands of society and the ability of culture to cater to its needs, leaving little or no room for such antisocial, unproductive cultural manifestations as lyric expression or, for that matter, for any form of cultural expression that did not conform to collective needs. Ultimately, Coutrot's aesthetic speculations led him to deeper reflection about the way collective life functioned in contemporary France and to a series of attempts to rationalize and organize it. Above all else, Coutrot was a man who delighted in collective enterprises, whether intellectual or purely technical, that involved marshaling the resources and talents of a wide range of individuals. As his own intellectual reputation grew, Coutrot began to envision a role for himself outside the realm of industrial activity. More and more, he saw his ideas about contemporary social life as potential catalysts for a new kind of social debate. Over time, Coutrot evolved into something of an intellectual impresario, orchestrating the comings and goings of an endless stream of influential figures from the worlds of religion, psychology, medicine, business, and the arts.

By the mid-1930's, he had begun to devote more and more of his time to the organization of a series of discussion groups designed to bring together friends and acquaintances from different parts of his life to discuss the contemporary social issues he found most pressing. His efforts culminated with the founding of the Centre d'Etudes des Problèmes Humains (CEPH) at the Abbaye de Pontigny. The CEPH was intended both as a center for the propagation of Coutrot's ideas about managerial psychology and as the locus for the development of a new humanistic social philosophy. Its associates included such luminaries as Teilhard de Chardin, Aldous Huxley,[34] Maria Montessori, and the Nobel Prize–winning eugenics advocate Alexis Carrel,[35] but the center also brought together lesser-known but still influential professionals from a wide range of fields.

Certain areas of inquiry were particularly well represented at CEPH gatherings: Coutrot's fascination with the problem of human motivation led him to invite a number of prominent psychologists to participate in the meetings, among them Dr. René Allendy, who helped to introduce psychoanalysis in France, Jean-Marie Lahy, an efficiency expert and editor of *Le Travail humain,* and Serge Tchakhotine, a well-known Russian émigré expert on the psychology of political propaganda. He also favored those with some degree of expertise in the visual arts, although his autocratic style as an organizer often brought him into conflict with his friends from the Parisian avant-garde who attended the meetings.[36] Coutrot had numerous contacts in the world of advertising, and worked closely with several of them, including R.-L. Dupuy, an important advertising executive who wrote for *Vendre* and edited *La Publicité* in the 1930's, and Lucien Augier, who also wrote for the major trade publications in advertising.[37] He invited economists and social commentators, including Hyacinthe Dubreuil, Alfred Sauvy, and André Siegfried, and friends and collaborators from the scientific management organizations, as well as a series of participants from the Catholic community, including some of the main organizers of the Semaines Sociales, notably Jean Brunhes and Maurice Ponthière.

What Coutrot had created at Pontigny was an odd cross-section of a very particular French elite. With the possible exception of some of his artistic friends, the majority of those he invited to participate in the meetings at Pontigny were highly trained professionals with expertise in a specific practical domain who were committed to the idea of scientific modernity. Coutrot's aim in creating the CEPH was not only to elevate the level of discussion about France's social problems, but to put together a team of individuals with the will and the technical know-how to transform French society, and to work with them to create a new science of social life that was beyond both ideology and politics.

From the outset, Coutrot declared himself opposed to communism, capitalism, and "statist socialism" as visions of the ideal society. Like Lucien Romier and other social Catholics, Coutrot had certain doubts about the benefits of industrial rationalization, if not in theory, then certainly as it had been implemented thus far in postwar France. In his view, while rationalization was surely a good thing over the long term, in the shorter term the drive for increased productivity had made industrial working conditions almost intolerable by heightening already existing tensions between workers and management. Conventional political debate only made the situation worse by reinforcing old patterns for thinking about the problem.

For Coutrot, the task of humanist managers and economic planners would be to devise a new way of conceptualizing the relationship between labor and management, abandoning the rigid certainties of earlier management techniques, and seeking ways to make it tolerable for workers to function within a hierarchy. The manifesto of the CEPH included among its demands the institution of the forty-hour week, the development of effective economic planning that would eliminate unemployment, and the creation of an extensive program of research in the human sciences, particularly psychology, in order to achieve the "rational and humane limitation of inequality."[38]

In his book on the general strike of 1936, Coutrot observed that worker unrest had grown out of a sort of collective nervous condition brought on by rising expectations. He suggested that talking about the "occupation" of factories was an error, since the term was a military one that brought to mind images of invasion by an enemy. Instead, he argued, factory owners and managers needed to learn how to see strikes as the manifestations of a dynamic psychological process. His alternative description of the events of May and June 1936, then, ran as follows: "Last week's work stoppage was above all a phenomenon of emotional disintegration brought on by two coinciding factors: a slight economic upturn which gave workers the impression of increased security and helped to alleviate their nervous depression and, of course, the election results, which opened the door to boundless, still mystical hopes."[39] For Coutrot, any attempt to explain labor unrest in terms of political divisions could only lead to mutual incomprehension between management and labor. In his vision of the future, the crude formulations of politics would eventually give way to psychological analyses, and technicians would resolve conflict by literally engineering it out of the system through the careful application of *psychotechnique*.

Similarly, Coutrot favored collective bargaining because of its psychological benefits for workers. No matter how hard managers tried to create an atmosphere of open negotiation in their talks with workers, only workers who possessed an official position as the representatives of their fellows would be able to "relax, leave their tensions behind, feel free from their inferiority complex, and allow their integrated personality to express itself openly in discussions with their superiors."[40] He also saw collective bargaining as a way of shifting the terms of the interaction between workers and managers from a scenario based on conflict to one geared toward the achievement of consensus.

He believed that with further research into human cognitive processes and the effects of fatigue and emotional disruptions on the job, the efficiency of workers could be increased almost infinitely. He was particularly interested in the psychology of communications developed by advertisers for conveying information as clearly and efficiently as possible; he looked forward to the day when advertising techniques would be put to use in the workplace as a means of improving communications in the workplace and worker morale.

Citing Raymond Satet's work on graphic representation in industry, Coutrot argued that images were an ideal means of communicating with workers because they were more readily grasped and easier to remember than verbal instructions. They also made it simpler for workers to learn how a machine (or a chain of command) worked and to assimilate numerical information quickly and in a way that allowed for comparisons between different elements on a graph. Coutrot also noted that graphics could be useful in industrial work because they made it less complicated for managers and workers alike to think about organizing time and space simultaneously. "We must rely on a spatial representation of time and appeal to the logic of solids that Bergson discussed," he wrote. "Our spirit combines the concepts just as our hands create solids that will keep their shape in space."[41]

Ultimately, psychology was to play a key role in all of these developments, for as Coutrot noted, the social sciences still awaited serious development for industrial applications. Coutrot looked forward to a future in which psychological techniques were put to use in everyday life as a means of reducing human suffering and eliminating needless conflict. In fact, he went so far as to imagine a time when revolutionaries would no longer need to use violence because they would be able to rely on their mastery of the techniques of psychological manipulation. "The maximum amount of violence that a methodical revolutionary could permit himself," he wrote, "would surely be a concentration camp, but one that avoided the use of privations or torture. A latter-day Sorel who had kept up with the progress of knowledge would design this camp as a temporary sanatorium with professors and nurses where those who remained unpersuaded [of revolutionary truth] could be isolated until the end of their cure to keep them from harming themselves or others."[42] Despite his protestations of humanism, Coutrot introduced this aside with a chilling bit of praise for the success of totalitarian regimes in using propaganda techniques to keep the social peace.[43] He also noted that such methods might be successfully put to use in business settings as a means of creating conditions of psychological "equilibrium."

One of the principal goals of Coutrot's economic humanism, then, was to use techniques from psychology and engineering to eliminate the unproductive and time-consuming debates that grew out of political conflict. As someone who opposed ideologies of every sort, Coutrot maintained that entrenched political divisions in France prevented the free circulation of ideas that might be useful across party lines. Thus, one of the projects he organized through his center was to rationalize the formation of public opinion (and especially the formation of elite opinion) through a special newspaper subscription, the "Abonnement Arc-en-Ciel," designed to provide its readers with opinions from every part of the political spectrum. Charter subscribers received a copy of a different newspaper every day from a list that included *L'Action française*, *L'Humanité*, *Le Populaire*, *L'Oeuvre*, and *La République*, while Coutrot hoped to expand the list of participating newspapers to include *Le Petit Journal* and *Le Figaro*.[44] In a later essay, he described this project as a step toward "the moral and intellectual disinfection of this country, [and] a preliminary stage of ground-clearing."[45]

Coutrot's dream of creating a society that could function without conflict and without politics bears a strong resemblance to the fantasies of control that motivated the development of scientific advertising techniques. Like Coutrot, advertisers hoped that the science of public persuasion would allow them to intervene in the public sphere in the objective certainty of creating order and predictability where chaos had flourished. His technocratic vision also calls to mind the aesthetic *dirigisme* of Le Corbusier's plans for forming and managing popular visual sensibilities.[46]

In the various reform projects outlined by Coutrot in *L'Humanisme économique,* several decades of progressive Catholic social thought came together with the most recent advances in French perceptual psychology and scientific management techniques. Coutrot's plans for the reorganization of French social and economic life perfectly embodied the contradictions embedded within French desires to integrate traditional values with modernity. As a Catholic and a defender of managerial paternalism, Coutrot saw himself as a defender of human values that were endangered, in his view, by the political free-for-all of the Third Republic. Those values could only be preserved under a hierarchical and paternalistic regime that made careful provision for the welfare of its people. Modernity simply provided the technical means for preserving social order and maintaining hierarchy in a humane fashion, without recourse to coercion.

Describing Nazi Germany, Jeffrey Herf has discussed what he calls "reactionary modernism" as a way of thinking that enabled Nazi ideologists and leaders to embrace the new with revolutionary zeal while persuading themselves and their followers that they were acting only out of the most conservative and nationalistic of cultural and political motives.[47] While Coutrot had no such stake in a specifically nationalist vision of France's future, the technocratic forms of industrial management and, eventually, social governance that he envisioned in his writings and promoted via the CEPH promised all the same to restore some version of "true France" in which the French nation's biological and psychological vitality was no longer hampered by the incessant chaos and conflict of democracy.[48] Despite his protestations of universalism and ideological neutrality and his uneasy relationship to Vichy,[49] Coutrot's concern for the health of France's social body (and social psyche) places him squarely within the bounds of French nationalist thought, both before the war and under Vichy.

As Chapter 1 suggests, Bergsonian vitalism was a common point of reference for most of the writers, industrialists, and organizers whose ideas are presented in this volume.[50] What began in the 1920's as a simple fascination with the physiology of human perception and the mechanics of attention, effort, and fatigue was transmuted in the writings of the social Catholics and Coutrot's collaborators at the CEPH into a rationalist and technocratic vision of social order that was firmly grounded in a biological interpretation of human action. In their pursuit of a stable vision of social order, then, Coutrot and his associates had radically reinvented the bases for national solidarity and national community. As authoritarian and conservative as their underlying intentions were, the technocratic innovators of the CEPH could only manage to salvage familiar social hierarchies by fundamentally recasting the most basic elements of social order—man, the community, the nation—in biological terms.

Conclusion

W alter Benjamin's 1936 essay, "The Work of Art in the Age of Mechanical Reproduction," is one of a few truly definitive texts in the literature of modern mass communications theory. The essay is perhaps best known for the distinction it draws between what Benjamin called "auratic" art and the more universal art of the modern age, detached from the specific context of its origin and ready to speak to audiences of disparate cultural backgrounds.[1] Auratic art, in his vision, was an art with roots. Its power derived from the fact of its singularity, its presence, and perhaps more than anything, its immersion within the realm of ritualized and traditional behaviors. By contrast, the art of the modern era was profoundly semiotic. Unlike auratic art, it could be easily copied and disseminated to a vast and unfamiliar audience without losing its ability to inspire deep emotion in its viewers. In fact, Benjamin predicted, art in its post-auratic state might well be the vehicle that would awaken the masses into a new era of political awareness and engagement.

For Benjamin, as for many of his contemporaries (and the numerous theorists who have followed in their wake),[2] the appearance of mass-produced and more broadly accessible media such as film and radio was critical to the emergence of cultural modernity. The new media promised to push aside tradition, ritual, and aura in favor of innovation, secularism, and a more graphic one-size-fits-all approach to aesthetic production and to other forms of communication as well. Moreover, Benjamin saw cultural modernity and political transformation as inherently linked. In his view, the new technologies of communication possessed the power to shock their audiences into a heightened awareness of their social circumstances.

Even more importantly, from his perspective, the new mass media had already succeeded in establishing their audience as a political force to be reckoned with. By the time Benjamin began to write about the effects of film on public consciousness, mass democracy was already an inescapable fact of political life, however tenuously so, in Third Republic France. Yet for traditional elites, the popular classes remained an unknown quantity, regardless of their newly expanded public role. As a result, the artists and editors, advertisers and managers who found themselves on the front lines of this encounter between the classes were drawn to experiment with modern forms of communication in the hope of finding a genuinely effective way of reaching out to, and eventually influencing, the masses.

The emergence of a broader urban audience for mass culture was a source of considerable anxiety for France's upper classes. For most traditionally educated elites, regardless of their political views, aristocratic ideals lay at the heart of French culture. Taste, wit, and style, or in a word, what Pierre Bourdieu has called *la distinction*,[3] defined French identity. Mass culture appeared to promote a very different set of values, encouraging aesthetic uniformity and a lack of subtlety that was utterly inimical to established notions of good taste. For the most part, then, interwar elites, including those who worked in fields like advertising and sales, looked askance at mass culture in all its aspects, from the proliferation of cheap mass-produced consumer products to the appearance of mass entertainments they viewed as essentially foreign and potentially disruptive. In the end, the very thing Benjamin had celebrated in mass culture, that is, its ability to denaturalize and delegitimize established cultural norms, was precisely what French elites feared most.

Benedict Anderson has argued that the advent of mass culture was critical to the emergence of new national identities in the form of "imagined communities" engendered by the press, the widespread availability of novels, and other forms of mass media.[4] However, it has been my contention in these pages that the emergence of a common cultural identity at the national level was never such a simple matter, nor was it ever so unproblematically aided by new technologies of communication. Far from serving as a unifying force in the formation of a new collective national identity, mass culture in interwar France proved alarmingly divisive, driving some members of the educated elite to denounce it as the source of all cultural ills. They blamed consumerism and mass entertainments for denaturing French culture, destroying traditional values, and corrupting well-established standards of taste. Of course, upper-class hostility to mass and popular culture was nothing new, and it would be easy to read much of the cultural commentary of the 1920's and 1930's as an ongoing exercise in elite self-justification through negative example. However, on closer inspection, a paradox emerges from these all-out attacks on mass culture and modernity, since quite often those who saw themselves as the guardians of tradition were among the most effective agents of cultural change.

The various elite groups and individuals whose activities are recounted here were united by the common conviction that if French culture as they knew it were to survive intact, it would have to be fundamentally rethought in modern terms. Even so, the figures I have discussed played down the more innovative and even revolutionary aspects of their ideas, choosing instead to present themselves as traditionalists whose projects were merely the logical outgrowth of what had come before. For the advertising community, this meant working to persuade skeptical French industrialists of the value of modern advertising techniques while at the same time pointedly rejecting American techniques as culturally inappropriate, and developing a theory of consumer behavior that was rooted in late nineteenth-century French academic psychology.

A very similar impetus led the pioneers of the French scientific management movement to embrace Taylorist theories with great enthusiasm, and then proceed to rewrite them from the ground up along even more socially conservative lines. Their aim, once again, was to rework American methods into a form that was better suited to the more hierarchical culture of the French workplace. When the social Catholics invoked "the renovation of tradition," at the Semaines Sociales, they too sought to place the latest insights of economics and sociology in the service of preserving a paternalist and hierarchical social order. Finally, for Jean Coutrot and his collaborators at the Centre pour l'Etude des Problèmes Humains, these conflicting sets of impulses culminated in his plans for "the humane management of inequality," a series of scientifically inspired programs for social reform and modernization that were designed to ensure the preeminent role of a technocratic elite in French society and eliminate the threat of mass politics once and for all.

Robert Paxton, Richard Kuisel, Charles Maier, and others have signaled the Vichy years as a period in which the French economy and the French state were fundamentally reshaped along technocratic lines.[5] Indeed, the years of collaboration with and eventually occupation by Nazi Germany made it inevitable that France's political and industrial leaders would adopt more corporatist policies for standardizing and streamlining the mechanisms of national economic and political affairs. However, the roots of that corporatist and technocratic vision of governance were already present in the complex and often contradictory reponses to modernity that were being worked out by French elites across the ideological spectrum during the 1920's and 1930's.

Both strong technocratic leanings and some degree of corporatism still characterize the French state and much of French industry today. By the same token, the educated elites of the 1920's and 1930's have been succeeded by a newer group with lesser cultural pretentions, *les cadres*, a broadly based managerial elite whose members form a highly trained corps of social engineers with the kinds of expert knowledge that make them indispensable to the smooth functioning of the modern corporate economy and the modern bureaucratic state.[6] However, unlike their predecessors, the cadres of the postwar period have already managed to forge an identity on the basis of their technical qualifications for leadership in combination with a well-developed sense of their social entitlements and a rather more circumscribed notion of their social responsibilities. By recasting themselves in the role of social engineers, the managerial experts and reformers of the 1930's largely succeeded in securing a stable position for themselves in the social hierarchy of modern

France, and even ensuring that their numbers would increase as the ranks of the technically educated swelled after 1945. However, in an odd Durkheimian twist, the increasingly specialized nature of their social function has meant that, for the most part, today's French technocrats can no longer pretend to the kind of cultural influence that had been the defining attribute of the elite under the Third Republic.

The legacy of the French elite's encounter with mass culture, then, is mixed and to some degree self-contradictory. Despite the inherent conservatism of French elites with regard to modernity and mass culture, their efforts to come to terms with the realities of the modern age led them, more often than not, into brave new worlds rife with unintended consequences. Often, these were largely benign, as in the case of the scientific advertisers. Despite their own attempts to establish themselves as technicians, as distinct from the artists who dominated advertising at the end of the nineteenth century, their visual and psychological investigations both inspired and, at times, echoed the aesthetic and commercial projects of the avant-gardist Le Corbusier. In other situations, unintended consequences were the stuff of comic irony: the paternalist plans for reform promoted by the advocates of Fayolist management principles, so carefully designed to keep deferential relations intact in the workplaces of the 1930's, were revived in the 1950's and 1960's as the basis for a new and more humanistic psychology of management.

However, some results were more troubling. The social Catholic movement, whose members were committed to defending the dignity of each human being, were also persuaded that the systematic application of observation techniques drawn from sociology would be the basis for the moral reform of French society. In the end, their concern for human particularity and individuality was overshadowed by their conviction that more extensive programs of social surveillance, especially among the poor, would be the key to improving their nation's social and moral hygiene. And so Christian humanism mutated into something more closely resembling Michel Foucault's notion of biopower.[7]

Perhaps most disturbing of all is the story of Jean Coutrot. Coutrot dreamed of founding a society designed to achieve human liberation by using psychology to identify the aptitudes and abilities of each individual and help each person to find his or her appropriate place in society.

Instead, his utopian vision devolved into an authoritarian nightmare in which dissent and rebellion would be engineered out of the social system through the judicious assignment of troublesome individuals to the latter-day equivalent of re-education camps. What was it then about the utopian dreams and technocratic fantasies of the interwar period that made the boundaries between social reform, social control, and outright repression so difficult to negotiate?

Walter Benjamin's famous essay, invoked earlier, wisely acknowledges some of the dangers as well as the benefits inherent in the new technologies of modernity. He warns prophetically in his epilogue that although the mechanical reproduction of images had undoubted revolutionary potential, it could also serve the ends of those who wished to disseminate reactionary messages. Worse yet, the very forms of modern mass culture could readily be perverted to fascist ends. While socialism and communism sought to use mass culture as a vehicle for awakening the political consciousness of the masses, he argued, fascism simply exploited it as a means of aestheticizing the political and thus neutralizing it as a force for change. For Benjamin, then, mass culture almost implicitly promised to leave the rhetorical forms of bourgeois liberalism behind. Instead, it would usher in the modern era, whose ultimate form still depended on the outcome of the ideological struggle between fascism and communism. This was, and is, a fairly stark alternative, and it is only in the intervening years since Benjamin wrote that we have fully come to fathom the broad spectrum of mass culture's social and political consequences. As a man of his time, Benjamin shared with many of his contemporaries a deep faith in the utopian and progressive possibilities of modernity. Modern technology, he felt, might serve as the foundation for a whole new social world, so long as one approached it with the correct ideological understanding of history and social processes. Most of the utopian reform projects discussed in these pages were organized around locating a set of techniques, psychological or otherwise, that could be put to use in the service of a particular social vision. However, this distinctively modern approach to the resolution of social problems had some serious drawbacks. Perhaps most ominously, problems that had once been seen as susceptible to solutions that could be hammered out in the public arena slowly began to fall more under the exclusive purview of scientifically trained experts. More often than not, the reformers of the 1930's sought out scientific, rather than political, solutions to the conflicts between classes and nation-states that threatened to tear the world apart. The wholesale abandonment of politics in favor of scientifically inspired techniques of social management by the various thinkers and managers portrayed here can thus be read as a sign of genuine crisis for French democracy during the interwar years.

How, then, can this crisis be characterized? Historians' assessments of the political health of Third Republican democracy during the interwar years are mixed and still contested. For Zeev Sternhell, the proliferation of antiliberal groups and technocratic visions that would transcend ideology was merely the fulfillment of a long history of French discomfort with democracy that dated back to the late nineteenth century.[8] In Sternhell's account, for which he has been roundly criticized,[9] fascism in France was no more than a natural outgrowth of French socialist and syndicalist thought as they were altered by the experience of war. For a host of earlier and more recent scholars, organizations such as Charles Maurras's Action Française, Colonel La Rocque's Croix du Feu, and Georges Valois's Faisceau show few, if any, signs of fully developed fascist ideology; if anything, French fascism emerges in their accounts as a vestigial phenomenon.[10] Indeed, one German historian, Klaus-Jürgen Müller, has provocatively, if a trifle optimistically, argued that the flourishing of ligues and extraparliamentary political organizations in the 1930's was simply evidence of the wide range of views that could be expected under a properly functioning democratic system.[11] Given such a lack of consensus on the precise nature of France's political difficulties in the interwar period, it seems that, at least for our purposes, the real issue may lie elsewhere.

In an essay on technocracy and democratic politics, sociologist Ian Varcoe identifies technocratic thinking as "symptomatic of a profound cultural crisis,"[12] which results from the distance that can grow up between the glittering images held out by technology's advocates of its promise to dramatically improve human life, and the more dismal social reality of advancing technological change that often follows in their wake. "Technocracy," he writes, "is . . . a phenomenon of lags; of the gaps of which it is painfully aware and from which its proponents seek to escape through the salvatory medium of science. . . . The technocratic utopia is one in which the tension between advanced technological processes and outmoded and retarded social and political arrangements has been removed."[13]

The French elites of the interwar period whose careers have been examined here were caught in an uncomfortable position, halfway between a world of privilege and social hierarchy that they deeply regretted and the promise of a utopian future that had been all too slow to manifest itself. The technocratic impulse in interwar culture, then, can perhaps best be understood as their attempt to respond to this historical malaise in a way that promised to secure a manageable future.

Ironically, the rationalist utopia envisioned by the architects, managers, engineers, and artists of the 1920's and 1930's did come into being after the Second World War, albeit scarcely under the ideal circumstances they had envisioned. Le Corbusier's vast housing projects became a model for urban planning in the France of the 1950's and 1960's, while the advertising profession flourished, and some of the CEPH's less revolutionary proposals began to make their way into the inner sancta of French corporate culture.[14]

In the end, the modernist enterprise of the technocrats and reformers of the 1920's and 1930's was an undertaking marked by their deep ambivalence toward the prospect of social transformation and their equally wholehearted, if often unwitting, embrace of cultural modernity. The interwar French elite, then, were reluctant modernizers who clung to the high cultural traditions of their past even as they stepped boldly, and blindly, into a new era.

Reference Matter

Notes

Introduction

1. See, e.g., Jean-François Lyotard, *The Postmodern Condition: A Report on Knowledge* (Minneapolis: University of Minnesota Press, 1984); David Harvey, *The Condition of Postmodernity: An Enquiry into the Origins of Culture* (Oxford: Blackwell, 1989); and Jürgen Habermas's essay in *Habermas and Modernity,* ed. Richard J. Bernstein (Cambridge: MIT Press, 1985).

2. See, e.g., Stephen Toulmin, *Cosmopolis* (New York: Free Press, 1990).

3. See the introduction to Matei Calinescu's *Five Faces of Modernity* (1977; Durham, N.C.: Duke University Press, 1987), 3. Calinescu suggests, however, that while the French moderns of the early Enlightenment era and their British counterparts were recognizably modern in their historical self-consciousness, their persistent belief in a transcendent idea of eternal beauty distinguishes them from their aesthetically relativizing successors of the nineteenth and twentieth centuries.

4. Karl Marx, *The Communist Manifesto* (New York: W. W. Norton, 1988), 57–58.

5. For an account of the necessary connection between modernity and memory, see Matt K. Matsuda, *The Memory of the Modern* (New York: Oxford University Press, 1996); and Michael Roth, *The Ironist's Cage: Memory, Trauma, and the Construction of History* (New York: Columbia University Press, 1995).

6. Max Weber, "Science as a Vocation," in *From Max Weber: Essays in Sociology,* ed. H. H. Gerth and C. Wright Mills (New York: Oxford University Press, 1946), 155. The essay was originally a speech given at Munich University in 1918 and was first published by Duncker and Humboldt in 1919.

rno and Max Horkheimer are the only Frankfurt School phi-
: views I purport to represent here, however summarily. Walter
ys on mass culture and technology adopt a very different inter-
/ork and reach radically different conclusions than Adorno and
regarding the liberating possibilities of mass-produced culture. It
ing briefly, though, that many of Benjamin's writings on the question o. .ernity concern themselves with the importance of memory and nostalgia in the constitution of the modern sensibility, and they devote considerable
attention to the notion of the *passé*, or the slightly outdated, as a source of evidence about the preexistence of the present. See, in particular, "Berlin Diary," in
Reflections: Essays, Aphorisms, Autobiographical Writings (New York: Harcourt
Brace Jovanovich, 1978).

8. See the chapter "The Culture Industry" in Adorno and Horkheimer's
Dialectic of Enlightenment, trans. John Cumming (New York: Verso, 1997).

9. See Jürgen Habermas, *The Structural Transformation of the Bourgeois Public Sphere* (Cambridge: MIT Press, 1989).

10. See, e.g., Matei Calinescu, *Five Faces;* David Frisby, *Fragments of Moder-
nity* (Cambridge: MIT Press, 1986); Renato Poggioli, *The Theory of the Avant-
Garde* (New York: Harper and Row, 1971); Peter Gay, *Weimar Culture* (New
York: Harper and Row, 1968); Jeffrey Herf, *Reactionary Modernism: Technology,
Culture, and Politics in Weimar and the Third Reich* (Cambridge: Cambridge
University Press, 1984); Andreas Huyssen, *After the Great Divide: Modernism,
Mass Culture, Postmodernism* (Bloomington: Indiana University Press, 1986);
Stephen Kern, *The Culture of Time and Space, 1880–1918* (Cambridge: Harvard
University Press, 1986); Alan Janik and Stephen Toulmin, *Wittgenstein's Vienna*
(New York: Simon and Schuster, 1973); Anson Rabinbach, *The Human Motor:
Energy, Fatigue, and the Origins of Modernity* (New York: Basic Books, 1990);
Romy Golan, *Modernity and Nostalgia: Art and Politics in France Between the
Wars* (New Haven: Yale University Press, 1995); Robert Jensen, *Marketing
Modernism in Fin-de-Siècle Europe* (Princeton: Princeton University Press,
1994); Ken Silver, *Esprit de Corps: The Art of the Parisian Avant-Garde and the
First World War, 1914–1925* (Princeton: Princeton University Press, 1989); Jef-
frey Weiss, *The Popular Culture of Modern Art: Picasso, Duchamp, and Avant-
Gardism* (New Haven: Yale University Press, 1994); or, for the period immediately preceding, Carl Schorske, *Fin-de-Siècle Vienna* (New York: Knopf, 1979),
and Debora Silverman, *Art Nouveau in Fin-de-Siècle France: Politics, Psychology,
and Style* (Berkeley: University of California Press, 1989).

11. Hence the title of Jürgen Habermas's *Strukturwandel der Offentlichkeit
[The Structural Transformation of the Public Sphere]* (1961) in its French translation: *L'espace public: Pour une archéologie de la publicité* (Paris: Payot, 1976).

12. See Daniel Pope, "French Advertising Men and the American 'Promised

Land,'" *Historical Reflections* 5.1 (summer 1978): 117–39, and Victoria de Grazia, "The Arts of Purchase: How American Publicity Subverted the European Poster, 1920–1940," in *Remaking History*, ed. Barbara Kruger and Phil Mariani (Seattle: Bay Press, 1989), 220–57.

Chapter 1: Advertising as Modernism

1. For an excellent account of the purists' artistic activities during and after the First World War, see Kenneth E. Silver, "Purism: Straightening Up After the Great War," *Artforum* 15 (Mar. 1977): 56–63, and Silver's 1989 book, *Esprit de Corps*.

2. Chambonnaud fails to note that this was a common business practice in France as well, where a smaller company would come along with an imitation that had a similar name and capture the market for the original product through a blitz of advertising. Hence the advertising slogan that appeared for years in every Chocolat Menier advertisement, "Evitez les contrefaçons" (Accept no substitute).

3. From Victor Cambon, *Notre avenir* (Paris: Payot, 1916), as cited in Louis Chambonnaud, *Les affaires nouvelles* (Paris: Dunod et Pinat, 1919), 9.

4. Octave-Jacques Gérin, "Quelques opinions," *La Publicité*, May 1909: 164, reprinted from an article that first appeared in *La dépêche coloniale*.

5. Pierre Clerget, "Les bases scientifiques de la publicité," *La Publicité moderne*, Oct./Nov. 1908: 1–6.

6. See Susanna Barrows, *Distorting Mirrors* (New Haven: Yale University Press, 1981); Rosalind Williams, *Dream Worlds: Mass Consumption in Late Nineteenth-Century France* (Berkeley: University of California Press, 1982); Jan Goldstein, *Console and Classify: The French Psychiatric Profession in the Nineteenth Century* (Cambridge: Cambridge University Press, 1987); or Debora Silverman's *Art Nouveau* for fuller accounts of the influence that the medical profession had on politics and culture in France between the 1848 revolution and the First World War.

7. Octave-Jacques Gérin, "Quelques opinions," *La Publicité*, May 1909: 163–64.

8. Octave-Jacques Gérin, "Quelques opinions," *La Publicité*, June 1909: 227.

9. Henry Ellenberger, *The Discovery of the Unconscious: The History and Evolution of Dynamic Psychiatry* (New York: Basic Books, 1970), 151.

10. See Gustave Le Bon, *Psychologie du socialisme* (Paris: Félix Alcan, 1898); Gabriel Tarde, *Les lois de l'imitation* (Paris: Félix Alcan, 1890).

11. Hippolyte Bernheim, *De la suggestion dans l'état hypnotique et dans l'état de veille* (Paris: Albin Michel, 1911), 18.

12. See Silverman, *Art Nouveau*, 87.

13. Bernheim, *De la suggestion*, 19–20.

14. Théodule Ribot, *La psychologie de l'attention* (Paris: Félix Alcan, 1889), 3 and 6.

15. Edith Weiler, *La publicité, sa psychologie, son organisation, et sa fonction économique* (Paris: Recueil Sirey, 1932), 17–18. Weiler specifically cites Ribot in this section.

16. Louis Chambonnaud discusses the use of Ribot's concepts in a similar way in *Les affaires et la méthode scientifique* (Paris: Dunod, 1928).

17. See Marcel Bleustein-Blanchet's autobiography, *La rage de convaincre* (Paris: Robert Laffont, 1970), 43–48, for an entertaining account of the excesses of early obsessional advertising.

18. Pierre Herbin, *Comment concevoir et rédiger votre publicité* (Paris: Editions de *La Publicité*, 1938), 228–31.

19. Jules Lallemand, "La conscience et ses lois: Applications publicitaires," *La Publicité* 18 (Feb./Mar. 1920): 39.

20. Henri Bergson, "Simulation inconscient dans l'état d'hypnotisme," *Revue philosophique* 22.2 (1886): 525–31. See also Ellenberger, *Discovery of the Unconscious,* 168; Silverman, *Art Nouveau,* 89; and Roméo Arbour, *Henri Bergson et les lettres françaises* (Paris: Librairie José Corti, 1955), 141.

21. Henri Bergson, *Essai sur les données immédiates de la conscience* (Paris: Presses universitaires de France, 1985), 11.

22. Ibid., 11–12.

23. For a more complete account of Bergson's discussion of mental images, see Arbour, *Henri Bergson,* and Emile Bréhier, "Images plotiniennes, images bergsoniennes," in *Les Etudes bergsoniennes* 2 (1949): 107–28.

24. Bergson, *Essai sur les données immédiates,* 9–10.

25. See Ellenberger, *Discovery of the Unconscious;* Silverman, *Art Nouveau;* H. Stuart Hughes, *Consciousness and Society,* rev. ed. (New York: Vintage Books, 1977); Stephen Kern, *The Culture of Time and Space, 1880–1918* (Cambridge: Harvard University Press, 1983); and Eugen Weber, *France, Fin de Siècle* (Cambridge: Harvard University Press, 1986).

26. Hughes, *Consciousness and Society,* 124.

27. Bergson, *Essai sur les données immédiates,* 12.

28. See Louis Aragon, *Le paysan de Paris* (Paris: Gallimard, 1926).

29. Victoria de Grazia, "The Arts of Purchase," in *Remaking History,* ed. Barbara Kruger and Phil Mariani (Seattle: Bay Press, 1989), 227.

30. See the advertisements in *L'Esprit nouveau,* nos. 11–12 (Aug./Sept. 1921).

31. Victor Basch, "L'esthétique nouvelle et la science de l'art," *L'Esprit nouveau,* no. 1 (Oct. 1920): 9.

32. Le Corbusier, "Programme de *L'Esprit nouveau,*" *L'Esprit nouveau,* no. 1 (Oct. 1920): 1 [n.b. this citation comes from a second printing of the manifesto in the October 1921 issue, p. 845].

33. Victor Basch, "L'esthétique nouvelle," 10.

34. Ibid., 11.

35. Amédée Ozenfant and Le Corbusier, "Sur la plastique," *L'Esprit nouveau*, no. 1 (Oct. 1920): 39.

36. Maurice Raynal, "Ozenfant et Jeanneret," *L'Esprit nouveau*, no. 7: 809. Raynal was also closely connected to the world of advertising, both as a designer of posters and as a regular contributor to the most influential graphic design publications in France during the 1920's and 1930's, *Arts et métiers graphiques*.

37. Louis Delluc, "La photogénie," *L'Esprit nouveau*, no. 5: 589.

38. Emile Vuillermoz, "Les films allemands," *L'Esprit nouveau*, no. 9: 1076.

39. Adolf Loos, "L'ornement et le crime," *L'Esprit nouveau*, no. 2: 160.

40. Adolf Loos, "Ladies' Fashion," in *Spoken into the Void: Collected Essays, 1897–1900*, trans. Jane O. Newman and John H. Smith (Cambridge: MIT Press, 1982), 102. This last discussion of Loos's ideas about aesthetics and economics draws heavily on Naomi Schor's account of his work in *Reading in Detail: Aesthetics and the Feminine* (New York: Methuen, 1987), esp. 51–53.

41. Le Corbusier, "Architecture: La prix de Rome," *L'Esprit nouveau*, no. 14: 1607. "The lesson of Rome," he says, "is for the wise, those who are capable of appreciation, resistance, and control. Rome is perdition for those who know too little. To send architecture students to Rome is to destroy them for life."

42. Ozenfant and Le Corbusier develop their ideas regarding the moral aspects of formal economy in "Esthétique et purisme," *L'Esprit nouveau*, no. 15: 1704–8.

43. Charles-Edouard Jeanneret and Amédée Ozenfant, "La formation de l'optique moderne," *L'Esprit nouveau*, no. 21 (1924): 1.

44. Ibid., 2–3.

45. For a concise and thorough account of advertisers' economic hopes and expectations, see Daniel Pope, "French Advertising Men and the American 'Promised Land,'" *Historical Reflections* 5.1 (summer 1978): 117–39.

46. Ozenfant and Le Corbusier, "Esthétique et purisme," *L'Esprit nouveau*, no. 15: 1706.

47. Ibid.

48. Le Corbusier, "Architecture: Pure création de l'Esprit," *L'Esprit nouveau*, no. 16: 1910.

49. Jeanneret and Ozenfant, "La formation de l'optique moderne," 1.

50. Paul Dermée and Eugène Courmont, *Les affaires et l'affiche* (Paris: Dunod et Pinat, 1922), 71.

51. Ibid., 72.

52. Ibid., 101.

53. Paul Dermée, "La découverte du lyrisme," *L'Esprit nouveau*, no. 1 (Oct. 1920): 29.

54. Ibid., 32. It is worth noting in this context that Pierre Janet made a strong connection between hysteria, automatism, and the visual in *L'automatisme psychologique*, where he wrote that the hysteric is a person who is dominated by images. See Pierre Janet, *L'automatisme psychologique, essai de psychologie expérimentale sur les formes inférieures de l'activité humaine*, 2nd ed. (1889; Paris: Félix Alcan, 1894), 206–7.

55. See Dermée's comments in *L'Esprit nouveau*, no. 28 (1925): 2324–25. Apollinaire is generally credited with inventing and popularizing the term *surrealism*. While Dermée may have been among the first to employ the term in his writings, his use of it was in no way as influential as Apollinaire's.

56. Paul Dermée, "Le panlyrisme," *L'Esprit nouveau*, no. 28 (1925): 2362. The article appears on pp. 2362–68.

57. Paul Dermée, "Poésie = lyrisme + art," *L'Esprit nouveau*, no. 3: 327.

58. Ibid., 329.

59. Ibid., 329–30.

Chapter 2: Commercial Warfare

1. See, notably, Comfort, "Nos affiches de guerre vues par les allemands," *La Publicité*, Nov. 1919: 367–70. The first time the French government employed professional advertisers for propagandistic purposes may have been under Vichy. Their work is collected in *Les publicitaires au service de la propagande française* (Vichy: Editions Séquana, 1943). However, advertising designers worked closely with the government to publicize such national commercial ventures as the tobacco monopoly (la SEITA) and prestigious events, such as the International Exposition of 1937.

2. For example, Paul Fussell's *The Great War and Modern Memory* (Oxford, 1975) or Jean-Jacques Becker's *Les français dans la grande guerre* (Paris, 1980).

3. Claude Bellanger, Jacques Godechot, Pierre Guiral, and Fernand Terrou, *Histoire générale de la presse française* (Paris: Presses Universitaires de France, 1972), 3:8, 12–13, 16.

4. The prewar trade journals are full of accounts like these. See esp. *La Publicité* (1903–13) and *La Publicité moderne* (1905–8). Law theses from the period also contain some intriguing accounts of fraud, notably G. Albucher, *La publicité commerciale au point de vue juridique* (Paris: Presses Universitaires de France, 1923) and *La publicité commerciale et son rôle économique* (Paris: Presses Universitaires de France, 1923).

5. See Henri Vathelet, *La publicité dans le journalisme* (Paris: Albin Michel, 1911), esp. 102–3, 149–51.

6. The *Procès-verbaux du conseil d'administration* available in the Agence Ha-

vas Archives provide numerous examples of contractual agreements reached between the Agence and various French daily newspapers.

7. Letter dated 4 Nov. 1889, from the Archives Nationales, 5 AR 133, as quoted in Michael Beaussénat Palmer, *Des petits journaux aux grandes agences: Naissance du journalisme moderne, 1863–1914* (Paris: Aubier, 1983), 130.

8. From a letter from Raffalovitch to Kokovtzev, dated 22 Nov. 1905, reprinted in Raffalovitch, "*. . . L'abominable vénalité de la presse . . .*" (Paris: Librairie du Travail, 1931), 111, and in Palmer, *Des petits journaux*, 224. For a more complete account of the negotiations surrounding the degree to which news would be suppressed or merely toned down, see Palmer, *Des petits journaux,* 220–29.

9. In a letter from Arthur Raffalovitch to de Witte dated 26 Oct. 1901, as cited in A. Raffalovitch, *"L'abominable vénalité,"* 7–8, and in Palmer, *Des petits journaux,* 221. This agreement was apparently still in effect during the Russo-Japanese War.

10. About 25 percent of French overseas investments went to Russia, as compared with about 10 percent to the colonies. See Gordon Wright, *France in Modern Times*, 3rd ed. (New York: W. W. Norton, 1981), 310–11.

11. Maurice Schwob, *Le danger allemand: Etude sur le développement industriel et commercial de l'Allemagne*, 2nd ed. (Paris: Flammarion, 1897), 53, 57–59.

12. Ibid., 22–23.

13. Léon Daudet, *L'avant-guerre: Etudes et documents sur l'espionnage juif-allemand en France depuis l'affaire Dreyfus* (Paris: Nouvelle librairie nationale, 1918). See the chapters entitled "Les messageries départementales par automobiles," 114–23, and "L'exploitation des mines de fer de Normandie par l'industrie allemande," 136–54, as well as 192 for the reference to the Société Française d'Electricité AEG.

14. Daudet, *L'avant-guerre,* see esp. 11–18. This account is picked up and elaborated in Paul de Mirecourt, *Le commerce français aux mains des allemands* (Paris: "Editions et librairie," 1915), esp. 17–19.

15. Daudet, *L'avant-guerre,* 17.

16. De Mirecourt, *Le commerce français,* 19.

17. Henri Hauser, *Germany's Commercial Grip on the World: Her Business Methods Explained,* trans. Manfred Emanual (New York: Scribner, 1917), 92. Among the sources for his discussion of cartels Hauser cites Paul de Rousiers, *Les syndicats industriels de producteurs* (Paris, 1901), Robert Liefmann, *Die Unternehmerverbände* (Freiburg, 1897), and Etienne Martin-Saint-Léon, *Cartels et trusts* (Paris, 1903).

18. Hauser, *Germany's Commercial Grip,* 94.

19. Ibid., 114.

20. Ibid., 165–67, 178–92.

21. Ibid., 201.

22. See Marius Vachon, *La guerre artistique avec l'Allemagne* (Paris: Payot, 1916), 26; and Norbert Lallié, *La guerre au commerce allemand, l'organisation allemande et ses résultats* (Paris: Recueil Sirey, 1918), 98–99.

23. Lysis was, in fact, a former businessman who had entered the journalistic arena as a way of publicizing his ideas about the need for a more technocratic approach to economic policy making on the part of the French government. Richard Kuisel identifies him as one of the earliest postwar technocrats in the Saint-Simonian tradition of combining capitalist ideals with socialist schemes for social organization. See Kuisel, "Technocrats and Public Economic Policy: From the Third to the Fourth Republic," *Journal of European Economic History* 2.1 (spring 1973): 63.

24. Lysis [Eugène Letailleur], *Les capitalistes français contre la France* (Paris: Albin Michel, 1916), 20–21.

25. See references to Raffalovitch's book, *"L'abominable vénalité,"* a collection of letters concerning his efforts to manipulate French reports about Russia.

26. Lysis, *Les capitalistes français,* 117.

27. Lysis [Eugène Letailleur], *Les allemands et la presse française* (Paris: "L'homme libre," 1918), 1–2, and Agence Havas, *Procès-verbaux du conseil d'administration,* register 8, pp. 87, 89, 106, and 252, entries for 8 Nov. 1910, 25 Nov. 1910, 25 Jan. 1911, and 14 Dec. 1912, which indicate that contracts were indeed signed with the Société Générale d'Annonces before the war.

28. Lysis, *Les allemands,* 4.

29. The years directly following the war also saw the organization of the Office de Justification des Tirages, an agency sponsored by the major newspapers and advertising agencies that was to verify the circulation figures for French publications so as to establish their worth for advertising purposes. In the trade journals of the period, advertisers attempted to fight *contrefaçon* and fraudulent advertising by promoting a *Good Housekeeping*–style program in which newspapers and magazines would only accept advertisements from products they were prepared to guarantee to consumers. The Chambre Syndicale de la Publicité also lobbied successfully for the introduction of advertising courses into the curriculum of the state business schools (the Hautes Ecoles du Commerce, or HEC) and the establishment of special schools where advertising professionals could be trained and receive a credential in advertising science.

30. Letailleur's wartime writings are collected in *Pour renaître* (Paris: Payot, 1917), *Vers la démocratie nouvelle* (Paris: Payot, 1917), *L'erreur française* (Paris: Payot, 1918), and *Demain* (Paris: Payot/Editions de la Démocratie nouvelle, 1918). After the war, Letailleur published a collection of essays on financial issues, *Politique et finance d'avant-guerre* (Paris: Payot, 1920). *La démocratie nouvelle* appeared from the end of the war until 1924.

31. Lysis, *Demain,* 24.

32. Lysis, *L'erreur française,* 206.

33. Lysis, *Vers la démocratie nouvelle*, 15–16.

34. Lysis was an advocate of accuracy in reporting despite the manifest inaccuracies couched within his own journalism. The number of establishments serving alcohol in Paris had remained stable over the preceding thirty years.

35. See *L'erreur française*, 243–46, where Lysis inveighs against liberalism in an aside on the coming of the Russian Revolution, observing: "We have been taken over by the dogma that all ideas have the same right to exist, and that we should allow them to spread freely and come into conflict with one another, since the most just and useful ideas will certainly triumph. . . . Experience has shown that imprecise and unhealthy ideas can win out over the others for some time. . . . Each time a people dies, it is because it has thought badly" (243). He further remarked, "Although we imagine ideas are inoffensive, they are the most dangerous things there are: drinking alcohol leads to *delirium tremens*, while by filling oneself with imaginary ideas, one becomes mad within a few years without even recognizing it" (244). His reference to Le Bon and his projects to reform French public opinion appears on p. 239.

36. Lysis, *Vers la démocratie nouvelle*, 188.

37. This account of the failure of newspapers and advertisers to reform their methods draws heavily on Marc Martin's research on the history of the advertising business in France. See Marc Martin, *Trois siècles de publicité en France* (Paris: Editions Odile Jacob, 1992), 191, 208–9.

38. For a detailed history of the advertising industry's continuing resistance to change in the interwar period, see Marie-Emmanuelle Cheyssel, *La publicité: Naissance d'une profession* (Paris: CNRS Editions, 1998).

Chapter 3: The Culture of Business

1. Anson Rabinbach has advanced this thesis in his book on the origins of European fatigue science, *The Human Motor: Energy, Fatigue, and the Origins of Modernity* (New York: Basic Books, 1990).

2. See Paul Devinat, *Scientific Management in Europe* (Geneva: International Labor Office, 1927), esp. 244–45. Devinat notes that both the press and the advertising community in France were distinguished by their willingness to experiment with rational organizational techniques in their day-to-day operations, as well as in their communicational strategies.

3. See Richard F. Kuisel, *Capitalism and the State in Modern France: Renovation and Economic Management in the Twentieth Century* (Cambridge: Cambridge University Press, 1981), esp. 98–104.

4. See Alexander Gerschenkron, *Economic Backwardness in Historical Perspective* (Cambridge: Harvard University Press, 1962); Charles Kindleberger, *Economic Growth in France and Britain, 1851–1950* (Cambridge: Harvard University Press, 1964); and David Landes, *The Unbound Prometheus* (Cambridge: Cambridge University Press, 1969), among others. Landes first developed his

ideas on the subject of backwardness in "French Entrepreneurship and Industrial Growth in the Nineteenth Century," *Journal of Economic History*, May 1949.
For an extreme formulation of these views in a discussion of twentieth-century
France, see Landes, "French Business and the Businessman: A Social and Cultural Analysis," in *Modern France*, ed. Edward Mead Earle (Princeton: Princeton University Press, 1951).

5. See Rondo Cameron, *France and the Economic Development of Europe,
1800–1914* (Princeton: Princeton University Press, 1961); and François Crouzet,
Capital Formation in the Industrial Revolution (London: Methuen, 1970).

6. Cameron was soon seconded in this view by François Crouzet in "French
Economic Growth in the Nineteenth Century Reconsidered," *History* 59 (June
1974): 167–79. Crouzet also remarked in passing that the tendency of British and
American scholars to dismiss French economic aptitudes betrayed a particularly
objectionable kind of "racialism" (174). He has pursued this subject as well as the
invidious comparison between France and Britain in greater depth in a more recent study, *De la supériorité de l'Angleterre sur la France: L'économique et
l'imaginaire, XVIIe-XXe siècle* (Paris: Librairie Académique Perrin, 1985).

7. Patrick O'Brien and Caglar Keyder, *Economic Growth in Britain and
France, 1780–1914: Two Paths to the Twentieth Century* (London: Allen and Unwin, 1978), esp. 196–98. They argue that industrialization was almost certainly
more tolerable for workers in France than in Britain due to better working conditions (e.g., higher percentage of laborers in smaller workshops rather than factories, and fewer hours worked per day and/or per week). They also maintain
that the French experienced less utter dispossession than the British, for more
French people owned some kind of property that allowed them to supplement
their wages, through gardening or some kind of independent productive activity for market.

8. Notably, the French tendency to invest overseas while leaving native enterprises to languish for want of capital. See Clive Trebilcock's account of this in
The Industrialization of the Continental Powers, 1780–1914 (New York: Longman,
1981). See also Patrick Fridenson and André Straus, eds., *Le capitalisme français
XIXe-XXe siècle: Blocages et dynamismes d'une croissance* (Paris: Fayard, 1987).

9. Landes, "French Business and the Businessman," 342–43.

10. Ibid., 341, 345.

11. Robert O. Paxton, *Vichy France: Old Guard and New Order* (New York:
W. W. Norton, 1975).

12. Georges Duhamel, *Scènes de la vie future* (Paris: A. Fayard "Le Livre de
Demain," 1934), 33–34.

13. Ibid., 23.

14. Ibid., 46.

15. Ibid., 35. Lawrence Birken entertains this hypothesis more seriously in

Consuming Desire: Sexual Science and the Emergence of a Culture of Abundance, 1871–1914 (Ithaca: Cornell University Press, 1988).

16. Duhamel, *Scènes*, 29.

17. Ibid., 78. For a full discussion of the theories of Taine and Le Bon, see Susanna Barrows, *Distorting Mirrors* (New Haven: Yale University Press, 1981).

18. André Sédillot, "La campagne du costume bleu; ou la manière dont les tailleurs américains mettent en application le système Taylor," *La Publicité*, Oct. 1931: 660.

19. Marcel Hercat, "Publicité américaine," *La Publicité*, Nov. 1931: 748. See also Emile Gautier's discussion of Duhamel on advertising in "Scènes de la vie future: Un ministère de la publicité," *La Publicité*, Mar. 1932: 177–78, where he announces that "every country has the advertising it deserves," and Robert Valéry, "En quoi l'esprit français s'oppose à la publicité," in *Mon Bureau*, Oct. 1926.

20. Paule de Gironde, "Si nous faisions une annonce américaine," *Vendre*, Mar. 1929: 175.

21. Rabinbach, *Human Motor*, esp. chapters 4 and 9.

22. Taylor, *Shop Management* (1903) and *On the Art of Cutting Metals* (1906).

23. Emile Pouget, *L'organisation du surmênage* (Paris, 1913), 13, as cited by Judith Merkle, *Management and Ideology: The Legacy of the International Scientific Management Movement* (Berkeley: University of California Press, 1980), 149n.

24. See Merkle, *Management*, 136–71, for a fuller account of the reception of Taylorism in France, and 149 and 152 for a discussion of Le Châtelier's role in the spread of his ideas. See also Patrick Fridenson, *Histoire des usines Renault*, vol. 1 (Paris: Editions du Seuil, 1972).

25. This advertisement appeared in *Mon Bureau* 5.48 (June 1913): 381.

26. Hyacinthe Dubreuil, *La république industrielle* (Paris, 1913), 65, as cited in Paul Devinat, *Scientific Management*, 153n.

27. Cross, *A Quest for Time: The Reduction of Work in Britain and France, 1840–1940* (Berkeley: University of California Press, 1989), 112; and Anson Rabinbach, "The European Science of Work: The Economy of the Body at the End of the Nineteenth Century," in *Work in France: Representations, Meaning, Organization, and Practice*, ed. Steven L. Kaplan and Cynthia J. Koepp (Ithaca: Cornell University Press, 1986), 507.

28. For the most part, contemporary accounts of workers' attitudes divide up neatly by political orientation. Those who sympathized with the position of management tended to portray workers as traditionalist and deeply resistant to change and to blame them for the failures of scientific management in France. Paul Devinat, a social Catholic who wrote an extensive report on the progress of scientific management in Europe, viewed workers as suspicious and basically regressive in their approach to scientific management. By contrast, Hyacinthe

Dubreuil of the CGT argued that they thought rationally about Taylorism and were willing to accept it. Similarly, in *L'organisation scientifique du travail* (Paris: Librairie Armand Colin, 1927), Georges Bricard suggested that working-class resistance to Taylorism was simply a response to the specific circumstances of its implementation in France, that is, improperly trained managers, poorly implemented systems, factory directors and engineers who were intellectually infatuated with the notion of rationalization and unable to make it work practically, and excessive greed and lack of concern for the welfare of employees on the part of owners (see Merkle, *Management,* 153, for the account of Bricard).

29. Alphonse Merrheim, "Le système Taylor," *La Vie ouvrière,* 20 Feb. 1913: 214, 224, and 5 Mar. 1913: 30. As cited in Cross, *Quest for Time,* 106.

30. Merkle, *Management,* 154. See also Cross, *Quest for Time,* 107, for a further account of the strike at Renault.

31. Rabinbach, "European Science of Work," esp. 481–84 and 498–506. See also his "The Body Without Fatigue: A Nineteenth-Century Utopia," in *Political Symbolism in Modern Europe: Essays in Honor of George L. Mosse,* ed. Seymour Drescher, David Sabean, and Allan Sharlin (New Brunswick, N.J.: Rutgers University Press, 1982), 42–62.

32. Rabinbach, "European Science of Work," 479–81; Cross, *A Quest for Time,* 111.

33. Etienne-Jules Marey, *Du mouvement dans les fonctions de la vie: Leçons faites au Collège de France* (Paris, 1868), 69, as cited in Rabinbach, "European Science of Work," 482–83.

34. Ernest Solvay, *Note sur des formules d'introduction à l'énergetique physio- et psycho-sociologique,* Institut Solvay, Travaux de l'Institut de sociologie, notes et mémoires (Brussels and Leipzig, 1902), 14, as cited in Rabinbach, "European Science of Work," 492–93.

35. Cross, *Quest for Time,* 112–13.

36. Among Jules Amar's works on work and fatigue were *Le rendement de la machine humaine* (Paris, 1909), *Le moteur humain et les bases scientifiques du travail professionnel* (Paris, 1914), and *L'organisation physiologique du travail et le système Taylor* (Paris, 1917). On Amar and his colleague Armand Imbert, see also Georges Ribeill, "Les débuts de l'ergonomie en France à la veille de la première guerre mondiale," *Mouvement social,* no. 113 (Oct.–Dec. 1980): 3–36.

37. Jean-Marie Lahy, *Le système Taylor et la physiologie du travail professionnel* (Paris: Masson, 1916), viii.

38. Ibid., ix, 179.

39. Ibid., vii.

40. Ibid., x.

41. Ibid., 13.

42. Jean-Marie Lahy, *La morale de Jésus, sa part d'influence dans la morale actuelle* (Paris: F. Alcan, 1911), 6–7.

43. Merkle, *Management and Ideology*, 156–57.

44. For an insightful discussion of what was at stake for workers in retaining control over the technical know-how they needed to do their jobs, see Stephen A. Marglin, "What Do the Bosses Do? The Origins and Functions of Hierarchy in Capitalist Production," in *Classes, Power, and Conflict: Classical and Contemporary Debates,* ed. Anthony Giddens and David Held (Berkeley: University of California Press, 1982), 285–98.

45. Bricard, *L'organisation scientifique*, 186.

46. Among the enterprises to adopt Taylor's methods were Michelin and the Penhoët shipyards. See Merkle, *Management and Ideology,* 152, 157, and Bricard, *L'organisation scientifique,* 195.

47. Fayol (1841–1925) was educated at the Ecole des Mines in Saint-Etienne and received his engineering degree in 1860. In 1866, he began to manage the Commentry Collieries, and he added the Montvicq coalfields to his responsibilities in 1872 before taking over as the firm's general manager in 1888. In addition to his expertise as an administrator, he commanded respect in the engineering community for his technical work on the geological formation of coal seams and techniques for extracting coal from beds that were situated at odd angles. See Henri Fayol, *Industrial and General Administration*, trans. J. A. Coubrough (London: International Management Institute, 1930), 4–5, for biographical details, as well as Devinat, *Scientific Management,* 31n.

48. Among them, *Exposé des principes généraux d'administration* (1908), *Administration industrielle et générale, prévoyance, organisation, commandement, coordination, contrôle* (1916), *Importance de la fonction administrative dans le gouvernement des affaires* (1917), *Sur la réforme des services publics* (1918), and *L'éveil de l'esprit public* (1918).

49. Fayol, *Industrial and General Administration*, 27.

50. Ibid., 52.

51. Besides its widespread use in state administrative schools, Fayolism provoked serious interest in the business community at large. See J. Billard, *Un essai de doctrine, le fayolisme* (Paris: Jouve, 1924), R. Desaubliaux, *Les origines biologiques de la fonction administrative* (Paris: Dunod, 1920), the articles by Gaston Ravisse and various anonymous authors in the March, May, and June 1926 numbers of *Mon Bureau*, and DuCrouzet, "Les développements actuels de la doctrine administrative," in the January 1925 issue of the social Catholic journal *Chronique sociale de France.*

52. Devinat, *Scientific Management,* 32.

53. See ibid., 43–44, for a discussion of some of the moral claims made by the scientific management movement in Europe.

54. On Taylor and Taylorism, see Robert Kanigel, *The One Best Way: Frederick Winslow Taylor and the Enigma of Efficiency* (New York: Viking, 1997); Daniel Nelson, *Frederick W. Taylor and the Rise of Scientific Management*

(Madison: University of Wisconsin Press, 1980); Charles D. Wrege, *Frederick W. Taylor, the Father of Scientific Management: Myth and Reality* (Homewood, IL: Business One Irwin, 1991); and Samuel Haber, *Efficiency and Uplift: Scientific Management in the Progressive Era, 1890–1920* (Chicago: University of Chicago Press, 1964).

55. See Donald Reid, "Fayol: Excès d'honneur ou excès d'indignité?" *Revue française de gestion,* no. 70 (Sept./Oct. 1988). My thanks to Robert Frost for bringing this essay to my attention.

56. On French taste in the decorative arts, see Leora Auslander, *Taste and Power: Furnishing Modern France* (Berkeley: University of California Press, 1996); Nancy Troy, *Modernism and the Decorative Arts in France: Art Nouveau to Le Corbusier* (New Haven: Yale University Press, 1991); and Debora Silverman, *Art Nouveau.*

57. See, notably, Kuisel, *Capitalism,* 101; and Merkle, *Management and Ideology,* 171.

Chapter 4: Catholicism and Modernity

1. As a central figure in French social Catholicism, René de La Tour du Pin generated a considerable amount of scholarly activity in the 1940's, 1950's, and 1960's. For more details on his life and thought, see Jacques Bassot, *Travail et propriété: Vers un ordre social d'après La Tour du Pin* (Paris: Georges and Roger Joly, 1942); Paul Chanson, *Autorité et liberté: Constitution de la France selon La Tour du Pin* (Paris: Editions du temps présent, 1941); and Robert Talmy, *Aux sources du catholicisme social: L'école de La Tour du Pin* (Tournai: Desclée, 1963).

2. See Henri Rollet, *L'Action social des catholiques en France,* vol. 1, *1871–1901* (Paris: Editions Contemporaines, 1949).

3. For a more comprehensive discussion of the social Catholic movement and its history, see Henri Rollet, *L'action sociale,* as well as the companion volume, *L'action sociale des catholiques en France,* vol. 2, *1871–1914* (Brussels: Desclée de Brouwer, 1958), as well as Georges Hoog, *Histoire du catholicisme social en France, 1871–1931* (Paris: Editions Domat et Monchrestien, 1946) and the more recent work by Gérard de Cholvy and Yves-Marie Hilaire, *Histoire religieuse de la France contemporaine, 1880–1930* (Paris: Edition Privat, 1986). Luc Boltanski also provides an interesting and useful account of social Catholic influences in business in *Les cadres: La formation d'un groupe social* (Paris: Editions de Minuit, 1982). Finally, my account of social Catholicism in its early days draws heavily on Paul Rabinow's discussion of the movement in *French Modern: Norms and Forms of the Social Environment* (Cambridge: MIT Press, 1989), especially its fourth chapter, "New Elites: From the Moral to the Social," 104–25.

4. Rabinow, *French Modern,* 122–23.

5. Christophe Prochasson, *Les années électriques, 1880–1910* (Paris: Editions La Découverte, 1991), 171.

6. Hubert Lyautey, *Le rôle social de l'officier* (Paris: Editions Albatros/Association Nationale Maréchal Lyautey, 1984), 77.

7. [Hubert Lyautey], "Du rôle social de l'officier," *Revue des deux mondes*, 15 Mar. 1891, p. 451.

8. Ibid., 451, 445–46.

9. On the Proudhonian tendencies of social Catholicism, see Adrien Dansette, *Histoire religieuse de la France contemporaine* (Paris: Flammarion, 1965), 491.

10. Jean-Marie Mayeur, *Catholicisme social et démocratie chrétienne* (Paris: Editions du Cerf, 1986), 121, 134–35. Mayeur notes that social concern could easily be linked to theological attitudes that were anything but forward-looking: "Intransigent [conservative] Catholicism aimed to be and was a popular movement. It accepted social democracy, but not political democracy. . . . Despite the French usage of the term, democracy is not necessarily tied to the liberal and Jacobin traditions nor to anticlericalism. In fact, one of the virtues of democracy [from this perspective] was its association with both ultramontane thought and Christianity" (121). See also Mayeur, "Le catholicisme social en France," *Mouvement social*, no. 77 (1970): 113–21.

11. The precise title of the sessions in 1939 was "Le problème des classes dans la Communauté Nationale." The Semaines Sociales also took on such wideranging issues as international economic and diplomatic relations and working conditions in industry and the social question in the colonies. Periodically, sessions were devoted to topics that engaged both sociological and metaphysical analysis, as for example in 1937 and 1938, when the themes announced were, respectively, "La personne humaine en péril" and "La liberté et les libertés dans la vie sociale."

12. Henri Lorin, "L'orientation sociale de la pensée catholique au XIXe siècle," as cited in Eugène Duthoit's own "Déclaration d'ouverture," reprinted in the *Semaine Sociale de France—XIe session—Metz, 1919* (Lyon: Chronique sociale de France, 1919), 20–21.

13. The citation here is from the conclusion of Durkheim's *Les règles de la méthode sociologique* (Paris: F. Alcan, 1895), as reproduced in Msgr. Deploige, "L'idée de responsabilité dans la sociologie contemporaine," *Semaine Sociale de France—Xe session—Versailles, 1913* (Lyon: Chronique sociale de France, 1913), 131.

14. Deploige, "L'idée de responsabilité," 142–43.

15. Maurice Deslandres, "La mode: Ses conséquences économiques et sociales," *Semaine Sociale de France—VIIIe session—Saint Etienne, 1911* (Lyon: Chronique sociale de France, 1911), 352–55.

16. Deslandres returned to this theme twenty years later in an article for the Semaines Sociales in which he condemned the temptations proffered by consumer society as a powerful force for social disruption. See M. Deslandres, "Les

consommateurs et la moralité des affaires," in *Semaine Sociale de France, Mulhouse, XXIIIe session, 1931—La morale chrétienne et les affaires* (Lyon: Chronique sociale de France, 1931), 437–58.

17. Deslandres, "La mode," 349 and 351.

18. Ibid., 356.

19. Etienne Martin-Saint-Léon, "Le contre-coup de la guerre et de l'après-guerre sur la consommation et le coût de la vie," *Semaine Sociale de France—XIIe session—Caen, 1920* (Lyon: Chronique sociale de France, 1920), 231–32.

20. Maurice Deslandres, "La participation des consommateurs à la vie des corps publics," *Semaine Sociale de France—XIVe session—Strasbourg, 1922* (Lyon: Chronique sociale de France, 1922), 364. Deslandres justifies his arguments, which he describes as a "réhabilitation du consommateur par la science économique moderne" (364) as an effort to make social science categories correspond more closely to contemporary social realities.

21. See Rollet, *L'action sociale*, 2:50–51.

22. See Eugène Duthoit, "La crise de la production et la sociologie catholique," *Semaine Sociale de France—XIIe session—Caen, 1920* (Lyon: Chronique sociale de France, 1920), 30–31.

23. Eugène Duthoit, "La crise de la probité publique et le désordre economique," leçon d'ouverture, *Semaine Sociale de France—XIIIe session—Toulouse, 1921* (Lyon: Chronique sociale de France, 1921), 17.

24. Ibid., 25–26.

25. On Taylorism in France, see Richard F. Kuisel, *Capitalism and the State in Modern France: Renovation and Economic Management in the Twentieth Century* (Cambridge: Cambridge University Press, 1981); Judith Merkle, *Management and Ideology: The Legacy of the International Scientific Management Movement* (Berkeley: University of California Press, 1980); and Charles S. Maier, *In Search of Stability: Explorations in Historical Political Economy* (Cambridge: Cambridge University Press, 1987).

26. Eugène Duthoit, "La crise de la production," 31.

27. G. Perrin-Pelletier, "Le rôle de la science et de la technique dans l'economie nationale," *Semaine Sociale de France—XVIe session—Rennes, 1924—Le Problème de la terre dans l'economie nationale* (Lyon: Chronique sociale de France, 1924), 319, 321.

28. Ibid., 320.

29. Ibid., 323.

30. Ibid., 324. Perrin-Pelletier complained that if contemporary French society was run by soulless technocrats, there was only the educational system to blame, for their training in the physical and social sciences excluded any systematic discussion of morality. "How could it be otherwise," he asked, "since official instruction offers no psychological, social, or moral doctrine and refuses to

adopt one on the pretext of preserving its objectivity? This attitude has lamentable consequences and is the result of anti-scientific [thinking]."

31. Le R. Père Danset, "Rationalisation . . . moralisation," *Semaine Sociale de France—XIXe session—Nancy, 1927—La femme dans la société* (Lyon: Chronique sociale de France, 1927), 379.

32. Ibid., 388.

33. Ibid., 396, 398, and 408.

34. Devinat, *Scientific Management*.

35. Paul Devinat, "L'organisation scientifique du travail," *Semaine Sociale de France—XXIe session—Besançon, 1929—Les nouvelles conditions de la vie industrielle* (Lyon: Chronique sociale de France, 1929), 192.

36. Eugène Duthoit, "La 'rationalisation' est-elle un progrès?" *Semaine Sociale de France—XXIe session—Besançon, 1929—Les nouvelles conditions de la vie industrielle* (Lyon: Chronique sociale de France, 1929), 40.

37. Ibid., 41, citing Ernest Mercier's report to the Association Française pour le Progrès Social, 1927.

38. Ibid., 62.

39. See John Hunter, "The Problem of the French Birth Rate on the Eve of World War I," *French Historical Studies* 2 (1962); Angus MacLaren, *Sexuality and Social Order: The Debate over the Fertility of Women and Workers in France, 1770–1920* (New York: Holmes and Meier, 1983); Karen Offen, "Depopulation, Nationalism, and Feminism in Fin-de-Siècle France," *American Historical Review* 89 (June 1984); Mary-Louise Roberts, *Civilization Without Sexes: Reconstructing Gender in Postwar France, 1917–1927* (Chicago: University of Chicago Press, 1994); Francis Ronsin, *La grève des ventres: Propagande néo-malthusienne et la baisse de la natalité française* (Poitiers: Aubier Montaigne, 1980); William Schneider, *Quality and Quantity: The Quest for Biological Regeneration in Twentieth-Century France* (Cambridge: Cambridge University Press, 1990); Joseph Spengler, *France Faces Depopulation: Postlude Edition, 1936–1976* (Durham, N.C.: Duke University Press, 1979); and Richard Tomlinson, "The Politics of Dénatalité in the French Third Republic," Ph.D. thesis, Cambridge University, 1983. On pro-natalism, see Francine Muel-Dreyfus, *Vichy et l'éternel féminin: Contribution à une sociologie politique de l'ordre des corps* (Paris: Editions du Seuil, 1996); Philip Ogden and Marie-Monique Huss, "Demography and Pronatalism in France in the Nineteenth and Twentieth Centuries," *Journal of Historical Geography* 8 (1982); Robert Talmy, *Histoire du mouvement familial en France, 1896–1939* (Paris: Union nationale des caisses d'allocations familales, 1962); Françoise Thébaud, *Quand nos grand-mères donnaient la vie: La maternité en France dans l'entre-deux-guerres* (Lyon: Presses Universitaires de Lyon, 1986); and Thébaud, "Maternité et famille entre les deux guerres: Idéologie et politique familiale," in *Femmes et fascismes,* ed. Rita Thalman (Paris: Editions Tierce, 1987).

40. Joseph Daniel, "Les crises du passé et la crise présente," *Semaine Sociale de France—XXIVe session—Lille, 1932—Le Désordre de l'Economie internationale et la pensée chrétienne* (Lyon: Chronique sociale de France, 1932), 92–94.

41. Ibid., 96.

42. Daniel cites an essay by one M. Brocard, "Le crédit," which appeared in the *Revue des deux mondes* for 15 Mar. 1932.

43. Robert Paxton, *Vichy France: Old Guard and New Order, 1940–1944,* 2nd ed. (New York: W. W. Norton, 1975), 256.

44. See Henri Moysset, "L'opinion publique, étude de psychologie sociale," *Semaine Sociale de France—VIIe session—Rouen, 1910* (Lyon: Chronique sociale de France, 1910), 135–58. Among the works cited by Moysset were Gabriel Tarde's *L'opinion et la foule* (1901), Gustave Le Bon's *La psychologie des foules* (1910 ed.), J. Arren's *La publicité lucrative et raisonnée* (1909), and Hippolyte Taine's historical essay, *Les origines de la France contemporaine,* vol. 1, *L'ancien régime.*

45. Moysset, "L'opinion publique," 140.

46. Ibid., 143.

47. Ibid., 151.

48. Ibid., 144.

49. In his discussion of contemporary management policies, G. Perrin-Pelletier made reference to "ingénieurs moraux" in some of the larger French corporations, claiming that several railroad companies had engaged them to contend with psychological impediments to increased efficiency in the workplace. Perrin-Pelletier, "Le rôle," 325.

50. *Vouloir, journal d'action économique et sociale,* Dec. 1918: 1.

51. See Raymond Clémang, "Une faute inutile: Les projets d'impôts sur la publicité," *Vouloir,* Nov. 1917: 13–14; and René Castelneaux, "'Casse Cou': L'étranglement de la poule aux oeufs d'or," *Vouloir,* no. 30 (Sept. 1918): 6. Similar articles appeared in *La Publicité* both before and after the war. See, e.g., "L'impôt sur la publicité," *La Publicité,* May 1919: 121.

52. See Raymond Clémang, "L'attention en publicité," *Vouloir,* no. 34 (Jan. 1918): 15–16; "La mémoire en publicité," *Vouloir,* no. 36 (Mar. 1918): 14; and "Les eléments psychologiques de la publicité," *Vouloir,* no. 45 (Dec. 1918): 7. Both Clémang and René Castelneaux began writing for *La Publicité* after the war.

53. The notice appeared in *Vouloir,* no. 44 (Nov. 1918): 4.

54. Many of those who wrote for *La Publicité* and *Vendre* also taught part-time at the Institut Catholique de Paris and the Catholic universities in Louvain (Belgium) and Lille. While the state delayed in setting up marketing and advertising curricula in its Hautes Ecoles Commerciales and lesser trade schools, the Catholic universities made a point of offering these courses and employing instructors who were at the forefront of the profession.

55. Marius Gonin, "L'aspect moral du problème de la publicité," *Semaine*

Sociale de France—XXIIIe session—Mulhouse, 1931—La Morale Chrétienne et les affaires (Lyon: Chronique sociale de France, 1931), 480. See also Colonel André Roullet, "La presse (Journal Filmé et T.S.F.) responsabilités educatives," *Semaine Sociale de France—XXVIe session—Nice, 1934—Ordre social et education* (Lyon: Chronique sociale de France, 1934), 383–408. Roullet worried about the effects of advertising on the public sphere, citing recent instances of fraud and misrepresentation, and the advertising industry's unwillingness to take responsibility for the social ills (indebtedness, needless consumption) engendered by intensive publicity. Typically, he concluded that "advertising still awaits moral regulation" (398).

56. Gonin, "L'aspect moral," 482.

57. Ibid., 485–86.

58. Ibid., 489.

59. Ibid., 491. The actual passage from Gérin reads as follows: "At the present time, there is no human being whose thoughts have not been engendered by the thoughts of others. None of our acts . . . escapes the influence of the thoughts and acts of those who surround us, who we affect in our turn."

60. Ibid., 489.

61. Ibid., 499. Gonin also cites here J. Hours, "La publicité," *Notes de doctrine et d'action*, Jan.–Mar. 1931.

62. Jean-Marie Mayeur expands on this point in *Catholicisme social et démocratie chrétienne* (Paris: Les Editions du Cerf, 1986).

63. Luc Boltanski, *Les cadres*, 65–66.

64. See Paxton, *Vichy France*, 269 n. 43.

65. Ibid., 269n, 271.

66. Lucien Romier, "La solidarité européenne," *Semaine sociale de France—XVIIIe session—Le Havre, 1926—Le Problème de la vie internationale* (Lyon: Chronique sociale de France, 1926), 515–28.

67. Lucien Romier, "La déprolétarisation des masses," *Semaine Sociale de France—XIXe session—Nancy, 1927—La Femme dans la société* (Lyon: Chronique sociale de France, 1927), 415.

68. Ibid., 417.

69. Ibid., 418.

70. Ibid., 423.

71. Ibid., 419.

72. Romier's two addresses at the Semaines Sociales provide a synopsis of the major themes in his essays from the period, *Explication de notre temps* (Paris: Grasset, 1925), *Qui sera le maître, Europe ou Amérique?* (Paris: Hachette, 1928), *L'homme nouveau, esquisse des conséquences du progrès* (Paris: Hachette, 1929), and *Si le capitalisme disparaissait* (Paris: Hachette, 1933. Romier believed that the western European nations were bound to modernize more successfully than the United States or the Soviet Union because of their greater respect for tradition.

Otherwise, he wrote, "The lack of tradition makes men unable to imagine life except as part of a 'futurist' evolution, and incapable of using any methods but those that distinguish the present from the past: technology and applied science" (*L'homme nouveau*, 108).

73. Paxton, *Vichy France*, 352–56.

Chapter 5: Coutrot and the Art of Social Engineering

1. See Anson Rabinbach, *The Human Motor: Energy, Fatigue, and the Origins of Modernity* (New York: Basic Books, 1990).

2. See Christophe Prochasson, *Les années électriques, 1880–1910* (Paris: Editions La Découverte), 1991, esp. chap. 5, "Le monde des revues," 155–94, and chap. 7, "Les congrès, lieux d'échange intellectuel," 223–50.

3. The classic account of these groups is Jean Loubet del Bayle, *Les nonconformistes des années trente* (Paris: Editions du Seuil, 1969).

4. For more on Le Corbusier and *L'Esprit nouveau*, see Ken Silver, *Esprit de Corps: The Art of the Parisian Avant-Garde and the First World War, 1914–1925* (Princeton: Princeton University Press, 1989); Nancy J. Troy, *Modernism and the Decorative Arts in France: Art Nouveau to Le Corbusier* (New Haven: Yale University Press, 1991); and Beatriz Colomina, *Privacy and Publicity: Modern Architecture as Mass Media* (Cambridge: MIT Press, 1994). On Le Corbusier's ties to technocratic reform movements, see Romy Golan, *Modernity and Nostalgia: Art and Politics in France Between the Wars* (New Haven: Yale University Press, 1995); and Mary McLeod, "Urbanism and Utopia: Le Corbusier from Regional Syndicalism to Vichy," vol. 1, Ph.D. diss., Princeton School of Architecture, 1985.

5. For more on X-Crise, see Gérard Brun, *Technocrates et technocratie en France, 1914–1925* (Paris: Albatros, 1985) and "Histoire d'X-Crise," in G. Brun, T. de Monbrial, A. Sauvy, and J. Ullmo, *De la récurrence des crises économiques* (Paris: Economica, 1981); Guy Desaunay, "X-Crise: Contribution à l'étude des idéologies économiques d'un groupe de polytechniciens devant la grande crise économique, 1931–1939," thesis, Université de Paris, 1965; and most recently, Olivier Dard, "Voyage à l'intérieur d'X-Crise," *Vingtième siècle* 47 (July–Sept. 1995): 132–46. See also Jean-Pierre Callot, *Histoire de l'Ecole Polytechnique* (Paris: Les Presses Modernes, 1958); Richard F. Kuisel, *Capitalism*, 105, 130; and R. Kuisel, *Ernest Mercier: French Technocrat* (Berkeley: University of California Press, 1967), 97n, 127–33.

6. My discussion of Coutrot is based primarily on my research in his personal papers, currently housed at the Archives Nationales as 468 AP 1–33. Olivier Dard's unpublished doctoral thesis, "Les novations intellectuelles des années trente: L'exemple de Jean Coutrot," Institut d'Etudes Politiques de Paris, 1993, provides an extensive overview of the archive's contents and places Coutrot's ideas within the intellectual context of the 1930's. Coutrot also figures

significantly as Le Corbusier's associate and collaborator in McLeod, "Urbanism and Utopia."

7. This account draws on a memorial speech by Robert Lelong, president of the Comité National d'Organisation Française, in A.N. 468 AP 32, dossier 3a, as well as Olivier Dard's thesis, "Les novations intellectuelles," 1:13–21. There is a slight discrepancy between their accounts: Dard has Coutrot's wife's maiden name as Blancan, whereas Lelong reports that it was Gaut.

8. Coutrot was doubtless influenced by reading Le Corbusier's *L'Esprit nouveau*, although the two men came into contact only in the 1930's, after Le Corbusier co-founded *Plans*. Similarly, Ernest Mercier's industrial lobbying organization, the Redressement Français, certainly played a role in Coutrot's intellectual development, although he was never a member of the group. The Redressement Français brought together technocratic and reform-minded industrialists to lobby government officials on behalf of new schemes for the rationalization of production. Mercier himself was right-leaning and no friend of the parliamentary process. He and his associates hoped to use their influence with deputies and ministers so as to leave more decisions regarding manufacturing and the national economy in the hands of technicians and experts, rather than in the hands of politicians. The definitive work on this subject is Richard Kuisel's *Ernest Mercier: French Technocrat* (Berkeley: University of California Press, 1967). Also of interest is his article "Technocrats and Public Economic Policy: From the Third to the Fourth Republic," *Journal of European Economic History* 2.1 (spring 1973): esp. 63–64.

9. Speakers at the group's events included some of the most progressive French industrialists and their advisers, notably Gaston Menier of Menier Chocolate, one of the first French companies to make a real commitment to advertising, André and Hugues Citroën, who first experimented with scientific management techniques, Jean-Marie Lahy, a pioneer in the psychology of work, and Jacques Worth of the Maison Worth, a family-owned couture firm that was attempting to apply modern insights to its business operations.

10. My source for Coutrot's activities with the CNOF draw on the dossier concerning the period when he helped organize the Fourth International Congress of Scientific Management in 1929. See A.N. 468 AP 1, dossier 2.

11. Tardieu formed a coalition of young politicians of the center and the right in support of an extended program of what he called *outillage national*, or "national retooling," geared toward bringing French industry to a level where it could compete with the United States. However, Tardieu was insufficiently the master of liberal politics, which he held in contempt as inefficient, to push his proposal through the French Assembly. Tardieu's government was voted out of power in the wake of a financial scandal before his plan came to a final vote in the fall of 1930. See Kuisel, "Technocrats," 67–68; and Dominique Borne and Henri Dubief, *La crise des années 30, 1929–1938* (Paris: Editions du Seuil, 1989), 75–80.

12. For more on Wilbois, see Bernard Kalaora, "Le mysticisme technique de Joseph Wilbois," in *Les chantiers de la paix sociale,* ed. Yves Cohen and Rémi Baudoui (Fontenay: Editions ENS, 1997), and for more on his roots in the thought of Le Play and Bergson, see Kalaora and Antoine Savoye, *Les inventeurs oubliés: Le Play et ses continuateurs* (Seyssel: Champ Vallon, 1989).

13. See Dard, "Voyage à l'intérieur d'X-Crise," 132–39.

14. Georges Valois's intellectual and political life is deftly summarized in Allen Douglas, *From Fascism to Libertarian Communism: Georges Valois Against the Third Republic* (Berkeley: University of California Press, 1992). Other useful accounts of his life and intellectual evolution appear in Yves Guchet, *Georges Valois: L'Action française, le Faisceau, la république syndicale* (Paris: Editions de l'albatros, 1975; reissued in 1990 by Erasme); Jules Levey, "Georges Valois and the Faisceau: The Making and Breaking of a Fascist," *French Historical Studies* 8.2 (fall 1973); and Robert Soucy, *French Fascism: The First Wave* (New Haven: Yale University Press, 1986). On Valois's corporatism, see Matthew H. Elbow, *French Corporative Theory, 1789–1948* (New York: Columbia University Press, 1953), and on his ties to Le Corbusier, see Mary McLeod, "Urbanism and Utopia."

15. Coutrot's archives include reading notes on de Man's *La joie au travail* (Paris: Alcan, 1930), first published in German as *Der Kampf um die Arbeitsfreude* (1927), and *Au delà du marxisme* (Paris: Alcan, 1929) (in German, *Zur psychologie des sozialismus* [1926]), a volume which advocated corporatist organization of industry and labor as a "third way" between the competing threats of untrammeled American-style liberalism and Soviet communism. De Man's theories served as a basis for later experiments with corporatist economic principles under Vichy. De Man was also the uncle of the future literary critic Paul de Man and probably encouraged the younger de Man's fascist sympathies in the 1930's and 1940's.

16. For more details of Valois's initial attacks on Coutrot, see Douglas, *From Fascism to Libertarian Communism*, 194; for their reconciliation, see 224–25. The harmony between them was, as before, very brief, for within months Valois had turned against his friend once again. Eventually, Valois was imprisoned for several months for plotting against the Vichy government, and upon his release in April 1941, he joined the French Resistance. He was imprisoned in May 1944 and deported, and he died in Bergen-Belsen in January 1945. See Douglas, *From Fascism*, 236–42.

17. See, e.g., Coutrot's essays on planning within industry: *Le système nerveux des entreprises, prévision et contrôle, coordination interne et planning* (Paris: Delmas, 1935), or *Planning, préparation du travail dans l'entreprise* (Paris: Dunod, 1939).

18. I use the term *man* here advisedly, but hasten to point out that through-

out his writings, Coutrot's theory of motivation is cast in strictly masculinist terms, despite the strong presence of women in factories and in a variety of other sorts of jobs throughout the 1920's and 1930's. His Centre pour l'étude des problèmes humains (CEPH) only began to concern itself with women's issues in the late 1930's, and even then, most of that discussion centered around the role of women in the home. This is probably the result of Coutrot's close ties to social Catholicism, which was strongly pro-natalist and mandated "la femme au foyer." For documents on the CEPH's attention to women's issues, see A.N. 468 AP 27, dossier 1. For more on the politics of women's work in the interwar period, see Laura Lee Downs, *Manufacturing Inequality: Gender Division in the French and British Metalworking Industries, 1914–1939* (Ithaca: Cornell University Press, 1995); Mary Louise Roberts, *Civilization Without Sexes: Reconstructing Gender in Postwar France, 1917–1927* (Chicago: University of Chicago Press, 1994); and Susan Pedersen, *Family, Dependence, and the Origins of the Welfare State: Britain and France, 1914–1945* (New York: Cambridge University Press, 1993).

19. For a detailed account of the strikes, which began before the Popular Front's accession to power, see Julian Jackson, *The Popular Front in France: Defending Democracy, 1934–1938* (New York: Cambridge University Press, 1988), esp. chap. 3, "The Social Explosion," 85–112. Jackson also cites J. Danos and M. Gibelin, *Juin 1936* (Paris, 1952); H. Proteau, *Les occupations d'usines en Italie et en France, 1920–1936* (Paris, 1938); S. Schwartz, "Les occupations d'usines en France de mai et juin 1936," *International Review of Social History* 2 (1937): 50–104; G. Lefranc, *Juin 36, l'explosion sociale du front populaire* (Paris, 1966) and "Problématique des grèves françaises de mai-juin 1936," in *Essais sur les problèmes socialistes et syndicalistes* (Paris, 1970), 127–40; and A. Prost, "Les grèves de juin 1936, essai d'interpretation," in *Léon Blum: Chef de gouvernment,* 2nd ed., ed. P. Renouvin and R. Rémond (Paris, 1981).

20. Socialist Charles Spinasse was one of the first French politicians to take a serious interest in rationalization and scientific management. He was involved with X-Crise as a speaker and discussant from its foundation in 1931, and would later invite several of the group's participants to work for him at the Ministry of the National Economy. In fact, the idea for COST grew out of his discussions with Jean Coutrot earlier in the 1930's, and Coutrot was invited to head COST as soon as it was created. For more on Spinasse and X-Crise, see Olivier Dard, "Voyage à l'intérieur d'X-Crise," 133. For more on the beginnings of COST, see Aimée Moutet, *Les logiques de l'entreprise: La rationalisation dans l'industrie française de l'entre-deux-guerres* (Paris: Editions de l'Ecole des Hautes Etudes en Sciences Sociales, 1997), 429–40. Richard Kuisel's "Technocrats" provides an excellent overview of competing and complementary intellectual tendencies in the 1930's and 1940's.

21. For details of Coutrot's business dealings with Delaunay, see A.N. 468 AP 10, dossier 3. In general, 468 AP 10 contains information about Coutrot's dealings with artists and critics in the earlier part of his career.

22. A.N. 468 AP 10, dossier 6.

23. Dard, "Les novations intellectuelles," 14.

24. Ibid., 13–14. See also André Grelon, ed., *Les Ingénieurs de la crise* (Paris: Ecole des Hautes Etudes en Sciences Sociales, 1986).

25. Jean Coutrot, "Minerve qui retrousse ses manches," *Orbes,* no. 2 (spring 1929), 71. The original quote appears in Blaise Cendrars, *Le plan de l'aiguille* (Paris: Au Sans pareil, 1927), 200, and reappears in Jean Coutrot, *De quoi vivre* (Paris: Bernard Grasset, 1935), 147.

26. Coutrot, "Minerve," 71. Later in the text, Coutrot draws on a source from the opposite end of the aesthetic and ideological spectrum, quoting Drieu La Rochelle in support of his argument that art and organization are one: Drieu notes quite simply that "what drives the head of a firm to his office cannot be the simple need to earn his mid-day meal, or silk stockings for his wife: it is the instinctive urge to create a world" (72).

27. Ibid., 72.

28. Jean Coutrot, "Le cinématographe et l'organisation scientifique du travail," part 1, *X-Informations,* 25 Oct. 1930: 91. Found in A.N. 468 AP 1, dossier 6a.

29. Jean Coutrot, "Le cinématographe et l'organisation scientifique du travail," part 2, *X-Informations,* 25 Nov. 1939: 113.

30. Jean Coutrot, *De quoi vivre,* 144.

31. The passage appears in Claudel's "Lettre à l'abbé Brémond sur l'inspiration poétique," an essay first published in 1927 that appears in P. Claudel, *Réflexions sur la poésie* (Paris: Gallimard, 1963), 92. Coutrot's undated notes on the essay are to be found in A.N. 468 AP 32, dossier 2a.

32. Jean Coutrot, notes on Claude's "Positions et propositions," and "Lettre à l'abbé Brémond," 1–2, in A.N. 468 AP 32, dossier 2a.

33. J. Coutrot, *De quoi vivre,* 167. Coutrot was quite serious about the development of a science of art, and he was a founding participant in the Congrès International d'Esthétique et de Science de l'Art during the 1930's, also serving on the editorial board of the (short-lived) *Revue d'art et d'esthétique,* which preceded the meetings. Conference papers covered a broad range of topics, but one common and frequently reiterated concern was to discover a physiological basis for aesthetic response that would make it possible to create visual works that would stimulate or calm its viewers as required.

34. Teilhard de Chardin and Aldous Huxley were apparently Coutrot's friends. See Boltanski, *Les cadres,* 118.

35. France's first Nobelist (1912), Alexis Carrel spent most of his career at the

Rockefeller Foundation in New York, returning to France only at the outbreak of war in 1914 and again in 1939. Of decidedly fascist sympathies, Carrel is perhaps best known for his tract on the perfectibility of the human species through eugenics, *L'homme cet inconnu* (1935), which was written simultaneously (and with significant variations) in English and French over the summers of 1933 and 1934. The work also appeared in English as *Man the Unknown* in 1935. Carrel was first introduced to Coutrot by one of his Polytechnicien associates, Félix-André Missenard. Coutrot and Carrel shared a vitalist perspective on human development, and Carrel was so taken by Coutrot's notion of a Center for the Study of Human Problems, that when he was offered the opportunity to found an institute for the study of demographics and racial biology under Vichy in December 1941, he named it the Fondation Française pour l'Etude des Problèmes Humains. The institute had more than a name in common with Coutrot's CEPH in that it employed several of Coutrot's former collaborators in the field of social psychology, among them Serge Tchakhotine, the propaganda expert, and Dr. M. Martiny, whose work on biotypes and the biology of aptitude had been a special interest of Coutrot's. For accounts of Carrel's life, see Jean-Jacques Antier, *Carrel cet inconnu* (Paris: Editions SOS, 1974), and Antier, *Alexis Carrel* (Paris: Wesmaal-Charlier, 1970). Alain Drouard's study of Carrel's foundation, *La Fondation Alexis Carrel* (Paris: Editions Maison des Sciences de l'Homme, 1992), is thorough and well documented, but it smacks faintly of apologetics. More critical and less cautious presentations appear in Hervé Le Bras, *Marianne et les lapins* (Paris: Olivier Orban, 1991), and Francine Muel-Dreyfus, *Vichy et l'éternel féminin: Contribution à une sociologie politique de l'ordre du corps* (Paris: Editions du Seuil, 1996), 300–350.

36. Cf. his exchange of letters with André Lhôte following an article published by Lhôte in the *Nouvelle revue française*, "Après vous, MM. les français moyens" (1 Sept. 1939: 518–19), criticizing Coutrot's direction of a meeting about the role of the arts in contemporary society, and Coutrot's response, which appears in the *NRF* on 1 Jan. 1940: 131–32.

37. Other advertisers who participated included Louis Damour, of Dam-Publicité and *Vendre,* and H.-L. Rumpf, a frequent contributor to *La Publicité.*

38. See the manifesto on the inside cover of the first issue of *L'Humanisme économique* (Sept. 1937) for a clear statement of these principles, as well as the concluding sections of *Les leçons de juin 1936,* where Coutrot enumerates the various ways in which the economy could be made more flexible and more humane (esp. 105–7).

39. Jean Coutrot, *Les leçons de juin 1936 — l'humanisme économique* (Paris: Centre polytechnicien d'études économiques, 1936), 19.

40. Ibid., 20. Coutrot returns frequently to the idea that managers should

become the analysts of their workers, struggling to "liberate" them from their collective "inferiority complex" for the sake of the common good. See also p. 23.

41. See Jean Coutrot, *Planning, préparation du travail dans l'entreprise* (Paris: Dunod, 1939), esp. 58, and R. Satet, *Les graphiques, moyen de direction des entreprises* (Paris: n.p., 1933). Satet was a member of the Comité National de l'Organisation Française and of the Taylor Society. He also published essays on advertising techniques in *La Publicité* and *Mon Bureau*.

42. Coutrot, *Planning*, 32.

43. Incidentally, one of Coutrot's chief collaborators at the CEPH was Serge Tchakotine, a left-wing propaganda expert whose widely read book, *Le viol des foules par la propagande politique* (Paris: Gallimard/NRF, 1939), argued that the left needed to master Nazi propaganda techniques in order to use them against fascism.

44. *L'Humanisme économique* 2.6 (Feb. 1938): 17.

45. Jean Coutrot, "Vers un transhumanisme: Pour le passant distrait," *L'Humanisme économique* 3.33 (Jan./Feb. 1937): 8.

46. There was more than just a structural similarity between the two men's views. Le Corbusier and Coutrot had both been associates of Georges Valois, Coutrot as a financial backer of *Chantiers coopératives* and Le Corbusier as a member of Le Faisceau in the late 1920's. Le Corbusier also became involved with Ernest Mercier's Redressement Français. See McLeod, "Urbanism and Utopia," 99–109. Le Corbusier's copies of Coutrot's *De quoi vivre* and *Les leçons de juin 1936—l'humanisme économique* on file at the Fondation Le Corbusier, show evidence of considerable annotation, and Jean Coutrot favorably reviewed Le Corbusier's journal, *Plans*, in the *Nouvelle Revue Française* when it first appeared in 1931 (*NRF*, 1 Sept. 1931: 510). When *Plans* published its "Plan du 9 juillet 1934," with a preface by Jules Romains, Coutrot was one of those who signed the manifesto. See Yves-Marie Hilaire, "L'ancrage des idéologies, 1900–1945," in Jean-François Sirinelli, *Histoire des droites en France*, vol. 1 (Paris: Gallimard, 1992). Coutrot and Le Corbusier also corresponded briefly in the late 1930's (A.N. 468 AP 23, dossier 2a), but never managed to work together.

47. See Jeffrey Herf's introduction to *Reactionary Modernism: Technology, Culture, and Politics in the Third Reich* (Cambridge: Cambridge University Press, 1984).

48. For a fascinating analysis of competing nationalist visions of France in the interwar period, see Herman Lebovics, *True France: The Wars over Cultural Identity* (Ithaca: Cornell University Press, 1992).

49. The nature of Coutrot's engagement with the Vichy regime remains somewhat vague and difficult to clarify. Although he was offered an official post during the Popular Front, Coutrot stayed on at the Ministry of the National Economy after Léon Blum's departure as prime minister, and he remained at COST until the summer of 1940. As Olivier Dard notes (see Dard, "Voyage,"

145 n. 3), shortly thereafter, Coutrot was pushed aside from any new governmental functions, and was finally named to a relatively unimportant post as a vice president of the accounting plan commission on 22 April 1941, only a few weeks before his suicide on 19 May. However, the circumstances surrounding Coutrot's death have led to considerable speculation about his involvement in an alleged plot by a secret organization known as the Mouvement Synarchique d'Empire to stage a coup d'état against Vichy and run the French state on technocratic lines. The myth of the synarchist plot circulated well into the 1960's. It was effectively debunked by Richard Kuisel in "The Legend of the Vichy Synarchy," *French Historical Studies* 6.3 (spring 1970). Speculations about the group, whose membership was largely recruited from X-Crise, have surfaced again in Limoré Yagil, "La synarchie ou le 'Mouvement Synarchie d'Empire' et Vichy, 1940–1944," *Guerres mondiales et conflits contemporains,* no. 165 (Jan. 1992) and have once again been laid to rest by Olivier Dard in *La synarchie* (Paris, 1998).

50. On Bergsonian vitalism and its transmutation into the basis for much of reactionary modernist thought, see Mark Antliff, *Inventing Bergson: Cultural Politics and the Parisian Avant-Garde* (Princeton: Princeton University Press, 1993), 14.

Conclusion

1. Walter Benjamin, "The Work of Art in the Age of Mechanical Reproduction," in *Illuminations,* ed. Hannah Arendt (New York: Schocken Books, 1968).

2. See, e.g., T. W. Adorno and Max Horkheimer, *The Dialectic of Enlightenment,* trans. John Cummings (1947; New York: Verso, 1997); Roland Barthes, *Mythologies,* trans. Annette Lavers (New York: Noonday Press, 1974); Jean Baudrillard, *Le système des objets* (Paris: Gallimard, 1968) and *La société de consommation* (Paris: Denoel, 1970); John Berger, *Ways of Seeing* (London: Penguin, 1972); Guy Debord, *The Society of the Spectacle* (Detroit: Black and Red, 1983); and more recently Donald Lowe, *History of Bourgeois Perception* (Chicago: University of Chicago Press, 1982); Jonathan Crary, *Techniques of the Observer* (Cambridge: MIT Press, 1990); Gilles Lipovetsky, *L'empire de l'éphémère* (Paris: Gallimard/NRF, 1987); and Mark Poster, *The Mode of Information: Poststructuralism and Social Context* (Chicago: University of Chicago Press, 1990).

3. Pierre Bourdieu, *La distinction: Critique sociale du jugement* (Paris: Editions de Minuit, 1979).

4. Benedict Anderson, *Imagined Communities: Reflections on the Origin and Spread of Nationalism* (London: Verso, 1983; 2nd ed. 1991). Anderson is primarily concerned with the role of the mass media as a unifying force for nationalist consciousness in developing societies, but some of his observations about the power of the media in the construction of a social imaginary are useful for our purposes as well. However, Anderson has been faulted for failing to recognize just how conflictual the process of forging a national consciousness can be in the

face of ethnic and gender differences that make any unified vision all but impossible. See Partha Chatterjee, "Whose Imagined Community?" in Chatterjee, *The Nation and Its Fragments: Colonial and Postcolonial Histories* (Princeton: Princeton University Press, 1993), 3–13.

5. See Robert Paxton, *Vichy France;* Richard Kuisel, *Capitalism and the State in Modern France: Renovation and Economic Management in the Twentieth Century* (Cambridge: Cambridge University Press, 1981); and Charles Maier, "Between Taylorism and Technocracy: European Ideologies and the Vision of Industrial Productivity in the 1920s," *Journal of Contemporary History* 5.2 (1970): 27–61, reprinted with alterations in *In Search of Stability: Explorations in Historical Political Economy* (Cambridge: Cambridge University Press, 1987).

6. For more on *les cadres* and their ascendancy in post-1945 France, see Luc Boltanski, *Les cadres.* Boltanski also traces the history of professional organizations for industrialists and engineers in the interwar years.

7. For Foucault's discussion of biopower and its emergence, see Foucault, *The History of Sexuality,* vol. 1 (New York: Pantheon, 1978). According to Foucault, biopower emerged with the demise of feudalism as a new form of sovereignty, in which power was no longer wielded by a single, identifiable ruler with the ability to directly coerce his or her subjects. The exercise of biopower, he claims, is an effect of language, and it can be recognized by its radically decentered and unlocatable quality. Biopower implies the redefinition of a subject population in purely biological, rather than political, terms so that technical discussions of biological and physiological issues come to substitute for conversations of a more open, contestatory, and ideological nature.

8. See Zeev Sternhell, *Ni droite, ni gauche: L'idéologie fasciste en France* (Paris: Editions du Seuil, 1983), published as *Neither Right nor Left: Fascist Ideology in France,* trans. David Maisel (Berkeley: University of California Press, 1986), esp. his introduction to the problem, where he argues that the First World War only served to accelerate proto-fascist tendencies that were already in existence well before the war (15, French ed.), and suggests that French fascism was a solidly constituted ideology by the 1930's (297, French ed.).

9. Most recently, see Pierre Milza, *Fascisme français: Passé et présent* (Paris: Flammarion, 1987), and Philippe Burrin, "Le Fascisme," in *Histoire des droites en France,* vol. 1, ed. Jean-François Sirinelli (Paris: Gallimard, 1992).

10. See René Rémond, "Y a-t-il un fascisme français?" *Terre humaine,* nos. 7–8, July–Aug. 1952; Ernest Nolte, *Three Faces of Fascism* (London: Weidenfeld and Nicholson, 1965); and Soucy, Robert, *French Fascism: The First Wave* (New Haven: Yale University Press, 1986) and *French Fascism: The Second Wave* (New Haven: Yale University Press, 1995) as well as Milza and Burrin, cited above.

11. See Klaus-Jürgen Müller, "French Fascism and Modernization," *Journal of Contemporary History,* no. 11 (Oct. 1976): 75–107, as well as "Protest-Modernisierung-Integration: Bemerkungen zum Problem faschistischer Phänomene in

Frankreich, 1924–1934," *Francia* 8 (1980): 465–524, and "'Faschisten' von links? Bemerkungen zu Neuen Theorien über 'Faschismus' und 'Collaboration' in Frankreich," *Francia* 17.3 (1990): 170–91.

12. Ian Varcoe, "Technocracy and Democratic Politics" in *Culture, Modernity, and Revolution: Essays in Honor of Zygmunt Bauman,* ed. R. Kilminster and I. Varcoe (New York: Routledge, 1996), 66.

13. Ibid., 67.

14. For the utopian aspects of French culture in the post-1945 era, see Kristin Ross, *Fast Cars, Clean Bodies: Decolonization and the Reordering of French Culture* (Cambridge: MIT Press, 1995). For the triumph of American-style marketing techniques, see Richard Kuisel, *Seducing the French: The Dilemma of Americanization* (Berkeley: University of California Press, 1993). The legacy of Coutrot's CEPH emerged in postwar French culture in at least two forms: first, a number of his collaborators, who went on to work for the Fondation Carrel (otherwise known as the Fondation Française pour l'Étude des Problèmes Humains) became the founders of the French national demographic study organization, the Institut National d'Études Démographiques (INED). Second, the CEPH's concern for biotypology, or the identification of aptitudes as a function of one's physical attributes, inspired by the work of Dr. Martiny, reemerged in the postwar period in the ubiquity of handwriting analysis in corporate personnel offices all over France.

Bibliography

I. Archival Materials

A. AGENCE HAVAS ARCHIVES, NEUILLY-SUR-SEINE

Procès Verbaux of the *Conseil d'Administration,* 1894–1940
Les Cahiers bleus, 1927, 1929, 1930, 1936
Les Propagandes Collectives, prepared by the Service des Etudes of the Agence Havas, 1931

B. ARCHIVES NATIONALES, PARIS

Series AP-468 AP Fonds Coutrot cartons 1, 2, 4, 7, 8, 10, 14, 16, 19, 21, 22, 23, 27, 29, 30, 32, and 33 (letters, assorted writings on scientific management, aesthetics, and film)
Series F21–F21 4691 (laws concerning the cinema, 1919–34)
Series F22–F22 315 (dossier on film import quotas)

C. ARCHIVES DÉPARTEMENTALES DE LA SEINE, PARIS

D 39 Z—publicity documents

D. BIBLIOTHÈQUE DE L'ARSÉNAL, PARIS

Collection Rondel, series RK—film history
　　RK 633—protection of minors
　　RK 634—cinema and the state
　　RK 733—the film public
　　RK 734—cinema publicity
　　RK 735—movie theaters

E. CENTRE NATIONAL DES ARCHIVES PUBLICITAIRES (CNAP)
collections of advertising films, 1897–1945

F. FONDATION LE CORBUSIER
Dossiers A 1 (19), A 2 (2, 4, 15, 16, and 18) on the early history of *L'Esprit nouveau*

II. Primary Source Periodicals

A. JOURNALS CONSULTED REGULARLY

L'Esprit nouveau (1920–25)
L'Humanisme économique (1937–38)
Mon Bureau (1910–13)
La Publicité (1903–39)
La Publicité moderne (1905–8)
Le Travail humain (1933–38)
Vendre (1924–39)

B. JOURNALS CONSULTED INTERMITTENTLY

Arts et métiers graphiques
Atlas
Chronique sociale de France
France et monde/Vouloir
Plans
Presse-Publicité
Revue des deux mondes
Revue internationale de l'étalage

III. Other Published Primary Sources

Achille-Delmas, F., and Marcel Boll. *La personnalité humaine, son analyse*. Paris: Flammarion, 1922.

Albucher, G. *La publicité commerciale au point de vue juridique*. Paris: Presses Universitaires de France, 1923.

———. *La publicité commerciale et son rôle économique*. Paris: Presses Universitaires de France, 1923.

Aragon, Louis. *Le paysan de Paris*. Paris: Gallimard, 1926.

Arren, J. *La publicité lucrative et raisonnée*. Paris: Bibliothèque des Ouvrages Pratiques, 1909.

Basch, Victor. "L'esthétique nouvelle et la science de l'art." *L'Esprit nouveau*, no. 1 (Oct. 1920): 8–12.

Bellet, Daniel. *Le commerce allemand, apparences et réalités*. Paris: Plon, 1916.

Bergson, Henri. *Essai sur les donneés immédiates de la conscience*. 1889. Paris: Presses Universitaires de France, 1985.

———. *Matière et mémoire.* Paris: Presses Universitaires de France, 1982.

———. "Simulation inconsciente dans l'état d'hypnotisme." *Revue philosophique,* 22.2 (1886): 525–31.

Bernheim, Hippolyte. *Automatisme et suggestion.* Paris: Félix Alcan, 1917.

———. *De la suggestion dans l'état hypnotique et dans l'état de veille.* 1884. Paris: Albin Michel, 1911.

Billard, J. *Un essai de doctrine, le fayolisme.* Paris: Jouve, 1924.

Bleustein-Blanchet, Marcel. *La rage de convaincre.* Paris: Robert Laffont, 1970.

Boettcher, H. *Comment protéger et défendre vos marques de fabriques, modèles et dessins.* 4th ed. Paris: Office des Marques de Fabrique, 1936.

Bricard, Georges. *L'organisation scientifique du travail.* Paris: Librairie Armand Colin, 1927.

Brockman, Léon. *Des millions gaspillés en annonces.* Paris: Nouvelle Librairie Commerciale, 1931.

Castelneaux, René. "'Casse Cou': L'étranglement de la poule aux oeufs d'or." *Vouloir,* Sept. 1918: 6.

Chambonnaud, Louis. *Les affaires nouvelles.* Paris: Dunod et Pinat, 1919.

———. *Les affaires et la méthode scientifique.* Paris: Dunod, 1928.

Charnay, Geoffroy de. *Synarchie: Panorama de 25 années d'activité occulte (avec réproduction intégrale du Pacte Synarchique).* Paris: Editions Médicis, 1946.

Clémang, Raymond. "L'attention en publicité." *Vouloir,* no. 34 (Jan. 1918): 15–16.

———. "La memoire en publicité." *Vouloir,* no. 36 (Mar. 1918): 14.

———. "Les eléments psychologiques de la publicité." *Vouloir,* no. 45 (Dec. 1918): 7.

———. "Une faute inutile: Les projets d'impôts sur la publicité." *Vouloir,* Nov. 1917: 13–14.

Clerget, Pierre. "Les bases scientifiques de la publicité." *La Publicité moderne,* Oct.–Nov. 1908: 1–6.

Comfort. "Nos affiches de guerre vues par les allemands." *La Publicité,* Nov. 1919: 367–70.

Coutrot, Jean. "Le cinématographe et l'organisation scientifique du travail." *X Informations,* 25 Oct. 1930: 91; 25 Nov. 1939: 113. Found in A.N. 468 AP 1, dossier 6a.

———. *De quoi vivre.* Paris: Bernard Grasset, 1935.

———. *Les leçons de juin 1936—l'humanisme économique.* Paris: Centre Polytechnicien d'Etudes Economiques, 1936.

———. "Minerve qui retrousse ses manches." *Orbes,* no. 2 (spring 1929).

———. *Planning, préparation du travail dans l'entreprise.* Paris: Dunod, 1939.

———. *Le système nerveux des entreprises, prévision et contrôle, coordination interne et planning.* Paris: Delmas, 1935.

———. "Vers un transhumanisme: Pour le passant distrait." *L'Humanisme économique* 3.33 (Jan./Feb. 1937): 8.

Daniel, Joseph. "Les crises du passé et la crise présente." *Semaine Sociale de France—XXIVe session—Lille, 1932.* Lyon: Chronique sociale de France, 1932.

Danset, le R. Père. "Rationalisation . . . moralisation." *Semaine Sociale de France—XIXe session—Nancy, 1927.* Lyon: Chronique sociale de France, 1927.

Daudet, Léon. *L'avant-guerre: Études et documents sur l'espionnage juif-allemand en France depuis l'Affaire Dreyfus.* 1913. Paris: Nouvelle librairie nationale, 1918.

Delluc, Louis. "La photogénie [excerpts]." *L'Esprit nouveau*, no. 5 (Feb. 15, 1921): 589.

Demortain, Lucien. *Les contrats de publicité.* Paris: Dalloz, 1925.

Deploige, Msgr. "L'idée de responsabilité dans la sociologie contemporaine." *Semaine Sociale de France Xe session—Versailles, 1913.* Lyon: Chronique sociale de France, 1913.

Dermée, Paul. "La découverte du lyrisme." *L'Esprit nouveau*, no. 1 (Oct. 1920): 29-37.

———. "Le panlyrisme." *L'Esprit nouveau*, no. 28 (1925): 2363-68.

———. "Poésie = lyrisme + art." *L'Esprit nouveau*, no. 3. (Dec. 15, 1920): 327-30.

Dermée, Paul, and Eugène Courmont. *Les affaires et l'affiche.* Paris: Dunod et Pinat, 1922.

Desaubliaux, R. *Les origines biologiques de la fonction administrative.* Paris: Dunod, 1920.

Deslandres, Maurice. "Les consommateurs et la moralité des affaires." *Semaine Sociale de France—XXIIIe session Mulhouse, 1931.* Lyon: Chronique sociale de France, 1931.

———. "La mode: Ses conséquences économiques et sociales." *Semaine Sociale de France—VIIIe session Saint-Etienne, 1911.* Lyon: Chronique sociale de France, 1911.

———. "La participation des consommateurs à la vie des corps publics." *Semaine Sociale de France XIVe session—Strasbourg, 1922.* Lyon: Chronique sociale de France, 1922.

Devinat, Paul. "L'organisation scientifique du travail." In *Semaine Sociale de France—XXIe session—Besançon, 1929.* Lyon: Chronique sociale de France, 1929.

———. *Scientific Management in Europe.* Geneva: International Labor Office, 1927.

Dubreuil, Hyacinthe. *Standards.* Paris: Bernard Grasset, 1929.

Duhamel, Georges. *Scènes de la vie future.* Paris: A. Fayard—"Le Livre de Demain," 1934.

Durkheim, Emile. *Les règles de la méthode sociologique.* Paris: Félix Alcan, 1895.

Duthoit, Eugène. "La crise de la probité publique et le désordre économique." *Semaine Sociale de France—XIIIe session—Toulouse, 1921.* Lyon: Chronique sociale de France, 1921.

———. "La crise de la production et la sociologie catholique." *Semaine Sociale de France—XIIe session Caen—1920.* Lyon: Chronique sociale de France, 1920.

———. "Declaration d'ouverture." *Semaine Sociale de France—XIe session—Metz, 1919.* Lyon: Chronique sociale de France, 1919.

———. "La 'rationalisation' est-elle un progrès?" *Semaine Sociale de France—XXIe session—Besançon, 1929.* Lyon: Chronique sociale de France, 1929.

Epstein, Jean. *Bonjour cinéma.* Paris: Editions de la Sirène, 1921.

———. *Le cinématographe vu de l'Etna.* Paris: Les Ecrivains Réunis, 1926.

———. *Ecrits sur le cinéma, 1921–1953.* Paris: Cinéma club/Seghers, 1974, 2 vols.

———. *Photogénie de l'impondérable.* Paris: Les Editions Corymbe, 1953.

Fayol, Henri. *Industrial and General Administration.* Trans. J. A. Coubrough. London: International Management Institute, 1930.

Feltaine, Edouard. *De la publicité commerciale.* Caen: E. Lanier, 1903.

Focillon, Henri. *The Life of Forms in Art.* New York: Zone Books, 1989 (originally published as *La vie des formes.* Paris, 1934).

Frémont, Louis. *La Publicité—son historique—sa technique—son importance dans l'économie moderne.* Verdun: H. Frémont et Fils, 1924.

Gautier, Emile. "Scènes de la vie future: Un ministère de la publicité." *La Publicité,* Mar. 1932: 177–78.

Gérin, Octave-Jacques. "Quelques opinions." *La Publicité,* May 1909: 163–64.

Gérin, Octave-Jacques, Etienne Damour, and Louis Serre. *Précis intégral de publicité.* Paris: Dunod, 1935.

Girardet, Philippe. *La connaissance des hommes (édition définitive).* 1932. Paris: Editions Gamma, 1950.

de Gironde, Paule. "Si nous faisions une annonce américaine." *Vendre,* Mar. 1929: 175.

Goblot, Edmond. *La barrière et le niveau.* Paris: Félix Alcan, 1925.

Gonin, Marius. "L'aspect moral du problème de la publicité." *Semaine Sociale de France—XXIIIe session—Mulhouse, 1931.* Lyon: Chronique sociale de France, 1931.

Hauser, Henri. *Germany's Commercial Grip on the World: Her Business Methods Explained.* Trans. Manfred Emanual. New York: Scribner, 1917.

Herbin, Pierre. *Comment concevoir et rédiger votre publicité.* Paris: Editions de La Publicité, 1938.

Hercat, Marcel. "Publicité américaine." *La Publicité,* Nov. 1931.

Jamakorzian, Roussignan. *De la publicité commerciale en France.* Paris: Larose, 1911.

Janet, Pierre. *L'automatisme psychologique, essai de psychologie expérimentale sur les formes inférieures de l'activité humaine.* 2nd ed. Paris: Félix Alcan, 1894.

Lahy, Jean-Maurice. *La morale de Jésus, sa part d'influence dans la morale actuelle.* Paris: Félix Alcan, 1911.

————. *La sélection psychophysiologique des travailleurs (Conducteurs de tramways et d'autobus).* Paris: Dunod, 1927.

————. *Le système Taylor et la physiologie du travail professionel.* Paris: Masson, 1916.

Lallemand, Jules. "La conscience et ses lois: Applications publicitaires." *La Publicité* 18 (Feb./Mar. 1920): 39.

Lallié, Norbert. *La guerre au commerce allemand, l'organisation allemande et ses résultats.* Paris: Recueil Sirey, 1918.

Lamirand, Georges. *Le rôle social de l'ingénieur.* 1932. 3rd ed. Paris: Plon, 1954.

Le Bon, Gustave. *La psychologie des foules.* Paris: Félix Alcan, 1895.

————. *Psychologie du socialisme.* Paris: Félix Alcan, 1898.

Le Corbusier [Charles-Edouard Jeanneret]. "Architecture: Le prix de Rome." *L'Esprit nouveau,* no. 14: 1607.

————. "Architecture: Pure création de l'esprit." *L'Esprit nouveau,* no. 16: 1910.

————. "Programme de *L'Esprit nouveau.*" *L'Esprit nouveau,* no. 1 (Oct. 1920): 1.

Les publicitaires au service de la propagande française. Vichy: Editions Séquana, 1943.

Liébault, Ambroise-Auguste. *Du sommeil et des états analogues considérés surtout au point de vue de l'action du moral sur la physique.* Paris: V. Masson, 1866.

Loos, Adolf. "L'ornement et le crime." *L'Esprit nouveau,* no. 2 (Nov. 15, 1920): 159–65.

Loustalan, Henri Albert Bernard. *La publicité dans la presse française.* Paris: G. Lescher-Montoué, 1933.

Lysis [Letailleur, Eugène]. *Les allemands et la presse française.* Paris: "L'Homme libre," 1918.

————. *Les capitalistes français contre la France.* Paris: Albin Michel, 1916.

————. *Demain.* Paris: Payot/Editions de la Démocratie Nouvelle, 1918.

————. *L'erreur française.* Paris: Payot, 1918.

————. *Politique et finance d'avant-guerre.* Paris: Payot, 1920.

————. *Pour renaître.* Paris: Payot, 1917.

————. *Vers la démocratie nouvelle.* Paris: Payot, 1917.

Man, Henri de. *Au delà du marxisme.* Paris: Félix Alcan, 1929. First published as *Zur psychologie des sozialismus,* 1926.

————. *La joie au travail.* Paris: Félix Alcan, 1930. First published as *Der Kampf um die Arbeitsfreude,* 1927.

Martin-Saint-Léon, Etienne. "Le contre-coup de la guerre et de l'après-guerre sur la consommation et le coût de la vie." *Semaine Sociale de France—XIIe session—Caen, 1920*. Lyon: Chronique sociale de France, 1920.

Marx, Karl. *The Communist Manifesto. 1848*. New York: W. W. Norton, 1988.

Mauduit, Roger. *La réclame: etude de sociologie économique*. Paris: Félix Alcan, 1933.

de Mirecourt, Paul. *Le commerce français aux mains des allemands*. Paris: "Editions et librairie," 1915.

Monod-Herzen, Edouard. *Science et esthétique, principes de morphologie générale*. Paris: Gauthier-Villars, 1927.

Moysset, Henri. "L'opinion publique, étude de psychologie sociale." *Semaine Sociale de France—VIIe session—Rouen, 1910*. Lyon: Chronique sociale de France, 1910.

Normand, Gilles. *La guerre, le commerce français et les consommateurs*. Paris: Perrin, 1917.

Nuel, Jean-Paul. *La vision*. Paris: Octave Doin, 1904.

Ozenfant, Amédée, and Le Corbusier. "Esthétique et purisme." *L'Esprit nouveau*, no. 15 (1922): 1704–8.

———. "La formation de l'optique nouveau." *L'Esprit nouveau*, no. 21: 1924.

———. "Sur la plastique." *L'Esprit nouveau*, no. 1 (Oct. 1920): 39–48.

Perrin-Pelletier, G. "Le rôle de la science et de la technique dans l'économie nationale." *Semaine Sociale de France—XVIe session—Rennes, 1924*. Lyon: Chronique sociale de France, 1924.

Platet, Jean-Louis. *L'industrie automobile française depuis la Guerre*. Paris: Presses Universitaires de France, 1934.

Raffalovitch, Arthur. ". . . *L'abominable vénalité de la presse* . . ." Paris: Librairie du Travail, 1931.

Raynal, Maurice. "Couleur dans le monde." *Arts et métiers graphiques*, 15 Aug. 1934: 3–6.

———. "Ozenfant et Jeanneret." *L'Esprit nouveau*, no. 7 (Apr. 15, 1921): 807–32.

Ribot, Théodule. *Essai sur l'imagination créatrice*. 7th ed. Paris: Félix Alcan, 1927.

———. *La psychologie de l'attention*. Paris: Félix Alcan, 1889.

———. *La vie inconsciente et les mouvements*. Paris: Félix Alcan, 1914.

Romier, Lucien. *Explication de notre temps*. Paris: Grasset, 1925.

———. *L'homme nouveau, esquisse des conséquences du progrès*. Paris: Hachette, 1929.

———. "La réprolétarisation des masses." *Semaine Sociale de France—XIXe session—Nancy, 1927*. Lyon: Chronique sociale de France, 1927.

———. "La solidarité européenne." *Semaine Sociale de France—XVIIIe session—Le Havre, 1926*. Lyon: Chronique sociale de France, 1926.

———. *Qui sera le maître, Europe ou Amérique?* Paris: Hachette, 1928.

———. *Si le capitalisme disparaissait.* Paris: Hachette, 1933.

Roullet, Colonel André. "La presse (journal filmé et T.S.F.) responsabilités éducatives." *Semaine Sociale de France—XXVIe session—Nice, 1934.* Lyon: Chronique sociale de France, 1934.

Satet, R. *Les graphiques, moyen de direction des entreprises.* Paris, 1933.

Sauret, Albert. *De la responsabilité des journaux en matière d'annonces.* Paris: Jouve, 1914.

Schwob, Maurice. *Le danger allemand: étude sur le développement industriel et commercial de l'Allemagne.* 2nd ed. Paris: Flammarion, 1897.

Sédillot, André. "La campagne du costume bleu; ou la manière dont les tailleurs américains mettent en application le système Taylor." *La Publicité*, Oct. 1931: 660.

Souriau, Etienne. *L'avenir de l'esthétique, essai sur l'objet d'une science naissante.* Paris: Félix Alcan, 1929.

Souriau, Etienne, et al. *L'univers filmique.* Paris: Flammarion, 1953.

Tarde, Gabriel. *Les lois de l'imitation.* Paris: Félix Alcan, 1890.

———. *L'opinion et la foule.* Paris: Félix Alcan, 1901.

Tchakotine, Serge. *Le viol des foules par le propagande politique.* Paris: Gallimard/NRF, 1939.

Tchernoff, Judah. *Traité de droit pénal financier.* Vol. 2, *Publicité financière.* Paris: Librairie Dalloz, 1931.

Toulouse, Edouard-Gaston-Dominique. *Au fil des préjugés.* Ed. Antonin Artaud. Paris: Editions du "Progrès Civique," 1923.

———. *Comment utiliser la guerre pour faire le monde nouveau.* Paris: La Renaissance du Livre, 1919.

Toulouse, Edouard-Gaston-Dominique, and R. Mourgue. "Des réactions respiratoires au cours de projections cinématographiques." Association française pour l'avancement des sciences: Compte rendu de la 44e session, Strasbourg, 1920.

Vachon, Marius. *La guerre artistique avec l'Allemagne.* Paris: Payot, 1916.

Valéry, Robert. "En quoi l'esprit français s'oppose à la publicité." *Mon Bureau*, Oct. 1926.

Vallet, Maurice, and M. de Roux. *Répertoire de l'avant-guerre.* Paris: Nouvelle Librairie Nationale, 1916.

Vathelet, Henri. *La publicité dans le journalisme.* Paris: Albin Michel, 1911.

Vuillermoz, Emile. "Les films allemands." *L'Esprit nouveau*, no. 9 (June 15, 1921): 1076.

Weiler, Edith. *La Publicité, sa psychologie, son organisation, et sa fonction économique.* Paris: Recueil Sirey, 1932.

Wilbois, Joseph. *Joie au travail et réformes de structure.* Paris: Bloud et Gay, 1939.

———. *La psychologie au service des chefs d'entreprise.* Paris: Félix Alcan, 1934.

IV. Secondary Materials

Adorno, T. W., and Max Horkheimer. *The Dialectic of Enlightenment*. Trans. John Cumming. New York: Verso, 1997. First published as *Die Dialektik der Aufklärungs*, 1947.

Albert, Pierre. *Histoire de la presse politique nationale au début de la Troisième République, 1871–1879*. Lille: Atelier Réproduction des Thèses, 1980.

Anderson, Benedict. *Imagined Communities: Reflections on the Origin and Spread of Nationalism*. London: Verso, 1983.

Antier, Jean-Jacques. *Alexis Carrel: La tentation de l'absolu*. Monaco: Editions du Rocher, 1994.

Antliff, Mark. *Inventing Bergson: Cultural Politics and the Parisian Avant-Garde*. Princeton: Princeton University Press, 1993.

Arbour, Roméo. *Henri Bergson et les lettres françaises*. Paris: Librairie José Corti, 1955.

Art et pub: Art et publicité, 1890–1990. Paris: Editions du Centre Pompidou, 1990.

Auslander, Leora. *Taste and Power: Furnishing Modern France*. Berkeley: University of California Press, 1996.

Barrows, Susanna. *Distorting Mirrors: Visions of the Crowd in Late Nineteenth-Century France*. New Haven: Yale University Press, 1981.

Barthes, Roland. *Mythologies*. Trans. Annette Lavers. New York: Noonday Press, 1974.

Bassot, Jacques. *Travail et propriété: Vers un ordre social d'après La Tour du Pin*. Paris: Georges et Roger Joly, 1942.

Baudrillard, Jean. *Amérique*. Paris: Editions Grasset et Fasquelle, 1986.

———. *La société de consommation*. Paris: Denöel, 1970.

———. *Le système des objets*. Paris: Gallimard, 1968.

Bauman, Zygmunt. *Legislators and Interpreters: On Modernity, Post-modernity, and Intellectuals*. Cambridge: Polity, 1987.

———. *Modernity and Ambivalence*. Oxford: Polity, 1991.

Becker, Jean-Jacques. *Les français dans la grande guerre*. Paris, 1980.

Becker, Jean-Jacques, and Serge Berstein. *Victoire et frustrations, 1914–1929*. Paris: Editions du Seuil, 1990.

Bellanger, Claude, Jacques Godechot, Pierre Guiral, and Fernand Terrou. *Histoire générale de la presse française*. Vol. 3. Paris: Presses Universitaires de France, 1972.

Benjamin, Walter. *Illuminations*. Ed. Hannah Arendt. New York: Schocken, 1969.

———. *Reflections: Essays, Aphorisms, Autobiographical Writings*. Trans. Edmund Jephcott. New York: Harcourt Brace Jovanovich, 1978.

Berger, John. *Ways of Seeing*. London: BBC/Penguin Books, 1972.

Bernstein, Richard J., ed. *Habermas and Modernity*. Cambridge: MIT Press, 1985.

Birkin, Lawrence. *Consuming Desire: Sexual Science and the Emergence of a Culture of Abundance, 1871–1914.* Ithaca: Cornell University Press, 1988.

Boltanski, Luc. *Les cadres: La formation d'un groupe social.* Paris: Editions de Minuit, 1982.

Borne, Dominique, and Henri Dubief. *La crise des années 30, 1929–1938.* Paris: Editions du Seuil, 1989.

Bourdieu, Pierre. *La distinction: Critique sociale du jugement.* Paris: Les Editions de Minuit, 1979.

———. *Reproduction in Education, Culture, and Society.* Trans. Richard Nice. London: Sage, 1977.

Bowlby, Rachel. *Just Looking: Consumer Culture in Dreiser, Gissing, and Zola.* New York: Methuen, 1985.

Bréhier, Emile. "Images plotiniennes, images bergsoniennes." *Les Etudes bergsoniennes* 2 (1949): 107–28.

Bürger, Peter. *Theory of the Avant-Garde.* Minneapolis: University of Minnesota Press, 1984.

Calinescu, Matei. *Five Faces of Modernity.* 1977. Durham, N.C.: Duke University Press, 1987.

Callot, J.-P. *Histoire de l'Ecole Polytechnique.* Paris: Les Presses Modernes, 1958.

Cameron, Rondo. *France and the Economic Development of Europe, 1800–1914.* Princeton: Princeton University Press, 1961.

de Certeau, Michel. *The Practice of Everyday Life.* Trans. Steven Rendall. Berkeley: University of California Press, 1984.

Chanson, Paul. *Autorité et liberté: Constitution de la France selon la Tour du Pin.* Paris: Editions du Temps Présent, 1941.

Chapman, Herrick. *State Capitalism and Working-Class Radicalism in the French Aircraft Industry.* Berkeley: University of California, 1991.

Chartier, Roger. *The Cultural Uses of Print.* Cambridge: Cambridge University Press/Editions de la Maison des Sciences de l'Homme, 1987.

———, ed. *The Culture of Print.* Trans. Lydia G. Cochrane. Princeton: Princeton University Press, 1989.

Chatterjee, Partha. *The Nation and Its Fragments: Colonial and Postcolonial Histories.* Princeton: Princeton University Press, 1993.

Cheyssel, Marie-Emmanuelle. *La publicité: Naissance d'une profession.* Paris: CNRS Editions, 1998.

Cholvy, Gérard, and Yves-Marie Hilaire. *Histoire religieuse de la France contemporaine, 1880–1930.* Paris: Editions Privat, 1986.

Clark, T. J. *The Absolute Bourgeois: Artists and Politics in France, 1848–1851.* London: Thames and Hudson, 1973.

———. *The Painting of Modern Life: Paris in the Art of Manet and His Followers.* New York: Knopf, 1984.

Cohen, J.-L., and H. Damisch. *Américanisme et modernité: L'idéal américain dans l'architecture*. Paris: Flammarion/EHESS, 1993.

Cohen, Yves, and Rémi Baudoui, eds. *Les chantiers de la paix sociale, 1900–1940*. Fontenay: ENS Editions, 1997.

Colomina, Beatriz. *Privacy and Publicity: Modern Architecture as Mass Media*. Cambridge: MIT Press, 1994.

Crary, Jonathan. *Techniques of the Observer: On Vision and Modernity in the Nineteenth Century*. Cambridge: MIT Press, 1990.

Cross, Gary. *A Quest for Time: The Reduction of Work in Britain and France, 1840–1940*. Berkeley: University of California Press, 1989.

———. *Time and Money: The Making of Consumer Culture*. New York: Routledge, 1993.

Crouzet, François. *Capital Formation in the Industrial Revolution*. London: Methuen, 1970.

———. *De la supériorité de l'Angleterre sur la France: L'économique et l'imaginaire, XVIIe-XXe siècle*. Paris: Librairie Académique Perrin, 1985.

———. "French Economic Growth in the Nineteenth Century Reconsidered." *History* 59 (June 1974): 167–79.

Dansette, Adrien. *Histoire religieuse de la France contemporaine*. Paris: Flammarion, 1965.

Dard, Olivier. "Les novations intellectuelles des années trente: L'exemple de Jean Coutrot." Thèse de troisième cycle, Institut d'Etudes Politique de Paris, 1993. 2 vols.

———. *La synarchie*. Paris: Perrin, 1998.

———. "Voyage à l'intérieur d'X-Crise." *Vingtième Siècle*, no. 47 (July–Sept. 1995): 132–46.

Dean, Carolyn. *The Self and Its Pleasures: Bataille, Lacan, and the History of the Decentered Subject*. Ithaca: Cornell University Press, 1992.

Debord, Guy. *Society of the Spectacle*. Detroit: Black and Red, 1983.

Deleuze, Gilles. *Cinéma 1: L'image-mouvement*. Paris: Les Editions de Minuit, 1983.

———. *Cinéma 2: L'image-temps*. Paris: Les Editions de Minuit, 1985.

Douglas, Allen. *From Fascism to Libertarian Communism: Georges Valois Against the Third Republic*. Berkeley: University of California Press, 1992.

Downs, Laura Lee. *Manufacturing Inequality: Gender Division in the French and British Metalworking Industries, 1914–1939*. Ithaca: Cornell University Press, 1995.

Drouard, Alain. *La Fondation Alexis Carrel*. Paris: Editions Maison des Sciences de l'Homme, 1992.

Ellenberger, Henry. *The Discovery of the Unconscious: The History and Evolution of Dynamic Psychiatry*. New York: Basic Books, 1970.

Ewen, Stuart. *All Consuming Images: The Politics of Style in Contemporary Culture*. New York: Basic Books, 1988.

———. *Captains of Consciousness: Advertising and the Social Roots of the Consumer Culture*. New York: McGraw-Hill, 1976.

Ewen, Stuart, and Elizabeth Ewen. *Channels of Desire: Mass Images and the Shaping of American Consciousness*. New York, 1982.

Foucault, Michel. *Discipline and Punish*. New York: Pantheon, 1975.

———. *The History of Sexuality*. Vol. 1. New York: Pantheon, 1978.

Fox, Richard W., and T. J. Jackson Lears, eds. *The Culture of Consumption: Critical Essays in American History, 1880–1980*. New York: Pantheon, 1983.

Fox, Stephen. *The Mirror Makers: A History of American Advertising and Its Creators*. New York: Morrow, 1984.

Freund, Gisèle. *Photographie et société*. Paris: Editions du Seuil, 1974.

Fridenson, Patrick. *L'Autre front*. Paris: Editions Ouvrières, 1977. Translated into English as *The French Home Front, 1914–1918*. New York: Berg, 1992.

———. *L'Histoire des usines Renault*. Vol. 1, *Naissance de la Grande Entreprise, 1898–1939*. Paris: Editions du Seuil, 1972.

———. "Le patronat." In *Histoire de la France*, ed. A. Burguière and J. Revel. Paris: Editions du Seuil, 1990.

———. "Le patronat français." In *La France et les français en 1938-1939*, ed. R. Rémond and J. Bourdin. Paris: Presses de la FNSP, 1978.

Fridenson, Patrick, and André Straus, eds. *Le capitalisme français XIXe-XXe siècle: Blocages et dynamismes d'une croissance*. Paris: Fayard, 1987.

Frisby, David. *Fragments of Modernity*. Cambridge: MIT Press, 1986.

Frost, Robert L. *Alternating Currents: Nationalized Power in France, 1946–1970*. Ithaca: Cornell University Press, 1991.

Furet, François, and Jacques Ozouf. *Reading and Writing: Literacy in France from Calvin to Jules Ferry*. Cambridge: Cambridge University Press/Editions de la Maison des Sciences de l'Homme, 1982.

Fussell, Paul. *The Great War and Modern Memory*. Oxford: Oxford University Press, 1975.

Gay, Peter. *Weimar Culture: The Insider as Outsider*. New York: Harper and Row, 1968.

Gerschenkron, Alexander. *Economic Backwardness in Historical Perspective*. Cambridge: Harvard University Press, 1962.

Golan, Romy. *Modernity and Nostalgia: Art and Politics in France Between the Wars*. New Haven: Yale University Press, 1995.

Goldstein, Jan. *Console and Classify: The French Psychiatric Profession in the Nineteenth Century*. Cambridge: Cambridge University Press, 1987.

de Grazia, Victoria. "The Arts of Purchase." In *Remaking History*, ed. Barbara Kruger and Phil Mariani. Seattle: Bay Press, 1989.

Grélon, André. *Les ingénieurs de la crise.* Paris: EHESS, 1986.

———. "L'ingénieur catholique et son rôle social." In *Les chantiers de la paix sociale,* ed. Yves Cohen and Rémy Baudouï. Fontenay: ENS Editions, 1997.

Guchet, Yves. *Georges Valois: L'Action Française, le Faisceau, la république radicale.* Paris: Editions de l'albatros, 1975.

Haber, Samuel. *Efficiency and Uplift: Scientific Management in the Progressive Era, 1890–1920.* Chicago: University of Chicago Press, 1964.

Habermas, Jürgen. The Structural Transformation of the Public Sphere: An Inquiry into a Category of Bourgeois Society. Cambridge: MIT Press, 1989. First published in 1961 as *Strukturwandel der Offentlichkeit.*

Harvey, David. *The Condition of Postmodernity: An Enquiry into the Origins of Culture.* Oxford: Blackwell, 1989.

Herf, Jeffrey. *Reactionary Modernism: Technology, Culture, and Politics in Weimar and the Third Reich.* Cambridge: Cambridge University Press, 1984.

Hobsbawm, Eric, and Terence Ranger. *The Invention of Tradition.* Cambridge: Cambridge University Press, 1983.

Hoog, Georges. *Histoire du catholicisme social en France, 1871–1931.* Paris: Editions Domat et Monchrestien, 1946.

Hughes, H. Stuart. *Consciousness and Society.* Rev. ed. New York: Vintage Books, 1977.

Huyssen, Andreas. *After the Great Divide: Modernism, Mass Culture, Postmodernism.* Bloomington: Indiana University Press, 1986.

Illich, Ivan, and Barry Sanders. *A B C: The Alphabetization of the Popular Mind.* New York: Vintage Books, 1989.

Jackson, Julian. *The Popular Front in France: Defending Democracy, 1934–38.* Cambridge: Cambridge University Press, 1988.

Janik, Alan, and Stephen Toulmin. *Wittgenstein's Vienna.* New York: Simon and Schuster, 1973.

Jay, Martin. *Downcast Eyes: The Denigration of Vision in Twentieth-Century French Thought.* Berkeley: University of California Press, 1993.

Jensen, Robert. *Marketing Modernism in Fin-de-Siècle Europe.* Princeton: Princeton University Press, 1994.

Kalaora, Bernard. "Le mysticisme technique de Joseph Wilbois." In *Les chantiers de la paix sociale,* ed. Yves Cohen and Rémi Baudoui. Fontenay: ENS Editions, 1997.

Kanigel, Robert. *The One Best Way: Frederick Winslow Taylor and the Enigma of Efficiency.* New York: Viking, 1997.

Kern, Stephen. *The Culture of Time and Space, 1880–1918.* Cambridge: Harvard University Press, 1986.

Kindleberger, Charles. *Economic Growth in France and Britain, 1851-1950.* Cambridge: Harvard University Press, 1964.

Kuisel, Richard F. *Capitalism and the State in Modern France: Renovation and Economic Management in the Twentieth Century.* Cambridge: Cambridge University Press, 1981.

———. *Ernest Mercier: French Technocrat.* Berkeley: University of California Press, 1967.

———. "The Legend of the Vichy Synarchy." *French Historical Studies* 6.3 (spring 1970): 365–85.

———. *Seducing the French: The Dilemma of Americanization.* Berkeley: University of California Press, 1993.

———. "Technocrats and Public Economic Policy: From the Third to the Fourth Republic." *Journal of European Economic History* 2.1 (spring 1973): 53–99.

Landes, David S. "French Business and the Businessman: A Social and Cultural Analysis." In *Modern France,* ed. Edward Mead Earle. Princeton: Princeton University Press, 1951.

———. "French Entrepreneurship and Industrial Growth in the Nineteenth Century." *Journal of Economic History,* May 1949.

———. *The Unbound Prometheus.* Cambridge: Harvard University Press, 1969.

Le Bras, Hervé. *Marianne et les lapins.* Paris: Olivier Orban, 1991.

Lears, T. J. Jackson. *Fables of Abundance: A Cultural History of Advertising in America.* New York: Basic Books, 1994.

———. *No Place of Grace: Antimodernism and the Transformation of American Culture.* New York: Pantheon, 1981.

Lebovics, Herman. *True France: The Wars over Cultural Identity.* Ithaca: Cornell University Press, 1992.

Lindenberg, Daniel. *Les années souterraines, 1937–1947.* Paris: Editions La Découverte, 1990.

Lipovetsky, Gilles. *L'empire de l'éphémère, la mode et son destin dans les sociétés modernes.* Paris: Gallimard/NRF, 1987. Translated as *The Empire of Fashion: Dressing Modern Democracy.* Princeton: Princeton University Press, 1994.

———. *L'ere du vide: essais sur l'individualisme contemporain.* Paris: Gallimard, 1983.

Lowe, Donald M. *History of Bourgeois Perception.* Chicago: University of Chicago Press, 1982.

Lyotard, Jean-François. *The Postmodern Condition: A Report on Knowledge.* Trans. G. Bennington and B. Massumi. Minneapolis: University of Minnesota Press, 1984.

MacCannell, Dean. *The Tourist: A New Theory of the Leisure Class.* New York: Schocken, 1976.

McKendrick, Neil, John Brewer, and J. H. Plumb. *The Birth of a Consumer Society: The Commercialization of Eighteenth-Century England.* London, 1982.

McLeod, Mary. "Urbanism and Utopia: Le Corbusier from Regional Syndicalism to Vichy." 2 vols. Ph.D. diss., Princeton School of Architecture, 1985.

Maier, Charles S. *In Search of Stability: Explorations in Historical Political Economy*. Cambridge: Cambridge University Press, 1987.

——. *Recasting Bourgeois Europe: Stabilization in France, Germany, and Italy in the Decade After World War I*. Princeton: Princeton University Press, 1975.

Marchand, Roland. *Advertising the American Dream: Making Way for Modernity, 1920–1940*. Berkeley: University of California Press, 1985.

Marglin, Stephen A. "What Do the Bosses Do? The Origins and Functions of Hierarchy in Capitalist Production." In *Classes, Power, and Conflict: Classical and Contemporary Debates*, ed. Anthony Giddens and David Held. Berkeley: University of California Press, 1982.

Martin, Marc. *Trois siècles de publicité en France*. Paris: Editions Odile Jacob, 1992.

Matsuda, Matt K. *The Memory of the Modern*. New York: Oxford University Press, 1996.

Mayer, Arno. *The Persistence of the Old Regime: Europe to the Great War*. New York: Pantheon, 1981.

Mayeur, Jean-Marie. *Catholicisme social et démocratie chrétienne*. Paris: Editions du Cerf, 1986.

——. "Le catholicisme social en France." *Mouvement social*, no. 77 (1970): 113–21.

Merkle, Judith. *Management and Ideology: The Legacy of the International Scientific Management Movement*. Berkeley: University of California Press, 1980.

Miller, Michael B. *The Bon Marché: Bourgeois Culture and the Department Store, 1869–1920*. Princeton: Princeton University Press, 1981.

Milza, Pierre. *Fascisme français, passé et présent*. Paris: Flammarion, 1987.

Moutet, Aimée. *Les logiques d'entreprise: La rationalisation dans l'industrie française de l'entre-deux-guerres*. Paris: Editions de l'Ecole des Hautes Etudes en Sciences Sociales, 1997.

——. "Une rationalisation du travail dans l'industrie française des années 30." *Annales ESC*, no. 5 (Sept./Oct. 1987).

Muel-Dreyfus, Francine. *Vichy et l'éternel féminin: Contribution à une sociologie politique de l'ordre des corps*. Paris: Editions du Seuil, 1996.

Nelson, Daniel. *Frederick W. Taylor and the Rise of Scientific Management*. Madison: University of Wisconsin Press, 1980.

Nolan, Mary. *Visions of Modernity: American Business and the Modernization of Germany*. New York: Oxford University Press, 1994.

Nolte, Ernst. *Three Faces of Fascism*. London: Weidenfeld and Nicholson, 1965.

Nord, Philip. *Paris Shopkeepers and the Politics of Resentment.* Princeton: Princeton University Press, 1986.

O'Brien, Patrick, and Caglar Keyder. *Economic Growth in Britain and France, 1780–1914: Two Paths to the Twentieth Century.* London: Allen and Unwin, 1978.

Palmer, Michael Beaussénat. *Des petits journaux aux grandes agences: Naissance du journalisme moderne, 1863–1914.* Paris: Aubier, 1983.

Paxton, Robert. *Vichy France: Old Guard and New Order.* 2nd ed. New York: W. W. Norton, 1975.

Pennelier, Paul. *La conception corporative de La Tour du Pin.* Paris: Domat-Montchrestien, 1937.

Poggioli, Renato. *The Theory of the Avant-Garde.* New York: Harper and Row, 1971.

Pope, Daniel. "French Advertising Men and the American 'Promised Land.'" *Historical Reflections* 5 (summer 1978): 117–39.

Poster, Mark. *The Mode of Information: Poststructuralism and Social Context.* Chicago: University of Chicago Press, 1990.

Prochasson, Christophe. *Les années électriques.* Paris: Editions La Découverte, 1991.

Rabinbach, Anson. *The Human Motor: Energy, Fatigue, and the Origins of Modernity.* New York: Basic Books, 1990.

———. "The European Science of Work: The Economy of the Body at the End of the Nineteenth Century." In *Work in France: Representations, Meaning, Organization, and Practice,* ed. Steven L. Kaplan and Cynthia J. Koepp. Ithaca: Cornell University Press, 1986.

Rabinow, Paul. *French Modern: Norms and Forms of the Social.* Cambridge: MIT Press, 1989.

Reid, Donald. "Fayol: Excès d'honneur ou excès d'indignité?" *Revue française de gestion,* no. 70 (Sept./Oct. 1988): 151–59.

Roberts, Mary Louise. *Civilization Without Sexes: Reconstructing Gender in Postwar France, 1917–1927.* Chicago: University of Chicago, 1994.

Rollet, Henri. *L'action sociale des catholiques en France.* 2 vols. Paris: Editions Contemporaines, 1949; Brussels: Desclée de Brouwer, 1958.

Ross, Kristin. *The Emergence of Social Space: Rimbaud and the Paris Commune.* Minneapolis: University of Minnesota Press, 1988.

———. *Fast Cars, Clean Bodies: Decolonization and the Reordering of French Culture.* Cambridge: MIT Press, 1995.

Roth, Michael. *The Ironist's Cage: Memory, Trauma, and the Construction of History.* New York: Columbia University Press, 1995.

Roudinesco, Elisabeth. *La bataille de cent ans: Histoire de la psychanalyse en France.* Vol. 1, *1885–1939.* Paris: Ramsay, 1982.

Schor, Naomi. *Reading in Detail: Aesthetics and the Feminine.* New York: Methuen, 1987.

Schorske, Carl. *Fin-de-Siècle Vienna.* New York: Knopf, 1979.

Schudson, Michael. *Advertising, the Uneasy Persuasion: Its Dubious Impact on American Society.* New York: Basic Books, 1984.

Seigel, Jerrold. *Bohemian Paris: Culture, Politics, and the Boundaries of Bourgeois Life, 1830–1930.* New York: Viking Press, 1986.

Sémichon, Roger. *Les idées sociales et politiques de La Tour du Pin.* Paris: Beauchesne, 1936.

Silver, Ken. *Esprit de Corps: The Art of the Parisian Avant-Garde and the First World War, 1914–1925.* Princeton: Princeton University Press, 1989.

———. "Purism: Straightening Up After the Great War." *Artforum* 15 (Mar. 1977): 56–63.

Silverman, Debora. *Art Nouveau in Fin-de-Siècle France: Politics, Psychology, and Style.* Berkeley: University of California Press, 1989.

———. *Selling Culture.* New York: Pantheon, 1986.

Sirinelli, Jean-François, ed. *Histoire des droites en France.* Vols. 1–3. Paris: NRF/Gallimard, 1992.

Soucy, Robert. *French Fascism: The First Wave.* New Haven: Yale University Press, 1986.

———. *French Fascism: The Second Wave.* New Haven: Yale University Press, 1995.

Soulez, Philippe, and Frédéric Worms. *Bergson.* Paris: Flammarion, 1997.

Sternhell, Zeev. *Ni droite, ni gauche: L'idéologie fasciste en France.* Paris: Editions du Seuil, 1983. Published in English as *Neither Right nor Left: Fascist Ideology in France.* Trans. David Maisel. Berkeley: University of California Press, 1986.

Sternhell, Zeev, with Mario Sznajder and Maia Asheri. *Naissance de l'idéologie fasciste.* Paris: Fayard, 1989.

Talmy, Robert. *Aux sources de catholicisme social: L'école de la Tour du Pin.* Tournai: Desclée, 1963.

Thépot, Andre, ed. *L'ingénieur dans la société française.* Paris: Editions Ouvrières, 1985.

Toulmin, Stephen. *Cosmopolis.* New York: Free Press, 1990.

Trebilcock, Clive. *The Industrialization of the Continental Powers, 1780–1914.* New York: Longman, 1981.

Troy, Nancy J. *Modernism and the Decorative Arts in France: Art Nouveau to Le Corbusier.* New Haven: Yale University Press, 1991.

Varcoe, Ian. "Technocracy and Democratic Politics." In *Culture, Modernity, and Revolution: Essays in Honor of Zygmunt Bauman,* ed. R. Kilminster and I. Varcoe. New York: Routledge, 1996.

Varnedoe, Kirk, and Adam Gopnik. *High and Low: Modern Art and Popular Culture.* New York: Museum of Modern Art, 1990.

Weber, Eugen. *France, Fin de Siècle.* Cambridge: Harvard University Press, 1986.

————. *Peasants into Frenchmen: The Modernization of Rural France, 1870–1914.* Stanford: Stanford University Press, 1976.

Weiss, Jeffrey. *The Popular Culture of Modern Art: Picasso, Duchamp, and Avant-Gardism.* New Haven: Yale University Press, 1994.

Williams, Raymond. *The Long Revolution.* New York: Columbia University Press, 1961.

Williams, Rosalind. *Dream Worlds: Mass Consumption in Late Nineteenth-Century France.* Berkeley: University of California Press, 1982.

Index

In this index an "f" after a number indicates a separate reference on the next page, and an "ff" indicates separate references on the next two pages. A continuous discussion over two or more pages is indicated by a span of page numbers, e.g., "57–59." *Passim* is used for a cluster of references in close but not consecutive sequence.

Voltaire, 131
Vouloir (journal), 132–43 *passim*, 136
Vuillermoz, Emile, 35–36

Weber, Max, 2–4
Weiler, Edith, 20–21, 41–42
Wilbois, Joseph, 149. *See also* Social
 Catholics

Worth, Jacques, 195n9

X-crise, 69, 139,146, 149–50, 194n5,
 197n20; and Coutrot, 146, 149–50; and
 technocracy, 69, 139, 146–50
X-Information, 149

Zola, Emile, 22

Library of Congress Cataloging-in-Publication Data

Beale, Marjorie A.
    The modernist enterprise: French elites and the threat of
modernity, 1900–1940/ Marjorie A. Beale.
        p. cm.
    Includes bibliographical references (…-…) and index.
    ISBN 0-8047-3511-5 (cl. : alk. paper)
        1. Elite (Social sciences)—France.   2. Social change—France.
I. Title.
HN440.E4B43   1999
305.5'2'0944—dc21   99-16483

This book is printed on acid-free, archival-quality paper.

Original printing 1999
Last figure below indicates year of this printing:
08 07 06 05 04 03 02 01 00 99

Typeset by John Feneron in 10/13 Galliard